THE

Fresh Start

DIVORCE
RECOVERY
WORKBOOK

**Other Fresh Start™ products available
from Thomas Nelson Publishers:**

Becoming Your Own Best Friend: Thomas Whiteman, Ph.D., and Randy Petersen

Flying Solo: Meditations for the Single-Again: Thomas Whiteman, Ph.D.,
and Randy Petersen

The Fresh Start Single Parenting Workbook: Thomas Whiteman, Ph.D.,
with Randy Petersen

Innocent Victims: Thomas Whiteman, Ph.D.

Love Gone Wrong: Thomas Whiteman, Ph.D., and Randy Peterson

Men Who Love Too Little: Thomas Whiteman, Ph.D., and Randy Petersen
(available February 1995)

Recovery from Divorce: Bob Burns

The Single Again Handbook: Thomas Jones

When Your Son or Daughter Is Going Through a Divorce: Thomas Whiteman, Ph.D.,
and Debbie Barr (available January 1995)

THE *Fresh Start*™

DIVORCE RECOVERY WORKBOOK

Bob Burns
&
Tom Whiteman

Thomas Nelson Publishers
Nashville • Atlanta • London • Vancouver

Published in Nashville, Tennessee, by Thomas Nelson, Inc., Publishers, and distributed in Canada by Word Communications, Ltd., Richmond, British Columbia.

Unless otherwise noted, the Bible version used in this publication is THE NEW KING JAMES VERSION. Copyright © 1979, 1980, 1982, Thomas Nelson, Inc., Publishers.

Printed in the United States.

ISBN 0-8407-9622-6   9 10 - 96

To

PAUL and PHYLLIS MALONE

whose commitment and labors
in the early years of Fresh Start
helped get us off the ground

and

whose continued efforts
serve as an example to
all who are involved
in the work.

Contents

Foreword

Although I've never been through a divorce, I know full well the emotional stages of grieving outlined in this workbook. Several years ago, I went through a devastating breakup of a very close personal and business relationship. I felt the deep pain and rejection you have experienced in going through an actual divorce. I experienced the anger, guilt, bitterness, and even depression you must be feeling, wondering if God is really out there and if He really cares.

I know many of you reading this workbook are in the midst of those emotions. You may even be wondering if life is still worth living. If that's your situation, let me say first that I empathize with you. Second, I'm glad you picked up this workbook. There *is* hope, and there *is* recovery from divorce. But it will be a slow and sometimes painful process.

Through my own recovery, I've learned a very simple truth that I believe you will also discover over the next year or two. Namely, God uses the most difficult circumstances in our lives to teach us the most important lessons. In my own case, I know the difficulties I endured deepened my faith and strengthened my character.

The *Fresh Start Divorce Recovery Workbook* is not a book you will browse through easily. It deals honestly with the approach to full recovery, not just spiritual Band-Aids to cover up the hurts. It's filled with hard-hitting, interactive material that will allow you to personalize the concepts presented and focus on specific areas you need help with. I believe it's the next-best thing to being at an actual Fresh Start Seminar.

The authors are men who not only hold the appropriate academic degrees (both have earned doctorates), but also know firsthand, through their own experiences, the trauma you face. They have traveled across the country, talking with literally thousands of separated and divorced individuals. They've opened up their lives in this workbook in order to share with you some of the pain that all divorced people face. I believe their experiences will not only be encouraging for you to hear, but also a challenge to you as you seek your own recovery.

If you take the time to read through this workbook and process the material, it will go a long way toward helping you out of your current crisis. May God bless you at this time of transition for you and your family.

Gary Smalley

Introduction

"Dear Diary,
     Today my husband asked me for a divorce..."
     Unless you've heard those words or words like them, it's hard to imagine the impact they have on your life. I (Tom) remember full well the intense emotion and overwhelming anxiety I felt during that time. Recovering from divorce took me several years. I tried to shut everyone out of my life. Not wanting to be hurt the same way again, I was convinced that the solution was to never love again, never trust again, and never let anyone into my life.
     I (Bob) have watched and worked with hundreds of people who faced the disruption of their marriages. Like Tom, I've known many who extended the time of their personal recovery from divorce because they didn't know of or weren't willing to appropriate the resources available for growth.
     The *Fresh Start Divorce Recovery Workbook* is designed to help you avoid those mistakes. We want to help you work through your present crisis as quickly and productively as possible. We believe there *is* life after divorce. We also feel that if you can learn from this crisis, God can actually help you come out of it better than you were before it happened.
     You may be thinking, *Better than before? Not in my case. That's impossible.* We've heard others express the same skepticism. Yet later we've heard those same people say, "I wouldn't wish divorce on my worst enemy, but I wouldn't trade anything for what I've learned having gone through it. I know I'm better off today in many ways."
     There *is* hope. God isn't done with us yet. To the contrary, He can do more in our lives over the next year or two than perhaps He has over the last ten! How can we make such a bold statement? Because as part of the Fresh Start team of speakers, we've had contact with thousands of people just like you who are going through divorce.
     This workbook will not merely present the experiences of one or two people as a guideline to recovery. Rather, it grows out of our interaction

with all those people in the Fresh Start seminars. Our goal is to present the conclusions of our eleven years of work, study, and experience with them.

Going through this workbook won't suddenly heal you of the divorce experience. The recovery process takes time and effort. You will, however, gain the tools needed to begin the journey. Thousands of evaluations indicate the Fresh Start program has helped individuals just like you to work through the issues of separation and divorce.

HOW TO USE YOUR DIVORCE RECOVERY WORKBOOK

Whether you're going through this workbook alone, as part of a small group, or in a Fresh Start Seminar, we have found that recovery is best achieved when you have someone else to talk to in the process—someone who understands you and what you're going through. That's why we have small groups as part of the seminar program. If you are going through this workbook on your own, you might want to ask someone in your church, neighborhood, or circle of friends who has been through a similar time of change to do it with you. It's best if you can find someone who is a little further along in the process than you. We all need encouragement as we sort through our emotions.

You may have generally recovered from a marital breakup already. We would encourage you to reach out to others by starting your own support group. Separated and divorced people live in every town in America. Becoming an instrument of God's healing in the lives of others will give you a tremendous feeling of purpose and worth.

Whether you're looking for a group or leading one, we'd love to hear from you at the Fresh Start office. We have compiled a list of our seminar alumni and support groups from around the country. Perhaps we can help you find a group or individual who can support you through the recovery process.

This workbook contains nine chapters. Most of them are divided into seven sections. If you'd like to go through the workbook in a systematic way, we recommend a section per day, or about a chapter a week. However, recovery from divorce is a very individual process. Therefore, you may need to go through some chapters slowly, skip through others quickly, or even put the book down for a while until you have the energy to move on.

The first seven chapters (excluding chapter two) make up the major part of the Fresh Start Seminar. They cover critical issues for every separated and divorced person. The remaining chapters on children of divorce and dysfunctional families also discuss critical issues, but they may not be applicable to all readers.

The articles at the end of the workbook are supplemental materials you might find helpful at any point of your journey through the divorce recovery process. They're written by the authors or others associated with the Fresh Start program.

A few comments on our writing style are in order. Throughout the text, we have used the pronoun *I* instead of *we*. We believe this makes for easier reading. Also, we have chosen to alternate feminine and masculine pronouns and references, and we hope we've done so fairly. We want recovering persons of both sexes to identify with what we're saying.

We've included numerous stories in the text. Our examples are based on actual individuals we have known or counseled. To protect the privacy of those individuals, we have changed names and some of the facts, as well as combining stories to make identification of any person virtually impossible. To all the Fresh Start alumni we have known, we say thank you for sharing your lives, your stories, and your inspiration.

If you are interested in knowing more about the Fresh Start Seminars or would like to find out how your church or organization can sponsor a seminar, write us at 63 Chestnut Road, Paoli, PA 19301, or phone 1-800-882-2799.

A special word of thanks goes to our friend and partner, Tom Jones. Tom has contributed to every aspect of Fresh Start and wrote chapter 5, "Sexuality," and the article "Letter to a Husband."

We also thank Randy Peterson for his helpful work in editing the interactive material. And the team at Nelson have done an outstanding job preparing our manuscript so that you, our reader, can benefit from it.

Finally, a special word of thanks goes to our wives (Janet and Lori) and our children (Rob, Chris, Elizabeth, Michelle, and Kurt). They generously gave up vacation and family time in order to complete this project. Each, in her or his own way, has contributed sacrificially to the work of Fresh Start and to the breaking of the cycle of divorce in our own family systems.

CHAPTER 1

THE STAGES OF DIVORCE RECOVERY*

What's the worst experience you've ever been through? Many people would refer to the death of a loved one or a serious illness. But if you've gone through a separation or divorce, your mind probably jumped to that experience.

That only makes sense. We're talking about the death of a relationship, the most-intimate human relationship. Naturally, that will cause a jolt to your way of life, and it will take some time to get over it. When a loved one dies, we observe a grieving process. It's natural for friends and family to be in mourning. Some cultures have traditions to mark this period, such as a widow's wearing of black. A divorce requires a grieving process as well. Researchers find the process typically takes at least two years. Yet we keep rushing things, wanting a quick cure-all for our intense pain, and we worry when the pain drags on month after month. But healing takes time.

> *Divorce recovery typically takes at least two years. So don't expect your emotions to stabilize right away. Take it step by step, day by day.*

*This chapter is developed and expanded in the book *Recovery from Divorce* by Bob Burns.

➤ How long ago did the shock of divorce or separation hit you? (We're not talking about the final legalities, but the first moment when you realized this marriage probably would not last.) _____

_____

➤ In most divorces, there is a period of limbo. The shock has hit. The marriage seems doomed. But you can't begin recovering yet, because nothing is final. There's still a glimmer of hope, however faint. This limbo can last for months, even years. How would you describe your situation? Are you still in limbo? _____

_____

_____

_____

➤ Can you pinpoint a date when the door was finally closed on this marriage? _____

➤ Two years is an average figure. Some recover faster, some slower. But let's pick a date about two years from the door-closing date you just listed. That's a target date for your emotional recovery. List that date here.

_____

➤ If that target date is already past or coming up too soon, feel free to adjust it. Choose a date a year or two from now. Adjusted Date:

_____

The purpose here is not to rush you by giving you a deadline you *must* meet. Instead, this should free you. You don't need to be kicking up your heels tomorrow or next week. You can take the time you need to get over this. And yet, it can be helpful to know where you are and where you're going.

THE SLIPPERY SLOPE

Emotions in the recovery process typically go down and then up. You'll feel awful at first, but then you turn a corner and things start to improve. There may be temporary setbacks along the uphill road to recovery, but you're moving in the right direction.

Looking at the following graph, which we call "The Crisis Time Line" or "The Slippery Slope," where would you say you are right now?

CRISIS TIME LINE
(THE SLIPPERY SLOPE)

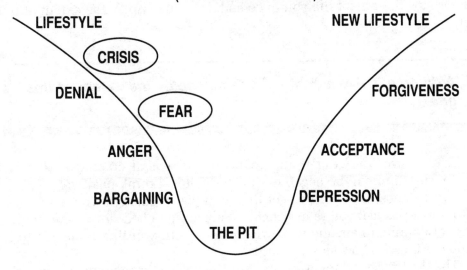

LIFESTYLE   NEW LIFESTYLE

CRISIS

DENIAL   FORGIVENESS

FEAR

ANGER   ACCEPTANCE

BARGAINING   DEPRESSION

THE PIT

A. Beginning to go downhill
B. Near bottom
C. Turning the corner
D. Going up
E. Temporary setback
F. Nearly there

Remember that divorce recovery, like grief recovery, is a *process*. It's not "wrong" to be at any particular point on that graph. We all go through stages.

If we take a closer look at the grieving process, perhaps you can better understand what you're going through right now, as well as the stages that lie ahead.

The Grieving Process

Elisabeth Kübler-Ross first popularized the stages of grief in her landmark book *On Death and Dying*. She highlighted five emotional levels people pass through as they deal with the death of a loved one—denial, anger, bargaining, depression, and finally acceptance. This theory has been immensely helpful, not only in dealing with grief, but also in coping with various tragedies, including divorce.

As we said before, a divorce is like a death. When a couple is torn apart, for whatever reason, that relationship dies. So the grieving process will be much like that after a loved one's death. Even if bitterness and anger keep you from missing your ex, you will still miss the intimate relationship and perhaps the way of life you once had. Don't downplay the extent of this grief.

> **A divorce is like a death. Don't downplay the extent of this grief.**

Getting over the grief is the goal. But for several crucial reasons, we have to work through the negative stuff and not just think positively.

For instance, let's say you get the flu. If you're like me, you won't see a doctor until you feel you're near death. So you lie in bed—moaning, aching, and complaining to anyone who will listen—until you finally decide to let the doctor tell you how sick you are.

The doctor says, "Yes, you do have the flu. It's been going around. I've had five people in my office this week with the same symptoms. You'll feel achy in your head and back, and you'll probably run a fever for a day or two. But if you get plenty of rest and drink lots of fluids, it will run its course in about forty-eight hours."

You drive home feeling a bit better about your situation. But why? What did the doctor do for you?

First, you learned that what you're going through is normal. In fact, many others have the same illness. That's reassuring. Second, you learned the normal symptoms of your illness—what you can expect to feel. Finally, and perhaps most importantly, you learned how long you can expect the pain to last. This information, combined with the practical advice about rest and fluids, helps you persevere through your illness.

So it is with our knowledge of the stages of grief. First, we learn that what we're going through is normal. You aren't alone; others are facing similar problems. That fact in itself offers immense encouragement.

Second, we learn to recognize our symptoms. They aren't physical but emotional. By labeling our emotional stages, we have a road map we can read to find out where we've come from and how far we still have to go. If your emotions are confusing or worrying you, this awareness can help a great deal.

Third, our knowledge of the grieving process helps us gain some idea of how long our pain will last. Unfortunately, it's not like the flu, lasting only a few days. That doesn't mean you'll be constantly miserable, however. It just means it may take a couple of years to restore a sense of emotional equilibrium, to "get back to normal." Nor does it mean that after a few years you'll be completely free from any sorrow or pain about your divorce. Especially if you have kids, the implications of the breakup will last and last. But after this recovery period, you should be strong enough to deal with most of the painful memories and difficult moments.

Don't be discouraged by this. You're facing a crisis. You have had a "nuclear bomb" dropped into your life. It will take a while for the fallout to settle, but you can survive if you take the proper steps. And you may even come out of all this a little smarter and stronger.

MAKE IT YOUR OWN

Does the prospect of being stable emotionally in about two or three years make you feel good, knowing there's light at the end of the tunnel; bad, because it will take so long; or something in between? Explain. _____

_____

_____

_____

➤ Which of the following is the most helpful for you to hear? Why?

_____

   a. "You'll be okay. Everything will be fine."
   b. "Your present feelings are normal and understandable. You're not going crazy."
   c. "Quit moping and start living."

➤ Is there a close friend you can tell about the kind of things you need to hear? Will it help to have this friend coach you through the recovery process? _____

➤ Who will this friend be?

_____

➤ Have you been aware of the grieving process in your own life? Do you think you are handling your grief better than average, average, or worse than average? Why? _____

_____

_____

_____

➤ How would your closest friends answer that question? Would *they* say you were handling your grief better than average, average, or worse than average? (You might try asking them.) _____

_____

_____

➤ What feedback have you received on how normal or unusual your feelings have been? _____

_____

_____

_____

THE SHOCK—"IT WILL NEVER HAPPEN TO ME"

When the wedding bells ring, no one is expecting a divorce. People are supposed to stay together forever, happily ever after. When divorce comes, it's a shock. Even if it comes slowly, as a creeping realization, and drags on for years, the entire divorce event is a jolt to our hopes, dreams, expectations, and beliefs. In the aftermath, many newly divorced people are literally in shock.

Before we examine the various stages of coping with the crisis, we must look at the shock itself. What emotional damage is done? The best way to approach this issue is for me (Tom) to tell my own story. Your story may be different, but you'll probably see similarities, especially in the emotions involved.

MY STORY

I was brought up in a loving and committed Christian family. We even had our own pew at the church: the third row back on the left side. You could count on our being there for every service.

From my earliest memory, I believed in Jesus Christ as my personal Savior. My parents faithfully taught me this truth. In junior high, I began to question the Christian belief system. Suddenly I wasn't content to take my parents' word for it. My period of questioning and rebellion lasted until high school. At that point I concluded that what my parents had taught me was true, and I recommitted my life to God. I also decided to go into Christian ministry.

I went on to Bible college. In my senior year, I married my high school sweetheart. We had dated for about four years, and she also wanted to go into Christian work. We both planned to spend our lives together forever, serving God. Even though we were young, we thought we would never get a divorce, because we knew God would bless our life together as long as we honored Him.

MAKE IT YOUR OWN

➤ So far in this story, what similarities do you find to your own experience? _____

_____

_____

_____

➤ What differences? _____

_____

_____

_____

➤ As a newlywed, I believed that God would protect our marriage from divorce because we were serving Him. To carry the idea a little further, I thought that divorce happened only to bad people. Since we were good people, we were safe.

When you first got married, did you believe you would be spared from the divorce trauma? On what basis did you believe that? Your love? Your maturity? Your family background? _____

_____

_____

➤ What were your beliefs about God and divorce? _____

_____

_____

➤ Did you assume God would keep such bad things from happening to you? Why? _____

_____

_____

THE FORMULA

I had a formula all worked out. It went something like this: as long as I committed my life to God and put Him first, He would bless me. I knew I'd have problems from time to time, but I'd be able to work through them. God would surely protect me from anything serious. This was very reassuring. In a way, it let me believe I could control my life. I just had to do my part, and God would do His.

This formula was reinforced in my thinking because it worked—at least it seemed to. I had a fairly easy life. I had loving parents, good friends, and now a fine Christian wife with whom I would share my life.

The formula also worked in reverse. I'd see other couples who were having problems in their marriages. Little by little, I'd notice that they weren't in church as much as they used to be. Soon, I wouldn't see them there at all. Then I'd hear through the grapevine, "Did you know about the So-and-so's? They're getting a divorce!"

"Well, that figures," I'd say. "That's what happens when you fall away from God." Or, "That's what happens when you don't have the right priorities." As long as I could explain why tragedy struck the other family, I could go on believing it would never happen to me. I was going to do things right in my marriage and life.

MAKE IT YOUR OWN

Take the following true-false test. But instead of putting *T* or *F*, rank your responses on a scale of 1 to 10; 1 is something you thoroughly disagree with, and 10 is something you thoroughly agree with.

1. Good people usually don't get divorced. _____
2. God generally gives us what we deserve. _____
3. If your spouse walks out on you, it means you've done something wrong. _____
4. If you pray hard enough, God will bring you and your ex back together. _____
5. Before my divorce, I was generally a good spouse. _____
6. I think my divorce was God's way of punishing me for something. _____
7. My divorce has made me question God's goodness. _____
8. In the first year of my marriage, I was sure divorce would never happen to me. _____
9. As I was growing up, my family (or church) taught me that divorce is very wrong. _____
10. Since my divorce, I feel closer to God than ever before. _____

DEBRIEFING

Divorce can shatter your belief system. Whether you're a Christian or not, and no matter what "brand" of faith you have, you hold certain basic beliefs about God and morality. A divorce cuts so close to the core of our being that it can sever our lines of faith. We no longer know how to find our way in the universe.

Looking at the quiz above, number 9 is foundational. As children, we pick up many values that we hold the rest of our lives. Our childhood truths are usually simplistic, true in the generalities but ignoring the exceptions. "Be good and good things will happen to you." That may usually work, but what about the biblical story of Job?

Numbers 1 and 2 fall into this category of simplistic truth. They are sort of true, but there are many exceptions. If you cling to those simplistic truths, it's natural to jump to the assumptions of numbers 3, 4, and 6. That is, "Something must be wrong with me, and if I'm good enough, maybe God will put it all back together." But that isn't the way life works. Many fine people have their spouses walk out on them through no apparent fault of their own.

Many of us develop a healthy belief in ourselves as basically good, moral people. But a divorce can shake that belief. We might begin to assume we must be bad because we're divorced.

If we manage to hang on to a belief in our own goodness, we can begin to doubt God. "How could He let this happen to me? What did I do to deserve this?"

Chances are, you answered numbers 5 and 7 similarly. If you're convinced you behaved well, you probably feel God betrayed you.

Some people find special comfort from God in times of hardship (see number 10). That makes sense, because God, too, is a sufferer. Both testaments of the Bible portray Him as one who sympathizes with those in trouble. But you may feel far from God, guilty or victimized. Those are common feelings.

It's not a bad thing to reexamine your beliefs. Much of the Bible contains such questioning. The result can be a good time of spiritual growth as you adjust your simplistic notions to allow for some of the complexities of life.

> *It's not a bad thing to reexamine your belief system. The jolt caused by your divorce may help you develop a more-mature way of thinking if you take the proper steps. You may come out of all this a little smarter and stronger.*

▶ To what extent have your beliefs been challenged by your divorce? Greatly, some, or not very much? Why? _____

_____

_____

▶ In a few words, describe what you believe about God right now. God is... _____

_____

_____

▶ In a few words, describe what you believe about yourself right now. I am... _____

_____

_____

STAGE 1—DENIAL

As you've already figured out, sooner or later all simplistic assumptions break down. The easy formula of "It will never happen to me because I'm good" falls apart.

For me it happened while I was working in a church, seeking to honor God. My wife came to me and said, "I'm not happy anymore, and I don't believe I love you." Eventually she said, "I found someone else, and I'm going to be leaving." I was entering the worst crisis of my life.

The news hit me like a ton of bricks. No one can fully prepare for an announcement like that. It took me entirely by surprise. I was happily married, or so I thought. If you had asked me just ten minutes before my wife broke the news, I would have told you everything was fine at home. Sure, we had our problems from time to time, but we could always work them out. After all, we were good Christians. That was all part of the formula.

It was like a bad dream, listening to my wife's explanations and reasoning. I kept thinking, *This can't be happening. She must have had a bad day.*

Then my thoughts turned into *How's God going to fix this mess?* Finally, I was able to accept that it *was* happening and it was a mess, but I was sure God would make it all better before I got into anything as bad as divorce. All those reactions indicated I was entering the first stage of grieving—denial.

➤ Think back to the first moment you realized your marriage was in trouble. Was it like being hit with a club, was it a slow, steady burn, or would you describe it differently? _____

_____

_____

➤ To what extent was denial a part of your reaction?

    a. I denied there was a problem.
    b. I denied the problem was serious.
    c. I denied it was serious enough to lead to divorce.
    d. Denial was not part of my response.
    e. Other? _____

    _____

➤ Was denial helpful or harmful (or both) as you dealt with the crisis? How so? _____

_____

_____

(*Note:* There is no "right" answer here. As we'll see, denial can be a helpful defense mechanism, numbing us to sudden pain. But it can also, if prolonged, keep us from dealing with a situation that needs attention.)

Active or Passive

In my story, I was the passive agent. The divorce happened to me; I didn't instigate it. But there are always two sides to such a story. Let's try to see it from the active agent's point of view.

My wife was aware of a problem in our marriage long before I knew anything was wrong. I'm not sure what was going on in her mind, but I can imagine she faced some sort of denial, too. When she first realized she wasn't happy in the marriage, she may have said to herself, *But I'm a Christian. I really shouldn't feel this way. I don't want to deal with this.*

Yet the problem just got worse. Her denial only served to make her feel more isolated.

➤ What problem in your marriage led to the divorce: alcohol or drugs? physical or emotional abuse? another woman or man? emotional neglect? If possible, write down in a few words the major factor(s) that caused your divorce. _____

_____

_____

➤ When did you first suspect this was a problem? In the last year or two? On the honeymoon? Maybe even while you were dating? As much as possible, pin down a specific time. _____

_____

_____

➤ How long, then, did you deny the problem? _____

_____

➤ When did you finally admit and confront it? _____

_____

➤ Date of confronting: _____

➤ Length of denial: _____

Look at the time line on page 27. Note that the active agent—the one who instigates the divorce—begins the grieving process well before the passive agent. In some cases, the active agent goes through the entire grieving process and reaches a point of acceptance before going to the passive agent and announcing the marriage is over. I've talked to some reluctant active agents who grieved through twenty years of marriage before finally confronting their spouses with "I can no longer live with...the abuse...the drugs...the affairs...the unhappiness."

At that point, the passive agent begins the grieving process. Often I find that passive agents are confused and bothered by the attitudes of their spouses. The passive one is in turmoil, while the active one seems carefree. The fact is, the active agent has probably gone through that turmoil already and has finally come to the point of acceptance and action.

MAKE IT YOUR OWN

➤ Would you consider yourself the active agent or passive agent in your divorce? _____

➤ Perhaps your roles have flip-flopped as you moved through the grieving process. Did you find yourself changing your mind about what you wanted, vacillating between reconciliation and divorce? Why? _____

_____

_____

➤ What prompted you to finally confront the problems in your marriage?

_____

_____

➤ What did you do about them? _____

_____

_____

TIME LINE OF THE DIVORCE EXPERIENCE

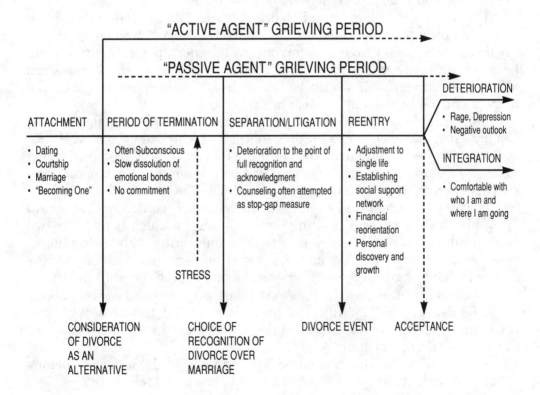

"ACTIVE AGENT" GRIEVING PERIOD

"PASSIVE AGENT" GRIEVING PERIOD

ATTACHMENT	PERIOD OF TERMINATION	SEPARATION/LITIGATION	REENTRY	DETERIORATION
• Dating • Courtship • Marriage • "Becoming One"	• Often Subconscious • Slow dissolution of emotional bonds • No commitment	• Deterioration to the point of full recognition and acknowledgment • Counseling often attempted as stop-gap measure	• Adjustment to single life • Establishing social support network • Financial reorientation • Personal discovery and growth	• Rage, Depression • Negative outlook INTEGRATION • Comfortable with who I am and where I am going

STRESS

CONSIDERATION OF DIVORCE AS AN ALTERNATIVE

CHOICE OF RECOGNITION OF DIVORCE OVER MARRIAGE

DIVORCE EVENT

ACCEPTANCE

Moving Through Denial

Is denial wrong? No. It's a natural and necessary first step in the grieving process. It provides us with the time we need to prepare for what comes next. But we mustn't stay in denial. We must move through it toward a healthy acceptance of what has happened.

Denial is a lot like the shock response your body goes through when you're injured physically. There's usually a numbness in the injured area. You are protected from the full pain of your injury as your body begins to prepare for healing. In the following hours and days, feeling returns to the injured area bit by bit. That's the normal healing process. But if the numbness remains, you have a more-serious problem. It's the same way with emotional denial.

So what keeps us in denial when we should be dealing with the crisis? Primarily fear. (See "The Slippery Slope" on p. 17). We fear what will happen to us.

Will I have to go back to work? What will happen to my kids? What will people think of me? These and hundreds of other fears flood us with more than we can handle. So we're tempted to stay in "la-la land," believing that somehow we'll never have to face the truth.

For me, my religious formula fed my denial. I didn't tell anyone what was going on, because I feared what they would think. I wanted to protect my image as "a good Christian," not only with others, but also with myself. I was sure God would work a miracle to save my marriage. I fantasized about how wonderful it would be when my wife repented and returned home, realizing how wrong she had been.

Some people use their religious faith to prolong denial far longer than is healthy. I met one woman at a Fresh Start seminar who had been divorced for about fifteen years. Her attendance at the seminar was a first step in trying to deal with the divorce. Her husband had left for another woman and married that woman as soon as the divorce was final. The jilted wife told me she had prayed for her husband's return for fifteen years, confident God would bring him back. The saddest thing was that she had also taught her two young children to pray every day that God would bring their daddy home. Now her kids were teenagers and she was at this seminar, realizing for the first time that her marriage was over and she had to move on with her life.

At a similar seminar on the West Coast, as the speaker was talking about denial, a wedding ring flew past his nose, hit the back wall, and rolled out onto the floor. He reached down and picked it up, saying, "Does this belong to someone here?"

A woman in the back row raised her hand and said, "It used to belong to me. I've been divorced for eight years, and I just now took it off."

That's denial extended to an unhealthy degree.

MAKE IT YOUR OWN

➤ For one woman, denial meant praying every day for her remarried ex's return. For another, it was hanging onto that wedding ring. What symptoms of denial appeared in your life? _____

_____

_____

➤ Are those now past, or are you still doing those things? _____

_____

➤ What fears are or were keeping you from moving on? (List up to three.)

a. _____

b. _____

c. _____

➤ Using a scale from 1 to 10, 10 being most fearful, go back to those three things and grade how afraid they made you.

a. _____

b. _____

c. _____

➤ Do you think God can work a miracle to undo the events that have caused you such pain? Why? _____

_____

_____

Depending on your current attitude, you may have answered yes or no. Either is fine, because God can work all sorts of miracles whether we expect them or not; the question is whether He will choose to do so in your life. He hasn't promised to protect us from painful experiences, despite what my "formula" said. He *has* promised to give us the strength to get through them.

It's not a lack of faith to accept reality. God can work a miracle, but to plan your life on the chance that He will is foolish. The greatest show of faith is to deal with your new reality in the confidence that God will give you strength to do so.

► As honestly as you can, estimate the chances that your marriage can be saved or resurrected apart from such a miracle (100% being "definitely can be"; 0% being "definitely can't be").

Action Point: What action can you take that will indicate you have moved out of denial and are accepting what has happened?

Suggestions:

✳ Removing wedding band

✳ Discarding (or shelving) other mementos

✳ Socializing again

✳ Improving your appearance

✳ Getting a job

✳ Getting involved in a church or community activity

✳ Throwing a party

✳ Talking with your children about the situation

Action Point: Choose some specific action, and write it here and on page 287 (appendix A). _____

_____

► When will you be ready to do it? List a target date here and on page 287. _____

STAGE 2—ANGER

Once I realized *Hey, she's really gone,* I was gripped with fear. I thought, *Oh, no, what am I going to do? How am I going to tell people? I'm in Christian ministry. What am I going to tell the kids in my youth group? What am I going to tell my parents?*

My belief in "the formula," as I described earlier, fed this fear. I was convinced that people would assume I had done something to deserve the problems I was facing. One conversation I had with a well-respected Christian leader confirmed that belief.

"Well," he said when I confided my problem, "what have you been doing wrong? What secret sins do you have in your life?" Those words were devastating. I was bleeding emotionally, and all around me, people were trying to figure out what I had done wrong.

As people began to find out my wife had left, I could no longer serve in a leadership position in my church. I had to resign. And as the word continued to spread, many of the things I feared came true. People were responding negatively to me. That finally helped me break through my denial and into the next stage of the grieving process, anger.

Some people say they waited months or years for their errant spouses to return. I wasn't that patient. After two weeks of trusting God to bring my wife back to me, I was enraged. At whom? Certainly at my wife. At those Christians who were trying to place blame. And at God. That's right. Sometimes I think I was more angry with God than with people. After all, I trusted Him. We had a deal. I was going to put Him first in my life, and He was going to take care of me. He didn't keep His end of the bargain, and I was fuming!

Not only had I lost my wife, but I'd also lost my job, my ministry. My ambitions were dashed. With a Bible college education, there wasn't a lot I was trained for besides Christian ministry. I had no future. I was convinced God could no longer use me.

To pay the bills, I found a job slicing lunch meat in a delicatessen. (I had paid my way through school by doing that type of work.) As you can imagine, that wasn't part of my life's plan. There was nothing wrong with the work itself, but I still resented having to do it. Each day as I went to work, I was reminded of how far I was from where I wanted to be. On many occasions, I shook my fist at God and yelled, "Leave me alone!"

That anger was often transferred to other Christians. I felt they were rejecting me. And if that's what Christianity was all about, I didn't want any part of it. As time passed, I became angrier and angrier.

MAKE IT YOUR OWN

➤ How angry are you? On a scale of 1 to 10 (10 being extremely angry), rate your level of anger over the last month. _____

➤ With whom are you angry? (Check all that apply.)

❏ Spouse/ex-spouse
❏ Friends/ex-friends
❏ Family
❏ Church
❏ God
❏ Yourself
❏ Add others if you wish: _____

➤ Using that same 1 to 10 scale, go back and rate how angry you are at each of the ones you checked above.

➤ How many of those did you check? Three? Four? Relax. You're normal. It's not uncommon for people who have been through what you've been through to be mad at everyone.

You'll find an anger inventory included as Appendix D at the end of this workbook. Now might be a good time for you to take the test and see how you score. You may even want to take it several times over the next year or so to see whether you're growing less angry.

➤ Is it wrong to be angry? The Bible offers some interesting insight: "Be angry, and do not sin" (Eph. 4:26; also Ps. 4:4). How would you put that in your own words? _____

_____

_____

➤ What about anger at God? Surely that's wrong, isn't it? How can we get mad at the all-righteous Ruler of the universe?

Yet the Bible shows many instances of people spouting off at God— many of them people portrayed as heroes of the faith. Abraham, Moses, David, Jeremiah, and others let God know what they were really feeling, even if they were steaming.

Many of the psalms—the hymns of ancient Israel—express anger and disappointment with God. In light of that, use the space below to write a letter to one of the objects of anger you checked above. It could even be a letter to God. This letter should honestly express your feelings of anger or whatever. *Do not send it, however.* This exercise will help you get some of your feelings out on paper. You don't need to confront others with it yet. (*Note:* If you have a hard time with pen and paper, get a cassette recorder and tape your letter.)

Dear _____,

_____

_____

_____

_____

_____

_____

Clearly, anger isn't necessarily wrong. It's a God-given emotion. It's how we *deal with* our anger that gets us in trouble. I believe in my heart that God understood why I was angry with Him.

As I cried out to Him, "Why did You do this to me?," He knew what was in my heart, and He forgave whatever needed forgiving. God understood my feelings because His own Son, Jesus Christ, yelled out as He hung on the cross, "My God, My God, why have You forsaken Me?" (Mark 15:34). Jesus understood the pain and rejection I was experiencing.

There are four basic ways for us to deal with our anger. The first two are negative, the other two positive.

1. *Rage.* We all know the devastating effects of rage. Most studies have shown that it leads only to more anger. It is certainly one way of venting your emotions, but it can compound your anger until you've lost control. (Interestingly, while women's anger may be just as intense, men tend to express it more often in rage.)

I remember instances when I vented my anger on a door, a wall, or my knuckles. In one case, I really thought I had lost it. The furniture was gradually being removed from our house. I would eventually be moving anyway, and I had agreed to all the changes. But still, each night as I saw the rooms grow more and more bare, the reality of my situation was eating away at me. One night I came home to a house completely empty except for the bedroom. My emotions erupted, and I overturned the mattress, knocked pictures off the walls, and generally dismantled the room. Then I lay there, totally exhausted. I looked around and thought, *Who's gonna clean up this mess?*

That's the problem with rage. It usually just gets us in trouble or creates more of a mess. That goes for relationships as well as objects. And it's usually easier to patch a wall than a friendship.

> **Anger, in itself, is not wrong. God understands how we feel.**

MAKE IT YOUR OWN

➤ On what occasions have you used violent rage to express your anger?

_____

_____

➤ How did you feel when it happened? _____

_____

➤ What were the consequences? _____
_____
_____

➤ If you could go back to those moments of rage, would you try to act differently? If so, how? _____
_____
_____

2. *Repression.* Repression seems to be a nicer option, but it can also be harmful. Instead of venting our anger, we hold it inside. When people ask how we're doing, we smile and say, "Just fine." But inside we feel as if our guts have been ripped out. I repressed my anger a lot longer than I should have. For at least six months, maybe a year, I felt as if somebody were wringing a dishrag in the pit of my stomach. The feeling was there when I got up in the morning and still there when I went to bed at night. I felt it for so long that I didn't remember what life was like without it.

I went to work, slicing lunch meat and mumbling to myself, "Why do I have to wait on these stupid people?"

Customers would say, "Could you cut that bologna a little thinner?"

I'd give them a big smile and answer, "I'd love to." But inside, I wanted to take the bologna and hit them over the head.

Isn't repression better than rage? Not necessarily. It's certainly not healthier. Studies have shown that repression reduces your body's ability to defend itself from disease, stress, and fatigue. You may be knocking years off your life. As I went through my divorce, particularly in the early stages, I had more colds, flu, headaches, and backaches than usual. All that repression was taking a toll on my body. Today I would guess that all that holding back probably shortened my life by about three years. I'll let you know when I'm seventy-five.

> **Repression may seem like a better option than rage, but in the long run it can be just as destructive.**

MAKE IT YOUR OWN

➤ How has your physical health been since the divorce crisis began? Normal? Better than normal? Worse than normal? _____

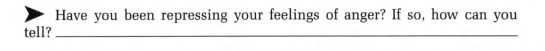

> Have you been repressing your feelings of anger? If so, how can you tell? _____

_____

_____

3. *Redirection.* A better approach is to take all your angry energy and redirect it into something positive or productive. Ultimately, in most cases of anger, the most-positive thing you can do is to go to the person with whom you're angry and resolve the problem. But let's face it—when you're going through a divorce, it's nearly impossible to resolve your anger with your ex.

Like many, your anger may be so intense that you can't even imagine having a civilized conversation, let alone resolving your disputes. Give yourself some time. Eventually, you should reach a point of acceptance and forgiveness. In the meantime, you can redirect your feelings into helpful activities.

Step 1: Start small. Some might join a health club to improve their physiques. Others might sink their energies into night school, their job, or some hobby. It can be extremely satisfying to do something positive with your life when everything else seems so bleak.

In my case, I knew I had to find something to take my mind off my troubles. I'd come home from work, eat a bowl of cereal, and watch TV. I couldn't sleep, so I'd toss and turn in bed or watch more TV. Then I thought, *I've got to do something. Well, I've always wanted to finish the basement. Why don't I make it into a recreation room?*

So after work, I'd come home and pound nails into the concrete walls. I'd work until 2 A.M. and then sleep like a baby. The next day I'd come home, pound more nails, and sleep some more. After about six months of work, I could look at something worthwhile that I had accomplished. I had turned my angry energy into something positive. I had redirected.

Step 2: Invest in people. There's a limit to the satisfaction a good physique or a finished basement can bring you. Eventually you need to get involved in the lives of other people.

Take, for example, the Fresh Start program. It was founded by a group of people who were angry about the way churches dealt with divorce. Instead of "torching" insensitive churches, they started seminars to help church people cope with divorce's trauma. Most of the people who volunteer their services to Fresh Start are divorced people who are redirecting their anger. Some lead support groups; others provide food. But they all tell me they get a tremendous feeling of fulfillment from helping others who are facing the same trauma they went through.

Another example would be MADD—Mothers Against Drunk Drivers—founded by women who've had children killed by people driving while intoxicated. Their grief would naturally have led to anger, and some might have been tempted to take a .357 Magnum and blow away the guilty driver. But they rechanneled their anger into more-positive outlets, changing laws and public awareness throughout the country.

MAKE IT YOUR OWN

➤ In what small way (step 1) can you begin to redirect your anger? Is there a project you could take on, a new hobby or activity? _____

_____

_____

➤ How can you redirect your energy to help other people who are hurting? (Suggestions: church involvement, inviting other divorced people to dinner, being aware of hurting people at work, Prison Fellowship, Habitat for Humanity, the Red Cross, other volunteer organizations) _____

_____

_____

➤ Do you feel ready to do this now? If not, when do you think you'll be ready? _____

_____

Caution: Don't rush into "people" ministry too soon. That may burn you out and not help anyone. Start your redirection in small, personal ways.

4. *Resolution.* The fourth way to handle anger, resolution, should be our ultimate goal. If you're newly divorced or separated, you may not be able to resolve things right now. It will take time. If you try too soon, you may just end up screaming at your ex or soaking yourself in guilt. But the time will come when you can resolve your anger with that person.

You'll find yourself saying something like, "I did a lot of things wrong. I would like you to forgive me. And I've also felt angry for a lot of things. May I share some of these feelings with you? Let me tell you what some of those were...."

That sounds like Mission Impossible, right? But you'll reach that point eventually.

➤ As you evaluate your angry feelings, which of the "4 R's" have you used most: rage, repression, redirection, or resolution? Why? _____

_____

_____

_____

➤ How has your anger (and the ways you've chosen to deal with it) affected: your relationships with friends? _____

_____

_____

➤ your family life? _____

_____

_____

➤ your daily work? _____

_____

_____

➤ your health? _____

_____

_____

➤ your attitude in general? _____

_____

_____

➤ your relationship with God? _____

_____

_____

➤ Can you reverse any of these effects through redirection or resolution? If so, how? _____

_____

_____

_____

_____

➤ List by name some of the people (besides your ex-spouse) you're angry with. _____

_____

_____

➤ Can you resolve those feelings with any of these? If so, how? _____

_____

_____

_____

➤ With whom will you start? _____

_____

EXAMPLE

Resolution might be as simple as this: "Marilyn, we used to do a lot of things together as couples. But since my divorce, it seems that you and Don have avoided me. I understand you probably feel uncomfortable about the breakup, but I've really needed your friendship. These have been rough times. I must admit I've felt pretty angry with you for shutting me out like that, and I may have said some unkind things in passing. But I'd like to patch things up and be friends again. What can I do to do this?"

BARGAINING

Before we discuss the third stage of grief, let me make something clear. The five stages don't necessarily occur *in the order presented here.* You could jump from denial to acceptance and then slip back to anger. It wouldn't even be unusual for you to go through all five stages in the same day.

The third stage, bargaining, can best be explained as trying to find a simple solution to a complex problem. It's like using a microwave for a crockpot recipe. We want to settle it all *right now.*

In my case, I found that denial wasn't helping and my anger only made things worse. I was desperate for answers. I hurt so much that I thought I would try almost anything to make the pain go away. Such desperation makes many people turn to drugs, alcohol, or shallow relationships.

How can I make this pain go away? I asked myself as I worked at the deli. I was smiling to the customers but dying inside. Finally I concluded that the solution was to get my wife to come back home. Everything would then be wonderful. My marriage would be saved. I could go back to church, and everyone would praise God for the miracle He had done in my life. And of course everyone would like me again. So I began to bargain.

I called my wife and gave her an offer she couldn't refuse. "Just come back home and I promise I'll never ask you about *him* again. In fact, we can go on from here as if the past year or so never happened."

You're probably thinking I was a fool to say that. And maybe I was. But many people find themselves in similar straits, desperate for a solution, grabbing at a fantasy. My fantasy was that we would live happily ever after. Our church would welcome us back. I would be the best husband ever and win her eternal love.

Reality, however, usually paints a different picture. Those trial separations rarely, if ever, work out.

You can probably predict the outcome of my efforts. My wife moved back in, and the first night was great. Candlelight dinner, flowers—all the things I knew she liked. We were well on the way to making this work—until day two, when she came home late from work.

"Where were you?" I asked.

"What do you mean, 'Where was I?' You told me you weren't going to ask."

"Well, I'm asking now. Where were you!"

"I'm not going to stand here and be interrogated about my day. It's none of your business where I was."

"None of my business? Well, if you think..."

You could write the rest of that script. The trial reconcilation lasted about one week. In fact, we had *three* trial reconciliations that each ended in similar disaster.

But shouldn't we work for reconciliation at any cost? That's a hard question. At Fresh Start, we believe that reconciliation is God's desire for our lives, but we also recognize it's a very difficult process. It takes two people who are willing to take a hard look at all their issues and then begin working on them one at a time with a counselor or other neutral party. The problems take years to develop; they certainly will not be solved in a few days.

And what *is* reconciliation? It's more than a plea to "just move back home." In fact, in many situations that can be a very negative, sometimes dangerous, option. When there has been abuse, drug use, alcohol abuse, or

---

True reconciliation requires changes in attitudes and behavior. It's not merely a matter of moving back in together.

even an affair, you shouldn't let your spouse move back in and pretend nothing has happened. Look beyond his or her words; watch for changes in behavior, along with a willingness to work on the issue. (The question of reconciliation is important and complex. We'll deal with it more fully in the next chapter.)

MAKE IT YOUR OWN

➤ In what ways have you bargained with your spouse (or ex-spouse)? Go through the following list, and put an M (for "me") next to any lines you've tried yourself. Then go through again, putting H (for "her" or "him") next to those your spouse tried with you.

_____ "I promise it will never happen again if you just love me."

_____ "I'll never take another drink (do drugs again) if you come home."

_____ "This time I'll put you first in my life if you just trust me."

_____ "I never realized how good I had it. I'll never take you for granted again."

_____ "I've really changed. My temper is under control now. Let me come home, and I'll prove it to you."

_____ "If you just go to two counseling sessions with me, I'll give you whatever you want."

_____ "Just let me have the kids. I'll sign any agreement as long as I can keep them."

What other lines could you add? _____

_____

_____

_____

➤ In general, how did this bargaining turn out?

_____ We both kept the bargain, and things turned out great.

_____ We both kept the bargain, but things fell apart anyway.

_____ I tried to keep my end of the bargain, but I was trading away important aspects of my identity. I couldn't do it.

_____ I just botched my end of the bargain.

_____ The other person reneged on his/her end of the bargain.

_____ It was a bad bargain to begin with. It fell apart.

Other: _____

_____

Bargaining with God

We don't bargain only with our spouses, we also bargain with God. "God, if You just help me through this, if You just solve this problem, I'll dedicate my life and my marriage to You." Such reasoning reminds me of the movie *The End*, starring Burt Reynolds. It's a comedy in which Burt's character wants to die, but he can't do anything right—even his attempts to kill himself fail. At the end of the movie, he's finally alone at the beach, and he decides to swim out to sea. He gets out rather far, takes a deep breath, and puts his head under water. But as he's waiting there, facing the reality of his own death, he realizes, *Hey, I don't want to die. I want to live!*

So he starts swimming to shore, but the current is against him. He looks toward the distant shoreline and cries, "Oh, God, please help me! Help me get back. I gotta get back to shore!"

The current continues taking him out to sea. In desperation, he pleads, "God, if you get me out of this one, I'll give 50 percent of everything I make to you, God. No, I'll give 80 percent of everything, and I'll..."

While he's still bargaining with God, the tide begins to shift directions, and he realizes he's being washed toward shore. As soon as he knows he's close enough to make it back, he says, "Never mind, God. I've got it now."

So is it wrong to bargain? Not necessarily. It's a natural way to deal with a crisis. We're trying to seize some control of an out-of-control situation. It can be a healthy step toward wholeness. But we should be careful not to make stupid mistakes at this stage. It's possible to trade away your fortune, your dignity, your self-esteem, and even your faith when you are in the desperate stage of bargaining. Such transactions seldom save a relationship. They merely impoverish the traders.

MAKE IT YOUR OWN

➤ Have you bargained with God about your marital troubles? If so, what have you offered Him? _____

_____

➤ What have you asked from Him? Has this bargaining process improved your relationship with God or hurt it? _____

_____

➤ How do you feel about God right now?

___ Angry ___ Confused ___ Cynical ___ Trusting
___ Humble ___ Doubting ___ Sympathetic ___ Hopeful
Other: _____

➤ What stupid mistakes do you need to watch out for in this bargaining stage? Or what stupid mistakes have you already made? _____
_____
_____
_____

➤ How would you describe your present situation?

___ I've been in denial, and I've been angry, and now I need to take control of things through bargaining.

___ I feel pretty sure that we both can make some changes and get back together.

___ Bargaining probably won't work, but I'm desperate.

___ What does he/she want? I keep searching for the right thing to make him/her love me again.

___ At this point, I'm not worth loving. He/she has used me and discarded me.

___ Does "getting run over by a Mack truck" mean anything to you?

DEPRESSION—THE FOURTH STAGE

What happens when we finally realize we can't bargain our way back to the blissful marriage we once had? Some go back to denial or anger, but many move on to depression. They hit bottom.

Has that happened to you yet? You realize all your efforts are futile. You're totally helpless to change the other person or your own situation. That's depressing!

In my case, I could no longer deny the reality of my impending divorce, and my anger only made me feel worse. Bargaining proved to me that I couldn't maneuver my way out of my problems, so I was left with the conclusion that nothing I could do made any difference. I wanted to give up on everything, including life.

I was convinced I would never be loved again. I would never be happy again. And I would never be used by God again. Basically, my life was over. So I resigned myself to mere existence. For the rest of my life, I wouldn't live; I would just *be*.

In much of the recovery literature, you will read the phrase "You've got to hit bottom before you can look up." That's also the way it is when you go through the grieving process. You must come to a point where you bottom out, where you just give up and say, "There's nothing more I can do."

The timing of this depression varies from person to person, and its length depends on your personality. For me, it hit about six months after my wife left. As I've mentioned, we had a few trial reconciliations, getting back together for a week, then splitting up again. That drew out the healing process; each time, I had a roller coaster ride of hope and despair.

Through it all, I learned I was helpless. I couldn't change my wife, my friends, my work situation, or the mortgage payment on my house. It all added up to more than I could handle by myself, and yet I couldn't bring myself to trust other people or God. Instead of reaching out to anyone, I withdrew all the more.

I stayed in my depression a lot longer than necessary. The lifestyle I chose wasn't helping any—go to work, come home, eat a bowl of cereal, go to bed. I didn't go out, use the phone, or make new friends. This formula kept me anchored in depression for at least a year. At times I thought I'd be better-off dead, and yet a part of me was determined to go on.

I also had this feeling that it was wrong for me to be so depressed. My Christian background had taught me the importance of joy. The gospel, I had learned, is good news for people in need. But during that year, the news was not good. Joy was far away. And I felt a bit guilty about that, which only added to my depression. I had slipped through the cracks of God's will. I was emotionally in a place where I did not belong.

This next statement may seem incorrect to you, but stay with me. *It is not entirely wrong to be depressed.* Depression, too, is a natural stage in the grieving process. It's a necessary "hitting bottom." It can be a time of rigorous self-examination, of a reordering of priorities. In depression, we learn we can't trust false promises or shallow friends. All the tricks we've tried to make people like us, to get by in this world, now seem useless because they *are* useless. To escape this, we need to get down to basics. We need to grow. As the narrator says in the play *The Fantasticks*: "We all must die a bit before we grow again."

I don't want to minimize depression or imply it's no big deal. It can be a very big deal, especially if there's a history of depression in your family, if you've had an extended period of depression, or if you've had serious suicidal thoughts. If any of those describes what you've been experiencing, you need to talk with a professional counselor as soon as possible. If you don't know of someone in your area, ask your physician or pastor for a referral. Or look in your phone book for a local mental health center.

If you're a Christian, you may be asking, "What about joy and good news and all that? Isn't it morally wrong to be in this depression?" No. the Bible portrays a range of emotions. Jacob, Moses, David, Nehemiah, Hosea, Jonah, Paul, and others sometimes showed signs of depression. The Psalms show clearly that we can be honest about our feelings. We'll all have ups and downs. God is with us throughout, even when He seems far away.

MAKE IT YOUR OWN

➤ In what ways might depression be good for you? _____

_____

_____

Some people are word people. Others are more visual. Here's a chance to play with your artistic side. On the next page you see a figure of a person. That's the beginning of a drawing you'll do entitled "My Depression." Don't worry about artistic excellence. No one is grading this. The drawing can be as abstract or realistic as you like. Draw how you feel.

Moving Through Depression

There are several very positive aspects of depression. That might sound strange, especially if you're in the midst of it, in which case it's hard to think of anything good in *any* area of your life. But let's put things in perspective.

In my case, depression was exactly what I needed. I had been striving for too long, convinced I was "going to do something about this." I needed a break from the stress and turmoil. Depression gave me that temporary pause, some much-needed rest, and some peace of mind.

In addition, it was the first stage in which I was dealing with my situation realistically. I was no longer denying. I was no longer blaming everyone else for my problem. I was no longer trying to bargain my way out. I was finally facing the truth. My marriage was over, and I needed to come to terms with that reality. It was a depressing thought, but it was the truth.

This is the point when many people seek help. They have exhausted their own efforts. Some lean on God in a special way. Some will now choose to see a counselor or open up to friends. I've talked to many who decided to attend the Fresh Start seminar only when they reached this stage.

Another positive aspect of depression is the self-examination that often occurs. Up to this stage, the focus is on everyone else.

* "If only she hadn't..."

* "If God would just answer my prayer,..."

* "Those hypocritical Christians, they..."

* "My in-laws started this whole mess."

I reached a point where I realized, *Hey, my wife was involved with someone else for six months before I even knew there was a problem. What kind of communicator was I? How much was I in touch with her needs and feelings? Maybe I wasn't the wonderful husband I thought I was.*

I'm not saying we should bathe ourselves in guilt. That does happen to people in depression when it goes too far. But we should get a realistic picture of what happened. We need to stop blaming other people and begin to look at ourselves. That can be a very positive step. After all, the *only* person you and I can really change is ourselves. I finally got to the point where I said, *Maybe there's something about me that I need to work on.* And that was my first step *out* of depression. I was learning to accept my breakup and move on.

MAKE IT YOUR OWN

► Since your marital troubles began, how much time have you spent in depression? _____

► Which of the following symptoms have you experienced? (Put a 3 if it's a severe problem, 2 if moderate, 1 for a slight problem.)

_____ trouble sleeping

_____ lethargy/boredom

_____ working too hard

_____ inability to concentrate on work

_____ loneliness

_____ inability to talk with other people

_____ need to be with others all the time

_____ susceptibility to colds, flu

_____ ulcer, digestion problems

_____ addictive/compulsive behavior

_____ spiritual apathy

_____ sudden weight gain

_____ sudden weight loss

Total your score. If it's ten or more, you probably need to seek some professional help from a doctor or counselor; six to nine, keep an eye on it.

► As you look back at your marital troubles now, what percentage would you say was your fault, what percentage was your spouse's fault, and what percentage was due to other factors?

You: _____   Your Spouse: _____   Other Factors: _____

► Explain what other factors were involved. _____

_____

_____

_____

▶ Cross out the numbers you listed for your spouse and other factors. There's nothing you can do about those. What was involved in the percentage of the problem that was *your* fault? What did you do wrong? (List no more than three things you did wrong.)

1. _____

   _____

2. _____

   _____

3. _____

   _____

▶ What can you do to improve in each of those areas. How can you make it less likely that you would do those things wrong again? Find one action step you can take in the next month to improve in each area. (Note that this step will probably not get rid of the problem totally, but it should make things somewhat better.)

Action Steps

1. _____

   _____

2. _____

   _____

3. _____

   _____

▶ Name one friend who might help by encouraging you to follow through on these steps. _____ When can you ask for that person's help? _____

ACCEPTANCE—THE FIFTH STAGE

Acceptance. It's easier said than done. Most people claim to be in the acceptance stage long before they actually are. We usually think we've arrived, or nearly arrived, when something comes along and throws us down the slippery slope again.

I finally moved out of depression by forcing myself to get out of bed and develop some new relationships. Most of my previous friends were married, and many were unsympathetic about my condition. I suppose there were several community activities where I could have chosen to get involved with new people, but I felt most comfortable in church. So I decided to start attending a church that had a strong singles program. I also heard they had a specific ministry to divorced people.

I really had no desire to attend programs for divorced people. In my mind, I was beyond all that. More than two years had passed since my wife had left. I was certainly over it—or so I thought. Besides, I didn't want to be associated with those who were down and out and probably hurting. So my attitude toward that group was ambivalent at first. But at least, I figured, they would have a heart for a divorced person like me.

You might think a hunger for spiritual growth drove me to find a church. No, it was nothing so noble. I just wanted to meet people again. I was coming out of hiding. I was going to take some risks again. This was a good sign that my depression was nearly ended.

Another good sign was that I was finally taking responsibility for my own healing. My attitude had changed from "Look what she did to me" to "Come on, stop lying around and *do something!*"

I was also gaining some objectivity about my wife and the divorce—even apathy. Some people think they're "over" their ex-spouses because they hate them. But the hate is a way of holding on. As long as your ex can ruin your day or still "push your buttons," you're still working through the matter. Freedom is found in a kind of indifference.

That may sound harsh, but it's necessary for divorced people to free themselves from the emotional ties to their ex-spouses. I remember when I first sensed my own freedom in this regard. In the beginning, I avoided going to the local mall, fearing I'd run into my ex-wife. Then one day, about two years after the breakup, I found myself shopping there. It suddenly occurred to me, *Hey, what if I see her here?* It was only a brief moment of panic, however, because I realized it didn't really matter. *If I see her here,* I told myself calmly, *I'll just say hi.* It was no big deal anymore. She no longer had the ability to upset my life.

Reaching this stage may be especially difficult if you and your ex are sharing custody of children. The kids often become weapons or battle-grounds in the continuing struggle between former spouses. There's a tendency to fight the same old battles over and over again.

For instance, the ex-husband brings the kids home late. The ex-wife thinks, *That's just like him, always late. Totally irresponsible. Just like when he left us for that other woman.* And the ex-husband thinks, *That's just like her, totally inflexible. Always nagging. I'm sure glad I got out of there.*

But if you've reached the point of acceptance, you don't need to rerun those scenes. The relationship is redefined. Your ex's personality flaws are not your problem anymore. You may need to deal with some issues of how the children are cared for, but you must carefully separate those issues from the original marital conflict.

Acceptance can probably be best summarized in the words of the apostle Paul: "I have learned in whatever state I am, to be content" (Phil. 4:11). That's a great survival strategy. If you're now divorced, you need to learn to be content. When you reach that point of acceptance, you will no longer be waiting for the damage of your divorce to be magically undone; you will no longer be raging at your ex; you will no longer be desperately bargaining to turn back the clock; you will no longer be down in the dumps, waiting for some far-off day when you'll finally be happy.

No, you will carve a contentment out of your present situation. You'll say to yourself, *I never would have chosen to be in this state, but now I accept it and move on. I will try to make the most of my life as a divorced person.*

Remember, this will take time. I'm not trying to jolt you into acceptance if you haven't yet dealt with your denial or anger. But acceptance is where you're headed. It may take two years. I've talked with people who took five to ten years to get there. The key to recovery is in making wise decisions now about how you're going to live and what you're going to believe about yourself. We'll deal with those questions in future chapters.

> **The key to recovery is in making wise decisions now about how you're going to live and what you're going to believe about yourself.**

MAKE IT YOUR OWN

➤ I just talked about finding freedom in indifference. How indifferent are you now about your ex-spouse? Rate yourself on a scale of 0 (totally indifferent) to 100 (he/she still affects my emotions greatly). _____

➤ When you do reach that point of acceptance (which may be another year or two down the road), what do you think your life will be like? In five to ten sentences, describe yourself at that future point. What will be different between then and now? _____

_____

_____

_____

_____

_____

_____

▶ Look back at the diagram of the slippery slope on page 17. Based on what you've read in this chapter, where would you put yourself *right now* on that chart? Mark the spot with an X.

▶ If you like, try to rate your progress through the past year (or since your troubles began). Where were you *a year ago*? Mark that with an A.

Where were you *six months ago*? Mark that with a B.

Where were you *three months ago*? Mark that with a C.

Where were you *one month ago*? Mark that with a D.

Note that many people do not progress through the stages of grief in an orderly manner. There's a lot of bouncing around. Sometimes this bouncing is caused by specific events that set you back or propel you forward. Mark any influential events of the past year that have affected your recovery.

▶ Despite those events and the bouncing they may have caused, you may still find a general pattern in your life over the past year. What can you learn from the chart you've just made? Are you moving forward or backward? Are you moving quickly or slowly? _____

_____

_____

_____

▶ Based on that chart, where do you think you'll be three months from now? _____

_____

POSTLUDE

To conclude my own story, little by little, I began to take chances and develop new relationships. I had to start trusting and believing in people again. And as I did, I also began to think that maybe God was still working in my life. Maybe God wasn't finished with me. I began to notice divorced people who were in Christian ministry. Their lives weren't over! In fact, because of what they had been through, they were doing even *more* to help people.

God has kept working with me, however, and healing me. Today, He has given me a ministry that goes far beyond my wildest dreams. Through my painful experiences, He's helping many other hurting people, children and adults. I can honestly say that I have gotten back much more than I lost. I pray that someday you, too, will be able to say, "I wouldn't wish divorce on my worst enemy, but I wouldn't trade anything for what I've learned going through it."

Action Point: Fill out the following adjective checklist, and see how you score. We'll have you fill out the same checklist again at the end of the notebook (see Appendix B) so you can chart your progress.

Place a checkmark next to all the adjectives that describe how you feel right now. Read through the list by reading across the columns from left to right.

☐ angry	☐ annoyed	☐ ambivalent	☐ amused	☐ attractive
☑ anxious	☑ bored	☐ apathetic	☐ brave	☐ bright
☐ ashamed	☑ cheated	☐ collected	☐ calm	☐ confident
☐ bitter	☐ confused	☐ hesitant	☐ contented	☐ delighted
☐ defeated	☐ dejected	☐ disinterested	☐ engaged	☐ excited
☐ depressed	☐ detached	☐ different	☑ funny	☐ fulfilled
☐ disgusted	☐ discouraged	☐ glib	☑ grateful	☐ glad
☐ foolish	☐ empty	☐ interested	☑ helpful	☐ happy
☐ guilty	☑ exhausted	☐ hopeful	☐ interested	☐ inspired
☐ hateful	☐ helpless	☑ impatient	☐ involved	☑ independent
☐ inferior	☐ hurt	☐ indifferent	☐ joyful	☐ jubilant
☐ insecure	☐ irritated	☑ judged	☐ loyal	☐ loved
☑ lonely	☑ jealous	☐ at peace	☐ optimistic	☐ overjoyed
☐ miserable	☐ misunderstood	☐ misguided	☑ neglected	☑ needy
☐ overwhelmed	☐ nervous	☐ neutral	☐ pleased	☐ powerful
☐ pessimistic	☐ phony	☑ preoccupied	☐ relieved	☐ resilient
☐ rejected	☐ puzzled	☐ quiet	☐ respectful	☐ satisfied
☑ resentful	☐ restless	☐ reluctant	☐ romantic	☐ secure
☐ sadistic	☐ sad	☑ sexual	☐ sexy	☑ smart
☐ stupid	☐ sorry	☐ shy	☐ supported	☐ strong
☐ suicidal	☐ selfish	☐ silly	☑ thankful	☑ touched
☐ terrible	☐ tense	☐ surprised	☐ tough	☐ trusting
☐ ugly	☑ unappreciated	☐ unsure	☑ useful	☐ whole
☐ unhappy	☐ upset	☑ weary	☐ welcome	☐ well
☐ violent	☐ worried	☐ questioning	☐ willing	☐ wise

To score:

1. Add all the checks in vertical column 1, and then multiply that number by (-4).
2. Add all the checks in vertical column 2, and then multiply that number by (-2).
3. Add all the checks in vertical column 3, and then multiply that number by zero. (Total for column 3 will always equal zero.)
4. Add all the checks in column 4, and then multiply the total by 2.
5. Add all the checks in column 5, and then multiply the total by 4.

Total your score from the five columns to see if your overall feelings are overwhelmingly negative (indicated by a high negative score), basically neutral, or overwhelmingly positive. This score may not reflect anything more than how you were feeling when you took the test. But it will be helpful to take the test again at the end of the book and compare the two scores.

Enter your total score here: ____6____

CHAPTER 2

THE SEPARATION/ RECONCILIATION STRUGGLE

"I can't believe it," Brian said. "My wife got a restraining order to kick me out of my own house."

Brian is a pastor friend of many years. I knew his marriage had been strained, but I had no idea it had come to the point of separation.

His experience is more and more common in the church and in society. There is no simple answer for why spouses separate. Every separation, like every divorce, is unique in character and reason.

If you're currently separated, you know the pain and confusion involved. This section of the workbook will help you confront some crucial issues.

If separation is now behind you and your divorce is final, you may still want to work through this section. Lingering feelings from the separation may still need to be worked through. Sometimes divorced people carry a residue of guilt for not "trying harder" during that time of separation, for "giving up hope too soon." If that's true of you, this chapter will help you deal with your own second-guessing.

If such issues are long past for you, however, feel free to skip to chapter 3.

LIVING IN NEVER-NEVER LAND

My pastor friend Brian quickly learned that separation is one of the most difficult and stressful experiences in life. On the slippery slope of divorce recovery, separation wraps up all the confusion of denial, anger, bargaining, and depression.

"Sometimes I feel like I'm having an 'out of body' experience," Brian said. "I really can't believe this is happening to me. To make matters worse, people don't know how to deal with me." Brian's experience is normal. Some friends consider your separation as a prelude to divorce. Others view it only as a time of marital difficulty.

"Who cares what others think!" I told Brian. "You're the one being torn apart by this never-never land of separation. You have to live between reconciliation and the death of your marriage."

Perhaps you're like Brian, emotionally strung out by your separation and needing to marshal your resources to cope with the circumstances. Unfortunately, your strength has been sapped by the difficulties of the moment. And your friends? Most of them mean well, but they tend to pull away, uncertain of what to say or how to act.

Making the Most of the Process

Making it through the separation process requires time and effort. And most of us aren't ready for that kind of work. As I said in the last chapter, when my wife left me, I was distraught. I was emotionally, physically, and spiritually drained. And I was defensive, often unwilling to receive any help.

Separation reminds me of an emotional roller coaster. Just when you think you're going to make it to the top, you slide even more rapidly back down into that emotional pit of despair. Then you determine once again that you're not going to let this problem defeat you, so you start climbing back up the hill again.

Through my own experience, and in working with many others, I've learned that it's easy to give in to our feelings and let them dictate how we act. However, that's not productive. Separation is a time to get a handle on our feelings and recognize our future well-being is not determined by the present circumstances. I well remember the feeling that I knew I could get through the next few days, but that when I thought about a year or two down the road, I couldn't imagine how I could make it that far.

The key is to begin by taking just one day at a time and making the most of our present situation. We do this by assuming personal responsibility for our future and making decisions that support this commitment.

When I explained this to Brian, he didn't know how to take it. "Wait a minute," he said. "I didn't want this separation. It's her decision. How can you say that I'm responsible for my future?"

I understood what Brian was feeling. A big struggle during separation is that one partner seems to be doing what he wants, while the other simply has to take it. I told Brian that while his wife made a decision to separate, he's still responsible for his attitude and his actions. She could not control or manipulate him in those areas. Brian and I then discussed the fact that responsible attitudes and actions develop from a good understanding of ourselves.

> *Even if the other person has instigated the separation or divorce, we're still responsible for our own attitudes and actions.*

MAKE IT YOUR OWN

➤ I describe the state of separation as a "never-never land." In what other ways would you describe it? _____

_____

➤ If you are now divorced, how long did your separation last? If you're still separated, how long has it been so far? (*Note:* I'm not concerned about legalities here. I want you to write down how long it was from the time you first felt separated to the moment you realized your marriage would not recover, or to the present moment if there's still hope.) _____

_____

➤ Understandably, many aspects of your present situation are due to the decisions of your spouse (or ex-spouse). But still it's important to *take responsibility for your own attitudes and actions.* What attitudes and actions am I talking about?

ATTITUDES	ACTIONS
1. To let go of past hurts.	1. Do not bring up the old issues whenever I see him/her.
2. _____	2. _____

ATTITUDES	*ACTIONS*
3. _____	3. _____
_____	_____
4. _____	4. _____
_____	_____

▶ How can you be responsible for those? _____

_____

_____

_____

UNDERSTANDING YOURSELF

As we've seen, the time of separation can produce a great deal of confusion. Therefore, as we move through this transition, it's important to understand and accept what we're going through. For example, I recently took a plane trip to a distant city. After I landed, I *intellectually* understood the change of my location. However, I still *felt* disoriented and out of sorts. It took a good night's sleep to reorient my body's equilibrium with my new location.

In a similar way, it's possible for you to understand the factual reality of separation while not gaining equilibrium between the facts and your feelings.

Facing the Facts

Therefore, the first step in understanding is to "own" where we are in the process of separation and be honest with ourselves about it. As some wise person once said, "No one can ever work on a solution until he is aware of the problem."

That means facing all the possible losses: your mate, your marriage, your way of life, and all the things you have claimed as your own. And it means facing the decisions that inevitably arise during separation. Some of these decisions include:

▶ Will I have to get a job?

▶ Should I retain a lawyer?

> Should I move out or stay in the house?

> Are my children going to stay in the same school(s) or transfer to a new school (or school district)?

> Can I talk to my estranged spouse's parents?

Those are only a few of the questions you might ask. However, until you face the truth of your situation, you can't handle the challenges of separation.

Facing the Feelings

The second step in understanding is to get in touch with your feelings. Separation is a time of great swings on the emotional pendulum. I remember talking to Cindy, who had initiated separation after her husband had a third affair. "One day I walked around the house and tore down every picture of Jack from the walls," she told me. "The next morning, I woke up and immediately saw the stack of pictures in the corner of my bedroom. I broke into tears. Then I found myself slowly rehanging all the pictures!"

There are good reasons for emotional mood swings like the one Cindy described. One reason is the reality of rejection. The separation struggle is often the rejection struggle.

Another reason for changing emotions is a breakdown in marital bonds. Characteristics of love begin to be replaced by characteristics of indifference.

Love has at least three characteristics. The **first** is *trust*. Trust is when you believe in your partner, in her character and her word. You have no need to question her truthfulness. Trust says, "I believe in this person even when the circumstances seem to dictate the opposite." The Bible says, "Love...always trusts" (1 Cor. 13:6-7).

During separation, trust begins to be replaced by mistrust. This is particularly true in cases of unanticipated separation or infidelity. The sense of commitment and loyalty is shattered. Most of the time the offending spouse will have lied to the wronged spouse. Indeed, a secret affair in itself constitutes a major deception. The result is an erosion of ability to believe anything the partner says or to trust your own ability to distinguish truth from falsehood.

The **second** characteristic of love is *idealization*. Before we get married, idealization is superficial. The engaged person thinks, *He is just the right one for me. He understands me. I've only known him for a short time, but I've been able to share more with him than I've ever been able to share with anybody in the world. He understands me!*

After marriage, it doesn't take long for this romantic fallacy to wear off. In a healthy marriage, however, idealization becomes the ability to desire and expect the best from your spouse. It lets you view the circumstances of your life together from the best possible point of view.

The opposite of idealization is disillusionment. You begin to question everything she does or says. You're able to point out all her faults. What would never bother you about others bothers you when you see it in your spouse. I remember talking to one couple who didn't just disagree about how to squeeze a tube of toothpaste—each was absolutely furious over the way the other handled it. Disillusionment had set in!

The **third** characteristic of love is *respect*. Respect implies an admiration of your partner. Even with all your differences, you genuinely appreciate who he is as a person.

The opposite of respect is disrespect or disdain. You question his motives. You don't really like to be around him. You might even question his worth as a human being. One separated spouse confided in me, "I believe my husband is an evil person! I believe he is the most selfish individual in the whole world. I can't even stand being in the same room with him."

During separation we feel a tremendous amount of emotional ambivalence, because we flip-flop between love and indifference. At times it seems as though we're chanting, "I love him. I love him not."

A lawyer who works primarily in the area of divorce, when he sees a new client, usually spends the first session collecting information on the case. He sits with a pad of paper and says, "Tell me your story. How has your marriage come to this point?" Then he takes notes on his client's response. He tells me, "Usually my client describes her spouse as the worst person in the world—a real clone of Adolf Hitler!"

With about ten minutes left in the session, my lawyer friend reviews his notes with the client. "You want to know what happens when I read back what she has been saying?" he says. "As I restate all the problems, the client begins to defend her spouse! She says things like, 'Oh, he's not that bad,' 'I don't appreciate that,' or 'Did I really say that?' When I first started doing divorce cases, this response floored me. Now I recognize it as part of the ambivalence of separation."

MAKE IT YOUR OWN

➤ Let's face facts. As you honestly appraise your situation, what are the chances that your separation will end in divorce? _____

_____

▶ If that happens, what specific changes will occur in your life? Check all that are likely:

- ❏ Lose custody of kids
- ❏ Have to move
- ❏ Financial loss/simplify lifestyle
- ❏ Lose friends
- ❏ Lose job
- ❏ Keep the kids but face major upheaval in their lives
- ❏ Other _____ —

  _____

▶ What decisions will you have to make if you do end up divorced? (You don't need to *make* those decisions now, just list them.) _____

_____

_____

▶ I talk about mood swings. It's common to feel paradoxical emotions in a time like this—feelings that just don't match: happy and sad at the same time, or proud and humble. What pairs of conflicting emotions have you been experiencing? _____

_____

_____

▶ It's natural to move from love to indifference in your feelings toward your spouse. On each of the following lines, put an X where you find yourself right now.

Trust _____ Mistrust
Idealizing _____ Disillusioned
Respect _____ Disdain

GETTING IN TOUCH

A little earlier I said that we must assume personal responsibility for our future. As we face the facts and feelings of our situation, we can do a number of things. A little later in this section we'll discuss making responsible decisions, but right now I want us to understand how to get in touch with our feelings.

As we move back and forth between feelings of love and disillusion-ment, our primary task is to get in touch with our feelings so they won't dominate or dictate our actions. Facing our feelings allows us to concentrate on truth and reality rather than fantasy and fear, to evaluate the validity of our emotions and choose responsible action.

That's not an easy task! It's like trying to grab Jell-O. It squirts and oozes around in your hand. There's nothing solid to hold. In a similar way, feelings tend to be undiagnosed, yet they hold great influence over us.

To illustrate the difficulty, let's look at a recent conversation in which I took part. Some comments were made that I believed were unjust and irresponsible. Unfortunately, the conversation ended before I had a chance to express my viewpoint, and for the rest of the afternoon, I carried unresolved feelings about the discussion. In the frustration that followed, I even found myself kicking doors and lashing out at people. After a few hours of this behavior, I sat down and said, *Why am I acting like this?* I traced it back to the undiagnosed feelings growing out of that conversation.

How can we pinpoint and understand our feelings rather than being controlled by them? The best practical method I know is to begin writing a daily, personal journal. Journaling is an opportunity to:

✳ Record the facts

✳ Reflect on the issues we're going through

✳ Examine the feelings we've had in the midst of those circumstances

✳ Consider the decisions and actions we've taken (or should take) as a result

It helps to find a consistent time in your schedule when you can sit down with your journal and record your thoughts. Some people set aside a time early in the morning. Others prefer late in the evening. Still others set aside two or three times during the day to make their entries. Whenever you chose to do it, the benefits of journaling are greatest when you do it daily.

And what are those benefits? Journaling can do at least three things for you.

First, it *provides a list of what you've been going through.* Your journal becomes a daily record of your experiences and circumstances during the separation. Most lawyers will request that you provide as thorough a ren-dering as possible of what has taken place in your marriage. The journal can provide that accurate data.

Second, journaling *lets you reflect on your circumstances with some clarity.* As you write down your experiences, you begin to think through them for a more-objective point of view. Journaling lets you pull back from the whirlwind of circumstances and review how you've responded to them—

how you've been thinking and acting. You can also consider alternate behavior.

Third, as you reflect on those things, *you can begin to anticipate how you might feel during similar circumstances in the future.* Based on this anticipation of feeling patterns, you can develop a plan for how to manage your feelings.

For example, take Frank, who copes with negative feelings by suppressing them. He acts as if he doesn't have those feelings. As he begins writing in his journal, however, he expresses the feelings on paper. Then he realizes his tendency to suppress his emotions. He acknowledges he's not being honest with himself, and he decides to begin managing his feelings by facing their reality.

Consider Janice, whose boss comes into the office every morning and acts as though she's not even there. Every day she tries to give a friendly greeting, but he just walks right by without comment. Of course, his actions cause her to feel rejection and perhaps anger.

As she writes those facts in her journal, she recognizes her boss's actions have been getting to her for a long time. But she has denied those feelings, hoping things would get better. She realizes she has come upon an important issue, so she begins asking herself questions like the following: How do I feel when the boss walks by and doesn't acknowledge me? Have I ever done anything to make him act like that? How should I respond to him? How would God want me to respond to him? Didn't Jesus teach that we should treat others as we would want them to treat us?

As she reflects on those thoughts, she realizes she feels angry at her boss. Yet she doesn't want her anger to make her treat him in a way that *she* wouldn't want to be treated. So, on the basis of her reflections, she develops a strategy that could include a number of options, including:

✳ Lowering her expectations of her boss.
✳ Praying for him.
✳ Asking him for a five-minute conference to discuss her concerns and see if she has done anything to merit his aloofness.
✳ Turning in her resignation, telling him she doesn't want to work for an insensitive jerk. But would he give her a good recommendation? (We have the freedom to say anything we want in a journal!)

You can see how a journal helps us anticipate our attitudes and actions in the midst of separation. We can begin to review how we'll handle things when our estranged spouse comes by to pick up the children, or how we'll deal with his refusal to pay certain expenses. In the meantime, we're also keeping a record of those circumstances.

Finally, we must understand that the emotional swings of ambivalence will eventually be resolved. Separation will either end in reconciliation or in divorce. Thus, any resolution will leave one set of feelings unsatisfied. If we're reconciled, we'll have to work through the feelings of disillusionment that have developed. If we're divorced, we'll have to face the sorrow of the loss of a bonded partner. Recognize that's the case, and prepare to face those feelings.

Notes on Journal Keeping

✸ Find a regular time each day.

✸ Try to find a place relatively free from distractions.

✸ Be completely honest. Don't judge yourself before you write. Let it all out.

✸ Don't worry about spelling, grammar, or style. Just pour the words from your heart to the page.

✸ Keep your journal private. You'll be more honest if you know you're the only one seeing those words.

✸ From time to time, go back to previous pages and evaluate where you've been and where you're going.

MAKE IT YOUR OWN

➤ What's the best time for you to write in your journal each day? _____

_____

➤ What factors might keep you from doing it? _____

_____

_____

➤ Write here or in your journal how you've been feeling today. _____

_____

_____

_____

_____

Note: This workbook may be a helpful journal starter for you. That is, you may get into the habit of journaling by working through this book a step a day. Then, when you've finished, you can keep the same schedule but be writing your journal instead.

I recommend, however, that you begin the journaling process *now*. Keep the journal *alongside* this workbook. Maybe you could devote your journal time two or three days a week to this workbook, but keep recording your honest feelings regularly.

BALANCED STEPS TOWARD RECONCILIATION

What can we do in the midst of the separation struggle to seek reconciliation responsibly? And how can we develop balanced expectations about whether reconciliation is a possibility? Specific steps can be taken that will either lead us toward reconciliation or show us that reconciliation won't happen.

But at this point you may be asking some moral questions. Is divorce *ever* the best option? Isn't reconciliation *always* the "righteous" choice, whatever the circumstances? I'll talk more about this later, but I need to make one point here. *God always asserts the priority of reconciliation over divorce.* However, as we review the balanced steps toward reconciliation, we need to know that *the rebuilding of a marriage is the choice of* two *people*. God will not hold a person responsible for what others do or fail to do. He holds each person responsible for what she does with her own life (see Ezek. 18).

Many who are separated assume that divorce is the only possible outcome of their circumstances. They're negative pragmatists who only await the completion of the legal process. On the other hand, some assume that reconciliation will inevitably occur. Regardless of the present problems, they maintain a "pie in the sky" optimism.

Pessimism	Hope

▲

Reconciliation must be pursued with expectations that are balanced on this seesaw between hope and pessimism. While affirming the truth that God can work in miraculous ways, we must face the reality of our present marital condition and the potential for divorce.

Even if you didn't initiate the separation, even if you feel you're a victim of circumstances beyond your control, you are not merely a passive participant in the process. You *can* take action. I want to give you a number of steps you can take to develop and maintain balanced expectations for reconciliation.

Rebuilding Self-Esteem

The first step is to work on your own self-esteem. In most marital breakdown, there's a serious lack of respect between the spouses. James Dobson did an outstanding job of explaining this problem in his book *Love Must Be Tough*. If you're separated and have not read that book, do so immediately! In the meantime, let me give you a synopsis of the book's theme by quoting from an earlier work by Dr. Dobson. He writes:

> It is of the highest priority to maintain a distinct element of dignity and self-respect throughout the husband-wife relationship. This takes us into a related area that requires the greatest emphasis. I have observed that many (if not most) marriages suffer from a failure to recognize a universal characteristic of human nature. We value that which we are fortunate to get; we discredit that with which we are stuck! We lust for the very thing which is beyond our grasp; we disdain that same item when it becomes permanent possession. No toy is ever as much fun to play with as it appeared to a wide-eyed child in a store. Seldom does an expensive automobile provide the satisfaction anticipated by the man who dreamed of its ownership....
>
> I must restate the principle: we crave that which we can't attain, but we disrespect that which we can't escape. This axiom is particularly relevant in romantic matters, and has probably influenced your love life. Now the forgotten part of this characteristic is that marriage does not erase or change it. Whenever one marriage partner grovels in his own disrespect... when he reveals his fear of rejection by the mate... when he begs and pleads for a handout... he often faces a bewildering attitude of disdain from the one he needs and loves. Just as in the premarital relationship, nothing douses more water on a romantic flame than for one partner to fling himself emotionally on the other, accepting disrespect in stride. He says in effect, "No matter how badly you treat me, I'll still be here at your feet, because I can't survive without you." That is the best way I know to kill a beautiful friendship.
>
> So what am I recommending... that husbands and wives scratch and claw each other to show their independence? No! That they play sneaky cat and mouse games to create a "challenge?" Not at all! I am merely suggesting that self-respect and dignity be maintained in the relationship.
>
> In short, personal dignity in a marriage is maintained the same way it was produced in dating days. The attitude should be, "I love you and am totally committed to you, but I only control my half of the relationship. I can't demand your love in return. You came to me of your own free will when we decided to marry. No one forced us together. That

same free will is necessary to keep our love alive. If you choose to walk away from me, I will be crushed and hurt beyond description, because I have withheld nothing of myself. Nevertheless, I will let you go and ultimately I will survive. I couldn't demand your affection in the beginning, and I can only request it now." (James Dobson, *What Wives Wish Their Husbands Knew About Women* [Wheaton: Tyndale, 1975] pp. 78–79, 82–84).

Five Criteria for Reconciliation

As you begin to anticipate all that's involved in reconciliation, remember that any plan should include the following points of reference.

1. Reconciliation Requires Two People

Some writers say one person can bring a marriage back together. Well, maybe one can start the process, but in the final analysis it takes two to tango, and it takes two to make a marriage. Most counselors report that when only one person comes for marital counseling, the result can be worse than if neither came. For any meaningful reestablishment of a marriage, both partners must express an equal commitment to that end. Mutual commitment brings mutual trust. One-way commitment brings uncertainty, fear, and constant questions about whether things will ever truly work out.

2. An Honest Evaluation of Past Problems and Personal Mistakes

Reconciliation requires that both partners evaluate personal mistakes. Each person must recognize how he or she has contributed to the present tension. As hard as it is to admit, you both contributed to the breakup. You must face what you've done and make plans to correct any destructive attitudes and behaviors.

3. Mutual Repentance and Forgiveness

Even though I discuss this step in a later chapter, it's important to mention here the need for both spouses to demonstrate a sincere repentance and mutual forgiveness for the problems acknowledged under point 1 above. Owning up to our mistakes is hard. But it must happen if we're serious about reconciliation. At the same time, offering forgiveness to our spouses can be just as hard. Repentance and forgiveness are critical, however, in moving responsibly toward reconciliation.

By the way, this step cannot be one-sided. When only one partner expresses repentance and forgiveness, there's no mutual sense of accountability for the problems. And there is no closure to the issues that created separation in the first place. To put it simply, there's no mutual honesty in the relationship, making the next step of trust rebuilding impossible.

4. Trust Rebuilding

Even after sincere repentance and forgiveness take place, when we have experienced a great deal of pain in a relationship, we can't expect to jump back into it as though nothing ever happened. Questions remain in our hearts: *Can I really trust this person after what we've experienced?*

Such concern is understandable and a normal part of the emotional adjustment process in reconciliation. It's not unlike taking a vacation to Great Britain. Once off the plane, you rent a car and are away on your holiday. However, you immediately feel disoriented, because you find yourself driving down the wrong side of the street! It takes a while to get accustomed to this difference in traffic flow. After a few days, you get used to it and feel rather comfortable driving on the left.

The necessary emotional adjustment in rebuilding trust is called limbic lag. It's the gap between what you *know* is right (like driving on the left side of the street) and what you *feel* is right. It takes a while for our emotions to catch up to our experience.

Whenever we have a problem with someone else—whether it be as small as a disagreement with a child or as major as a marital separation—a resolution will always include limbic lag. Even when we know we're doing the right thing, it takes time for our feelings to catch up to our experience.

At the same time, rebuilding trust implies more than just feeling better about our estranged partner. We also need to reestablish a foundation for mutual respect and trust in the relationship. As we noticed before, separation disintegrates the love that forms the foundation of marital commitment. When that foundation has been torn down, it must be rebuilt before healthy reconciliation can occur. Reconciliation is more than just getting back together; it's the gradual rebuilding of a committed, trustworthy relationship.

Such a process requires time and accountability. Some history has to be built into the renewed relationship; we need to see our spouse's responsible behavior backing up his commitments.

It's easy for a partner to say she'll change. "If you let me come home, I'll get a job." "If you let me come home, I'll stop drinking." "If we get back together, I'll listen to you." You fill in the "promise" blanks. My point is that it's easy to verbalize promises. But as an old cartoon once stated, "If you don't walk the walk, don't talk the talk." The only way we'll know if our partner is serious about a renewed marital commitment is if we see her walking her talk. Lifestyle speaks louder than words. And lifestyle must be observed over an extended period of time.

5. Reconciliation Takes Time and Effort

It's not unusual for reconciling couples to find themselves falling into the same old patterns that led to separation in the first place. That's because reconciliation is usually viewed simplistically as getting back together. As my wife and I found in our several attempts at reconciliation, our living arrangements changed, but our lifestyles didn't.

Reconciliation is a decision to work for something far more meaningful than the two of you had before the separation. What you're looking for is not the resuscitation of a dead marriage but the resurrection of a new, vibrant, committed relationship.

Reconciliation requires time, energy, and a commitment to breaking out of old patterns and establishing new ones. I'm reminded of Larry and Joan Monroe, a couple who separated after seventeen years of marriage. For a long time, Larry couldn't understand Joan's dissatisfaction with their marriage. He was comfortable with things the way they were. After they separated, it took him months to realize that a healthy marriage would require him and his wife to change their patterns. Following a few weeks of accountability to some new commitments, Larry said, "Hey, this stuff takes work! But I'm already seeing the difference it can make. It's hard, but I like it."

MAKE IT YOUR OWN

➤ How has your separation affected your self-esteem?

❑ Improved it. I feel more confident now.

❑ Hasn't affected it.

❑ Worsened it a bit. I'm doubting myself more.

❑ Worsened it a lot. I'm a worm.

❑ Other _____

_____

➤ Do you think your chances for reconciliation would improve if you had better self-esteem? Why? _____

_____

_____

➤ Which of the following is true for you?

❑ My spouse has better self-esteem than I do.

❑ My spouse prefers it when I have a low self-image.

❑ My spouse would find me more attractive if I had a better self-image.

❑ My spouse takes every opportunity to tear me down.

❑ I generally try to enhance my spouse's self-esteem.

❑ Lately I've been trying to make my spouse think less of himself/herself.

➤ Finish this sentence: I would feel a lot better about myself if it weren't for _____.

➤ What can you do to improve your self-esteem? _____

_____

_____

Now is a good time to go to the back of this book and read Article # 1 entitled "Developing a Positive Self-Image." Do that; then continue here.

➤ How many of your ideas listed in answer to the preceding question did you find in the article? _____

_____

➤ Which of the following criteria for reconciliation are present in your case? (Mark Y for "yes" if it's present. Mark L for "likely" if it's not there yet but it's likely that it will be. Mark P for "possible" if it's not likely but still possible. Mark I for "impossible" if you feel it will never be true.)

❑ Both partners want reconciliation.

❑ We're honestly evaluating past problems and personal mistakes.

❑ There is mutual repentance and forgiveness.

❑ Trust between the partners is beginning to rebuild.

❑ Both partners are willing to invest time and effort in the reconciliation process.

CRITERIA FOR RECONCILIATION:
1. *It takes two*
2. *Honest evaluation of past problems and personal mistakes*
3. *Mutual repentance and forgiveness*
4. *Trust rebuilding*
5. *Takes time and effort*

PAM'S STORY

What steps could you take to work toward reconciliation? I would like to suggest a strategy some couples have found helpful in their attempts to rebuild their marriages. I'll do this by telling the story of my friend Pam.

Before I relate her story, however, I want to stress that anyone considering reconciliation needs the objective perspective of a third party with whom he can discuss and evaluate his plan and its results. The process of reconciliation is demanding, and it's easy to get caught up in emotional mood swings. An objective third person (such as a counselor or pastor) can help you maintain balance and realism in the midst of those changes.

For two years, Pam's husband had been living at his girlfriend's apartment during the week and at the family house over the weekend. At home, he would do all his household chores and pay the bills. Then on Monday, he would go back to work and to his girlfriend.

Over and over Pam heard her husband say, "I want to be married to you and be the father of our children. But I'm working through this stage in my life. You've got to give me space and time to get through this."

Pam believed her husband was sincere and wanted the marriage. But after two years, she had endured just about all she could take! So she came and asked me, "What can I do?"

1. List your expectations.

We began by having Pam write out a list of her expectations. I encouraged her to make the list as long and detailed as she liked, including anything she believed would make the relationship healthy. "Don't restrict yourself only to things you believe *could* happen," I said. "Include everything you feel *should* be taking place in your marriage."

2. Evaluate your expectations.

Pam came up with quite a list! Then we spent a great deal of time evaluating the list. We tried to distinguish between realistic expectations and those that were simply dreams. We also worked at understanding which expectations were fair and which ones stemmed from anger or frustration. Finally, we sought to focus on the issues that were vital to an honest, growing relationship. At the end of this evaluation, we really had two lists. One was a bare-bones list of critical issues for the health of the marriage. The other was a "dream sheet" listing things Pam agreed she would like to see happen but were not vital.

3. Prioritize your expectations.

For the moment, we decided to work only on the bare-bones list of critical issues. I asked Pam to do two things with that list. First, she was to grade the items according to their importance: an A for those of highest priority, a B for ones less critical, and so on. Next, I asked her to consider which expectations had to take place before the others could occur.

With those lists, Pam was able to develop some realistic expectations. She didn't have to mortgage her future on a hope that somehow, someday her husband might "snap out of it." Instead, she was beginning to build an understanding of what was truly important to her and what must reasonably take place for the marriage to be rebuilt.

4. Develop a Gameplan.

Next, Pam and I worked out a reasonable time line for what needed to take place in a reconciliation. We decided Pam would take one expectation at a time and put a realistic time frame to it. Then she would present her concern to her husband for interaction and negotiation.

The first thing Pam felt needed to happen was for her husband to move out of his girlfriend's apartment. He didn't need to move home, but he needed to demonstrate his seriousness in rebuilding the marriage by terminating the relationship with the other woman.

How long did Pam feel she could give her husband to think about her request and move out of the apartment? After a few moments she said, "I could wait up to two months."

5. Negotiate.

Later in the week, Pam went out to lunch with her husband. (We decided negotiation would best take place in a public facility, where feelings would need to be controlled.) After talking for a while over mutual interests, Pam presented her first concern for discussion. Note that she didn't dump the whole list of expectations on her husband. That would have been too much for him to take.

Pam said to him, "I know you love me and want to be my husband and the father of our children. I believe you when you say that. However, we've been separated now for two years, and it would be very helpful for me to understand where our marriage is going. So, I would like you to show me the sincerity of what you've been saying by cutting off your relationship with this other woman. You don't have to move back into the house if you're not ready. However, I believe you sincerely want our marriage to work, and this would give me tangible proof of your interest."

Pam's real purpose in this meeting was to get an understanding of her husband's willingness to work on their relationship. Further, she was checking to see if he respected her enough to take her request seriously.

He was furious. "Are you kidding?" he said. "Who do you think you are, trying to take away my freedom and telling me how to live?"

"Wait a minute," Pam replied. "You're the one who said you want to remain married to me. You also said you want to be the father of our children. I'm not telling you what to do. I just want to see if you want an honest partnership."

When Pam's husband said "Forget it," she still didn't act in anger. She would not allow him back in the home over the weekends, but she remained gracious to him while waiting for two months to see if he would change his mind. A phone conversation at the end of the two months convinced her that he wasn't interested in the marriage. He wanted his own way. The following week, she filed divorce papers against him.

Pam's story doesn't have the happy ending you might have expected. The purpose of the plan Pam and I developed was reconciliation, and that didn't happen. Yet the strategy clarified her expectations and provided her with a realistic understanding of her situation. Our responsibility in reconciliation is not to control or manipulate the other partner. However, we *can* expect him to exhibit respect and commitment to the marriage if he truly wants it to work.

The actions Pam took clearly demonstrated her desire to save the marriage. And they forced her husband to demonstrate his intentions. In that way, she was able to take an active role in her situation, not merely be a victim of his whims.

MAKE IT YOUR OWN

▶ What do you think of Pam's story? What would you have done differently? _____

_____

_____

_____

▶ How might her actions at this point affect the way she recovers from her divorce? Will she feel guilty for actually filing the divorce papers? Or will she feel comfort in the fact that she did her best to save the marriage? How would you feel? _____

_____

_____

_____

▶ Does Pam's strategy fit your situation? _____ If so, let's go through it. List all the things you want your marriage to be (and what your spouse needs to do to make this happen). _____

_____

_____

_____

_____

_____

_____

_____

➤ Now go back through that list, marking some items with N for "necessities" and some with D for "dreams." Relist all those marked N. _____

_____

_____

_____

_____

➤ Now grade them A to F in order of importance. Relist any you've judged as A needs. _____

_____

_____

➤ Of these, which needs to happen first? What's the time frame in which this needs to happen? _____

_____

_____

➤ How will you tell your spouse you need this to happen? Write a practice speech here. _____

_____

_____

_____

_____

_____

_____

_____

➤ When and where will you talk with your spouse about this? _____

_____

IN THE MEANTIME

While we're separated, we need to work out *guidelines for our own emotional protection*. We're vulnerable during this time, and it's possible to open ourselves to all kinds of hurts.

For example, though we're still married, if we allow ourselves to continue having sexual relations with our spouses (who may be having sex with others as well), we could be setting ourselves up for more pain. Continued sexual relations build the expectation of reconciliation. And a spouse may simply be using the opportunity to fulfill his own physical desires. By sharing ourselves sexually, we allow an estranged spouse to experience the joys of marriage without the accompanying responsibilities. That means sacrificing personal emotional stability for the sake of another's pleasure.

This self-sharing can work in other ways as well. For example, will you allow your spouse to come over to the house at any time? When can he see the children? When are you willing to talk together? Answers to such questions form the framework for our emotional protection. I don't mean to sound harsh, because we need to be as concerned for our spouses as we are for ourselves. We need to protect ourselves, however, from emotional violation. It's time for us to develop—and expect—some respect for ourselves before we open ourselves up for any more hurt.

During separation, we also need *a healthy social network*. One of the greatest problems we face when separated is that we're in a no-man's land between marriage and divorce. We wonder if we should spend time with singles: *Am I in the single's scene now? I sure don't feel single!* At the same time, we don't feel comfortable with married people. So what are we to do?

There's no doubt we need friendships; we need a network of safe friends with whom we can share ourselves and not be afraid of the expectations they might have for us. We need people who understand us. That's why I've included an entire chapter called "Reentry into the Single Life." Even if you're reconciled, it's important for you to work through that chapter, because it will help you know how to develop and maintain healthy relationships while separated.

Speaking of friendships, what about dating? Is it okay to date while separated? A number of points need to be made here.

First, we need to remember that dating is a prelude to remarriage, not a therapy for reconciliation. While we need friends, in a one-on-one relationship with the opposite sex, we can suddenly find ourselves in an emotionally compromising situation. If we begin to date, we may develop deepening ties to this new person that put any hope of reconciliation at risk. Furthermore, even if we didn't initiate the separation, we may find ourselves speeding up the divorce process in order to be free for our new relationship.

We also need to remember we're still married. Many people say, "If I'm going to be divorced, it's only a matter of time until the legal paperwork is completed. Why can't I date while I'm waiting?"

Remember, however, that there are at least three stages to divorce. First is the *emotional stage* of divorce. Many think the termination of marriage is at separation, because it disrupts the structure of one's social and emotional life.

But there's also the *spiritual stage* of divorce. When we marry, we make a vow before God stating our fidelity and commitment. The Bible tells us that God oversees that commitment and holds people accountable to their marriage vows (see Mal. 2:13-16). We must recognize our responsibility to maintain integrity and self-respect by being faithful to our vows, even if our spouses are unfaithful. Until the divorce has been completed before God, we must remain true to our commitment.

Such faithful commitment can deeply strengthen our character. When a man maintains faithfulness until the final termination of marriage, he forms a foundation on which future commitments can be built with full conviction and proven integrity.

After a few dates with the woman I would later marry, she began to ask about my former marriage and divorce. Then she asked this heavy question: "After your wife left you, did you start dating others, or did you keep your commitment to her even when she was unfaithful?"

I was relieved to be able to tell her I hadn't dated while I was separated.

Later she said, "I know you're a person who keeps his word. You remained faithful when it was the most difficult."

Finally, there is the *social (or legal) stage* of divorce. The Bible teaches that we are to "be subject to the governing authorities" (Rom. 13:1). Like it or not, in the eyes of the state, we're still married until the divorce decree. Perhaps it's just a matter of paperwork to the government. But you weren't allowed to get married without a marriage license, and, legally, you aren't divorced until the judge says so.

Therefore, until we're emotionally, spiritually, and legally divorced, we're still married. And a married person ought not to date others. However, a separated person still needs friends, and other options are available for personal support. As I said before, we'll look into healthy alternatives in the next chapter.

MAKE IT YOUR OWN

➤ What emotional guidelines do you need to set up during your separation? I'll list some possibilities here that you should consider. There may be many others.

Will you still sleep with your spouse?

Will you allow your spouse to visit whenever he or she wants?

How involved will your spouse be in your children's lives?

If there is "another woman" or "another man," how will you (or your children) deal with that person (if at all)?

Are you always available to talk with your spouse, or are there some times when you need to turn off that pressure? _____

_____

➤ What sort of social network can you develop? List the friends you can rely on for support. _____

_____

_____

➤ How do you feel about what I've said about dating? Why? _____

_____

_____

➤ What alternatives to dating can you think of? _____

_____

_____

WHERE IS GOD IN THIS MESS?

It's not unusual for a separated person to ask a question something like this: "I thought that when I got married in the context of the church, God was supposed to bless our union. After all, He created marriage in the first place. Now my marriage is falling apart. I feel God has failed me. Where is He in all this mess?"

Others ask questions like "Does God promise that if I do certain things my marriage will come back together?" and "Why would God allow something like this to happen?"

We'll look at God's perspective on marriage and divorce in a later chapter. However, as we consider where God is in the midst of marital separation, one important point needs to be made. God's first desire is always for reconciliation. He did not design marriage to end in divorce. The New Testament makes it clear that for a Christian, the grounds for divorce are rather narrow. And even when a believer is married to an unbeliever, Paul said the general rule is for a couple to remain married unless separation is initiated by the unbelieving spouse (see 1 Cor. 7:12-16).

Does God Promise Reconciliation?

Some teachers imply that all you must do is follow certain biblical patterns and your marriage will be reconciled. "After all," they say, "God is for marriage. Therefore, your obedience will release the power of God to bring your family back together again."

I don't believe the Bible teaches that kind of simplistic answer. Note, for example, the relationship between God and His "bride" Israel as described in Jeremiah 3. God drove home the point that Israel had abandoned her relationship with Him. God experienced marital separation!

Now, in Jeremiah 3, God said He desired reconciliation with his "spouse." But His call for reconciliation wasn't a method of bargaining! He didn't say, "Israel, please come back to Me and I'll act as though nothing ever happened in our relationship. If you come back, everything will be wonderful, and I'll never talk about our problems again."

No way! God cried out for reconciliation on the basis of correcting wrong, destructive behavior. Listen to what He said: " 'Return, backsliding Israel,' says the Lord, 'and I will not cause My anger to fall on you....Only acknowledge your iniquity, that you have transgressed against the Lord your God, and have scattered your charms to alien deities under every green tree, and you have not obeyed My voice,' says the Lord" (Jer. 3:12a-13).

God told Israel He desired reconciliation, but only on the basis of honesty. He refused to play the bargaining game, passing over the hurts and failures as if they had never happened.

The use of bargaining in reconciliation is seen in the story of Mike and Doris Bridges (see Bob's book *Through the Whirlwind*). "We separated after nine years of marriage," Doris said. "We have never spent one night apart these last nine years, and now we are finding it harder to be separated than we ever expected."

She went on, "I left home because of my husband's frequent unemployment, alcohol abuse, and cocaine addiction. I figured we were bad for each other since we seem to feed into each other's addictions. Since leaving, I've cleaned up my act. Now Mike wants me to come back. I know he has a long way to go, but I feel like I need him in my life again. Perhaps I can help him through his problems."

Mike explained, "Doris is right. I've been a bum. But now I know I can't go on alone. I told her if she will move back in, I'll stop the drugs and booze and get a job. This separation has made me realize how much I need her. I know when she comes back we will work it out together."

Doris moved back in with Mike, but soon they lapsed into the same destructive tendencies that caused the separation. The Bridges were trying to get it back together without honestly facing their mistakes, assuming everything would work out okay.

Unlike the Bridges, God would not play the bargaining game. He called His estranged wife to repentance, which simply means an honest recognition of mistakes and a commitment to accountable living in the future. Repentance is more than just remorse over the past. It implies a change of attitude and conduct for the future.

The point I'm making is this: God never promises a simplistic reconciliation. Throughout the Bible, we read that reconciliation happens only when one acknowledges his wrong attitudes and behavior, coupled with forgiveness and a commitment to work on a healthy, honest relationship. (In chapter 7, I'll say more about the process of forgiveness in separation and divorce.)

Reconciliation cannot be expected without those elements. Because Israel did not repent, God wasn't reconciled to her. And neither does He promise reconciliation to all who want it. You can't hold on to a spiritualized pipedream that reconciliation will inevitably occur.

However, saying reconciliation *may* not happen is different from saying it *will* not happen. God is at work doing more than we can ask or imagine (See Eph. 3:20). Reconciliation is not beyond His power.

Will God Heal My Marriage?

It helps to view reconciliation as similar to physical healing. I believe God can heal people. I remember a time in my church when a little girl had a serious problem with parasites. The doctors tried everything to get rid of them. But all their treatments were unsuccessful. It was so bad that the little girl could have died from the disease. The only alternative was to use a drug so strong that besides killing the parasites, it could also give her cancer.

At that point the girl's parents brought her to the elders of the church.

They asked us to lay hands on her and pray for healing. Now, none of the elders claimed to have the gift of healing. And we didn't promise a healing if we prayed for her. We simply obeyed God's instruction to pray for healing (see James 5:14-15), and we believed He had the power to do so if it was in His plan.

When the girl was taken for her last round of tests prior to administering the stronger drug, they discovered the parasites were gone. Who could explain it? The only answer was that an all-powerful God worked for His glory in healing her.

I have seen God heal marriages as miraculously as He healed that little girl. I'm reminded of a friend who had recently left his wife. He was driving through the rain one night on a business trip to a nearby community. Suddenly his car went out of control. When he regained consciousness, he was lying on the side of the road. His car was in the ditch, and he was viewing the scene by the flashing lights of a tow truck, an ambulance, and a police car. The car was pulled out of the ditch, and, after an examination by paramedics, my friend was able to get into his car and resume his trip.

He didn't continue to his original destination, however. Instead, he drove back to his house, walked up to his wife, and said, "I've been acting like an idiot. Would you please forgive me for hurting you?" Since that day they have worked at their marriage, and today it's a strong, healthy relationship. And it all began with the "miracle" of his car going off the road.

But God doesn't always heal physically by performing a miracle. Sometimes He heals through the hard work of professionals: doctors, nurses, therapists, and others in the medical profession.

I have a friend named Glenn who, while at the beach, dove into an oncoming wave. Misjudging the depth of the water, he broke his neck by hitting the shore bottom. Fortunately, he lived. And after an extended period of operations and therapy, he has regained the ability to walk and maintain an active lifestyle. A slight limp is the only visible sign of the accident.

I've also seen marriages healed through the hard work of professionals: counselors, psychologists, psychiatrists, and pastors working to create understanding and renewed commitment within couples whose marriages were on the brink of ruin.

That was the case with Paul and Diane. Both of them had been involved in affairs. Their separation seemed to drive a deeper wedge of mistrust and alienation between them until Paul asked if he could meet with Diane's counselor. Over the months, repentance turned to rebuilding. Now, with their commitment renewed, Paul and Diane work with alienated couples in their church, sharing a hope for honest reconciliation.

Miracles *can* happen. And professionals can facilitate healing. But the fact remains: *Not* all illnesses are cured, and not all marriages are put back together.

Take, for instance, the well-known story of Joni Eareckson Tada. Like my friend Glenn, Joni broke her neck while diving. Only in her instance there was no physical healing, no miracle. And though she received excellent care from physicians, Joni did not recover the use of her limbs.

However, Joni has devoted her life to expressing a message of courage and hope to thousands. Why? Because she had a healing that wasn't physical. Rather, she was healed in her soul. Through the power of God, she learned the strength of acceptance. And then she began to spread the good news of the lessons she learned to other people. According to the Bible, she learned to "comfort those who are in any trouble, with the comfort with which we ourselves are comforted by God" (2 Cor. 1:4). In her own way, Joni received a healing just as real and significant as the work of a doctor or a physical healing from God.

Likewise, I have seen people go through separation and divorce and never experience reconciliation. However, through their divorces they have experienced an inner healing of the soul so that they're stronger persons today. That's not because their divorces were good or something they really wanted. Rather, it's because God has used their divorces as a context for their growth and maturity.

Where is God in this mess? God does heal the separated. He doesn't always heal the way we expect or want, however. We can't control the actions of the loving, caring God. Nor will we be able to put all the pieces of the puzzle together and understand the way He works. But we can hold on and believe that He uses our pains to make us into healthy people who can honor Him.

MAKE IT YOUR OWN

➤ How has your separation affected your relationship with God? _____

_____

➤ What sort of miracle would you like to see happen? _____

_____

_____

➤ If God decides not to do that, what's your second choice? _____

_____ _____

_____

➤ If you like, write out a prayer to God in the space below. Be honest about your desires, your frustrations, your dreams, and your doubts. Be bold enough to ask for a miracle, but humble enough to yield to His ways. _____

_____

_____

_____

_____

Hope for the Future

Separation is a time of turmoil and uncertainty. While God desires reconciliation, there are no guarantees it will take place. The way you handle this crisis, however, can determine the future of your marriage and the stability of your life.

God is involved in the lives of His children who are separated. While the "all things" that work together for good (see Rom. 8:28) don't always work out the way we would like, we can call all things good because of His promise that nothing shall separate us from His love (see Rom. 8:29). That's a reality we can count on forever.

CHAPTER 3

REENTRY INTO THE SINGLE LIFE

Let's talk chronology. We started this workbook by looking at the stages of recovery. Then we discussed separation. When do the stages of grieving start—during separation, or after the divorce, or when?

It all depends. The stages of denial, anger, bargaining, and so on may start even *before* the separation. A friend tells of her struggles with an alcoholic husband. She went through all the stages with that, and the process *ended* with her asking for a divorce. She had come to a point of accepting what she felt she had to do.

The case of Pam, from the last chapter, is similar. She went through those stages *during* the separation. Finally, she came to terms with what was happening, asked her husband to take responsibility for his role in the marriage, and ultimately accepted the situation by filing for divorce. The timing of your stages of recovery depends largely on when the shock hits you.

You may go through an entire separation blithely assuming you'll get back together, and the recovery process begins only when that doesn't happen.

But let's suppose you've made it through most of the stages of recovery and you're moving on toward a point of acceptance. As I've said before, you'll slip back down the slippery slope every so often, but you've generally come to terms with your divorce. What's next?

Reentry. Somehow, you have to resume your life. And it will be a different life from what you're used to. You're single again. You're also older, wiser, and injured. The climb up the slippery slope toward acceptance is only half the struggle. Rebuilding your self-image and relationships and faith—that's what needs to happen next.

WHO AM I, ANYWAY?

I never had much sympathy for people who complained about "identity crises." They would whine, "I don't know who I am anymore!"

I thought that was the silliest thing I'd ever heard. "It's obvious who you are," I'd say, and I'd go on to say a few things I knew about them. I had very little patience for their emotional disorientation.

But then I had one of my own—a massive identity crisis. I didn't know who I was.

Oh, I could still fill out the forms: name, address, Social Security number. But deep inside me, it seemed there was no bedrock anymore, no place where I could put my foot down and it wouldn't move. Everything was in transition. *This is where I want to be*, I'd think, but then it wouldn't be what it used to be.

My sense of who I was had been forged by my relationships, my work, and my faith. With my divorce, that all had vanished. No wife, no job, very little faith, and only a couple of old friends. Everything that made me *me* was gone.

That's not unusual. Any crisis shakes our self-awareness to some extent, but especially the ripping apart of our most-intimate relationships. This is especially true of women, who often learn to define themselves in terms of their connections with others. But when the other goes away, what's left? If you're not Mrs. Smith anymore, who are you?

Thus, the first struggle of reentry is for a new *identity*. You must radically redefine yourself. That takes some reorientation, some digging, some shoring up. It sounds hokey these days to say you have to "get in touch with yourself," but that's the idea. You need to take the time to listen to yourself, to pay attention to your unique interests, talents, desires, and personality traits—to gain a new awareness of yourself completely apart from the old relationship.

Am I Any Good?

Many of us reenter life with a poor self-concept. Putting our identity back together makes us painfully aware of our shortcomings. After all, we've just been rejected by the ones who supposedly knew us best. We must not be worth much, or so we tend to think.

In my case, I felt like a complete failure. The most-important thing in my life—my family, my home—had fallen apart. And I thought to myself, *If I couldn't keep that together, what can I do? What good am I?*

I'm not talking about a week or a month after my wife left. I'm talking about *years* later. I had finally accepted my situation and *still* this self-doubt afflicted me. I felt like a total washout.

That attitude affected everything I did. I walked into every new situation feeling like a failure. Have you experienced that, too? You walk into a room, and you think, *These people don't care about me. They don't want to hear what I have to say. This person doesn't care how I feel. Everything I say is so stupid.* In the normal ebb and flow of life, every insult gets magnified a hundred times. And we tend to downplay whatever praise and affirmation we get.

As we rebuild our lives, we must not only find a new identity, but we must also accept ourselves. We may have reached the stage of acceptance by accepting our *situation*. But accepting *ourselves* is a different story; it may be even harder.

This low self-esteem hobbles us as we try to reenter society. We're not seeing anything—the world, ourselves, or even God—as it really is. We're skewing everything to conform to our negative view of ourselves. That can lead to twisted relationships as we rebound into encounters with those who affirm us, yet we never really trust them. We tend to use others and let them use us. Such unhealthy relationships are frequent in the lives of the newly separated and divorced.

You may know people who are stuck in low self-esteem. They have never rebuilt their self-image after a divorce, and now they're bitter, timid, withdrawn, desperate, and extremely vulnerable.

So be careful. Stay away from the voices that will tear you down. Find friends who will build you up. Start your own inner pattern of encouragement. When you look at yourself in the morning, say aloud, "I'm not a failure. I'm a unique individual, created in God's image. I have a lot to offer!" (See article 1 at the end of this book for further information on developing a positive self-image.)

The Elijah Syndrome

Divorce is an incredibly lonely experience. That's ironic when you consider that nearly half the marriages in the U.S. end in divorce. But when you're splitting up, you're sure no one else feels as you do.

I call that the Elijah Syndrome. In the Bible, the prophet Elijah was struggling against an evil king and queen. Queen Jezebel was out to kill him, and Elijah was hiding. He was also severely depressed. "There is no one," he complained, "who is not worshiping idols. I am left alone, and they're trying to murder me!" (1 Kings 19:10, my paraphrase).

Maybe you're not dodging assassination plots, but you probably know the feeling. *No one understands what I'm going through!* The irony is that, with the divorce, you've lost the person closest to you. The person who *should* be there to understand you, to commiserate with and support you, is gone—and that's the whole problem. It gets worse when people try to give you advice. "What are you moping around for? It's been six weeks now. Come on. Get on with your life."

And you think, *I must be crazy, because it's been six weeks, and I'm still heading downhill.*

If you watch anything on television about people who've been through divorce, you feel even stranger. It's so far from reality. I wish they'd put on a program that showed the reality of divorce. Most divorced people on TV are separated one day and then back in action the next. They seem free to enjoy this great single life. Hundreds of eligible people of the opposite sex are just dying to go out with them. There's no loneliness, no pain, and no strings attached to the relationships they enter.

Yet you're going home to your empty home, sinking into your easy chair with a bowl of cereal, and flicking on reruns of "The Love Boat." On the tube, every passenger is finding the love of his life in one weekend cruise. And you're thinking, *I must be weird. My life isn't like that. I'm dying inside. There must be something wrong with me.*

Remember Elijah, sitting and complaining? God answered him by assuring him there were six thousand people in Israel who were on his side. He wasn't alone after all.

As I speak in Fresh Start seminars, I sometimes stop and ask whether anyone is relating to the feelings I'm describing. Invariably, a sea of hands goes up. Then I ask people to look around. "Here are people feeling the same frustrations you are," I say. "You are not alone." That in itself is worth the price of admission.

If you've been thinking you're the only one who's not out having a good time, you've been watching too much TV. I've done many Fresh Start Seminars, and I've worked with six thousand divorced people, and they're

> **More than 1 million Americans go through divorce every year.**

not going on cruise ships and finding the men and women of their dreams. They're working through recovery. And that takes a long time and a lot of work.

So relax. You're not crazy. You're not alone.

MAKE IT YOUR OWN

➤ Do you feel you're ready for reentry? That is, have you passed through the stages of recovery and reached a point of acceptance of your new life-style? How do you know? _____

_____

_____

➤ If not, when would you estimate you'll be ready for reentry? Why?

_____

_____

(*Note:* It's important that you not hurry things. Going through this section of the workbook may tempt you to rush into reentry when you're not ready. You may want to skim this section now and return to it later.)

➤ Who are you? Start writing some things about yourself: name, age, job, schooling, address, interests, and so on. _____

_____

_____

_____

_____

➤ What personality traits do you have? List three things you like about yourself, and then three things you don't like or wish you could change.

Likes   Dislikes

1. _____   1. _____

2. _____   2. _____

3. _____   3. _____

➤ Between the likes and dislikes you just recorded, which list was easier for you to write? Why? _____

_____

Your answer may give you some insights into your self-image.

➤ What activities do you enjoy? What are your talents? _____
_____
_____
_____

➤ What are your most-important relationships? _____
_____
_____

➤ Choose one of the people you just listed. In twenty-five words or less, how would that person describe you? Call the person and ask for that brief description. Write it down here. _____
_____
_____
_____

➤ What's your best personal quality? (Some options, among many, are loyalty, love, humor, tenacity, good listener, intelligence, humility, spirituality.) _____
_____

➤ Is there some area of knowledge in which you know more than the average person? What is it? _____
_____

➤ On a scale of 1 to 10, (10 being extremely) how lonely have you felt since your divorce? _____

➤ Have you talked to others recently in similar situations? If so, who?
_____

➤ If we called together one hundred people at random from your town, how many of them do you think would understand how you feel right now? _____

➤ How many do you think would be experiencing the same amount of emotional pain or worse? _____

➤ How many of them do you think would consider themselves failures?

_____

TORN BETWEEN TWO TROUBLES

So what's the cure for loneliness?

Being with people, right? But if you're in those early stages of recovery or reentry, you know better. There is nothing *more lonely* than being in a crowd and feeling you're totally alone. The party may go on around you, but you're not a part of it. You may even be talking and laughing with people, but inside you're thinking, *They don't really know me. I don't belong here.*

I went through that. For quite a while, I felt this tremendous sense of ambivalence. I needed people desperately, but they scared me to death.

This tension stems from two God-given instincts. On the one hand, we need to be loved and considered valuable by others. On the the other hand, we need to protect ourselves. We've just been clobbered emotionally by divorce, and all our instincts tell us to run and hide. People can hurt.

I would find myself at some social event, feeling very "out of it." I'd walk into a room full of people and immediately look for the exits. I always wanted to sit near the edges or in the back so I could make a quick getaway if things got uncomfortable.

I found myself dealing with others on a surface level; I wasn't investing myself in anyone. That would be too dangerous. I was terrified that someone would ask me a probing, penetrating question like "How are you?" I felt as if I had a big, red D on my chest and that everyone was avoiding or pitying me because I was *divorced*.

So the whole event would be unsatisfying to me. It was teasing me. People were close enough to offer the love and affirmation I needed, but I couldn't let them do that because I'd have to open up my heart, and I might get clobbered again. The two opposing instincts taunted me. It was like having somebody knock on the front door and the back door at the same time. You don't know which way to turn.

Often I would leave social events early just to get out of that pressure. But then where would I go? Home? To my lonely place? No love and affirmation would be found there. Sometimes I just drove around and around as my emotions went around and around on the inside. My ambivalence had me trapped.

Do you know those feelings? There's a kind of fatigue that goes with them. Constantly being pulled one way and then the other wears you out.

The Way We're Made

What's the answer? It starts by accepting both feelings as gifts from God. You may feel very odd when you're dealing with the conflicting emotions, but that's the way God made you.

The need for other people was built in when God created us. The Bible says we're created in His image (see Gen. 1:26-27). In part that means this: God is a Trinity—Father, Son, and Holy Spirit—wrapped up in one being. The three Persons are constantly communing with each other. So God is a God of fellowship, a God of relationships. To be made in God's image, then, is to *need relationships*. There's nothing wrong with that!

We get another clue a chapter later in Genesis. God had created the world, at each stage declaring it "good." Then He made Adam and put him in charge of it all. But suddenly He said, "It's not good for the man to be alone" (2:18, my paraphrase). And so He made Eve. From the start, then, God intended for human beings to relate to each other. Remember, Adam walked with God in the Garden of Eden, but he still needed other people in his life. (By the way, that doesn't mean God wants everyone to be married, as Scriptures like 1 Cor. 7:7-8 prove.)

So when people say, "All you need is God. You're a single parent, but don't worry about it. God will be there for you"—well, that's nice, but they don't understand. You need other people in your life. You may not need a new spouse, but you need *friends*, people to talk to and listen to, people who will love and appreciate you.

But God also gives us the wisdom to shield ourselves from emotional disaster. We've been wounded, and we need to recover. If you break your arm, what does the doctor do? She puts it in a cast. Why? To immobilize it. It needs to heal. It needs to be out of action for a while.

Similarly, your heart has just taken a pounding. You might even say it's been broken. You need to put it in a cast, to immobilize it for a while. That means drawing back, protecting, shielding yourself from involvement in relationships.

Sometimes you'll see people who try to deal with their divorce without this self-protective instinct. They say, "Hey, I'm so glad I finally got that divorce out of the way. I can dive right into life again. I'm going to have a blast." You can see the denial a mile away. They need to pull back, but they're out there saying, "No problem! It's been a whole two months since my divorce. I'm okay!"

They're not okay. In fact, they're in *more* danger because they refuse to accept their "injuries" and immobilize their wounded hearts. If you try to use your broken heart in new relationships, the result will be the same as when you try to use a broken arm—it will cause you more pain.

If you find yourself putting up walls of self-defense, great! That's a healthy option at this point. You're extremely vulnerable. Proper healing requires that you understand your vulnerability and allow for it.

Vulnerability

In my case, I found that I was extremely sensitive emotionally. I suddenly had an overkeen sense of justice. *I had been wronged,* so I felt moral indignation at every act of injustice I learned about. I couldn't watch the evening news. It would stir me up to hear Dan Rather talking about dictators mistreating peasants or a murderer getting off on a technicality. I'd throw things, I'd pace up and down, and I'd think, *This world stinks.*

The same sensitivity crept into my personal life. I was quick to feel mistreated over the slightest misunderstanding. You may be like that now, or you may know others like that. We go around with a chip on our shoulders, daring the world to knock it off. The healing process involves a slow putting down of the boxing gloves. Slowly, we learn to give people the benefit of the doubt.

During my reentry, I was also quick to feel sorrow. I couldn't watch "Little House on the Prairie" without bawling like a baby. At the time I thought, *I must be going crazy. I can't control myself.* Any little thing could push a button. All I'd have to see was a happy family with a dog by the hearth, and right away I'd start crying.

That can be cyclical. Our emotional instability makes us think we're crazy, which further convinces us we'll never have a home like "Little House." The healing process involves a certain distancing from those things that make us cry. *It's only a TV show,* we can say to ourselves. *My life is different from that, but it's okay.*

It may sound silly, but you may need to stop watching upsetting TV shows or going to weepy movies for a while. Don't toy with your vulnerability. As you ease your way back to health, you can resume some of those "normal" activities. But in the meantime, recognize your need for protection, and avoid stimuli that will wound you further.

Recognize also that your sense of self-protection may make you very selfish for a while. You'll be focusing on your own needs (and probably unaware of the needs of others). That happened to me, and it strained one of my best friendships.

Through my whole ordeal, I had this one friend who stayed with me. He kept calling me and didn't let me get away with locking the doors and unplugging the phone. He kept calling and saying, "Why don't you come over? You can watch TV, have dinner, talk if you want, sleep here if you want, do whatever you want. Just come over." He kept bugging me, and little by little, as I began to go over and pour out how unfair everything had been, how people had hurt me, and how God was a terrible God to allow such things, my friend simply listened.

Looking back on that, I realize I never once said, "Well, how are *you* doing?" All I was focusing on was me. That's part of that self-protection. I was very needy, very vulnerable. My friend must have provided me with twenty or more meals, and I never said, "Hey, how about you guys coming over my place, and I'll cook you a meal?"

One of the first signs of my healing was that I became aware of my selfishness. I suddenly began to say, "You know, if I ever get healthy again, I'd like to do something for these friends of mine." I was already planning my road to recovery.

Thinking again of the arm-breaking analogy, when you first break your arm, it hurts a lot. Then, as it heals in a cast, it just feels uncomfortable. Initially you also find yourself complaining a lot; you're focusing on your own pain, your own inconvenience. But that's okay. You have a right to complain. Then suddenly you turn a corner; you start counting the days until the cast comes off. You start thinking about what you'll do when you have the use of your arm again. That's where I was as my emotions were healing.

One other expression of self-protection is pride. That seems illogical when so many suffer from low self-esteem. But the mind plays funny games with us. We tend to overcompensate for our internal self-hate with an external self-assurance.

In my case, I found it hard to admit I needed help. I was hiding out at first. I was going to a singles group at the new church I was attending, and I knew about the Fresh Start program for divorced people, but I didn't go to their meetings. I was determined to make it on my own. It was safer that way. I was going to shut everyone out of my life. I was a rock; I was an island. No one was ever going to hurt me again.

I was compensating for my pain with bravado. I didn't want to admit my weakness, my need for help. I still felt too vulnerable.

MAKE IT YOUR OWN

➤ Of the two instincts—the need to relate to others and the need to protect yourself—which is stronger now? _____

_____

➤ When have you most recently sensed your need to relate to others?

_____

➤ When have you most recently sensed your need to protect yourself?

_____

➤ In what ways are you vulnerable? _____

_____

_____

➤ What examples of selfishness have you been noticing in your life?

_____

_____

➤ What examples of pride have you noticed? _____

_____

_____

➤ Do you think those are understandable, considering what you've been through, or do you think they're excessive? Why? _____

_____

_____

➤ As you look forward to the time when you're healthy again, what would you like to do for someone else? Be specific. _____

_____

_____

Action Point: As you think about the kind of friend you are now and compare that with what you'd like to be when you're more healed, what do you need to change about yourself? Be specific. _____

_____

_____

Write this same goal on page 287 for future reference, as well as part of your personalized action plan.

THE BALANCING ACT

How can we deal with all this vulnerability? How do we balance our need for others with our need to protect ourselves? We have to learn how to take calculated risks. Emotional wholeness comes to those who learn how to balance proper risks with proper cautions. Let me emphasize: *proper risks* and *proper* cautions. Many take foolish risks (like rebound romances) or observe needless cautions (like hiding away for years). But by keeping the two instincts in balance, we can edge our way back to wholeness.

The first risk you may have to take, as I did, is *seeking help.* Maybe that starts with this workbook. It might involve going to a Fresh Start seminar, getting involved with a church, or seeing a counselor. It may be difficult, but it's a risk worth taking.

As I mentioned, I was too proud (or too vulnerable) to seek help. And as things turned out, I never had to. Ironically, the first time I came to Fresh Start, I came to help others. The singles pastor asked me to help out, not even knowing I had been through a divorce. You see, I was a "closet divorcé."

I was convinced that if people knew I was divorced, they would reject me. So I just wanted to blend into the singles group. But the pastor said, "We're looking for facilitators for Fresh Start. We usually like for them to have gone through divorce, but we'd like for you to come and help out anyway."

Not knowing what to say, I gave the good Christian answer: "Well, let me pray about that and get back to you." I didn't tell him I was in fact divorced until later—after doing a lot of soul searching. I was afraid that if he knew, he would suddenly feel differently about me. There was that needless caution again. It made no sense! He was *looking for* divorced people to help lead, and I was afraid to tell him I was divorced.

I finally did consent to come, and I finally told him I had been through divorce. I remember his reaction. "You have?" he said. "That's great! Boy, now that I know that, we could use you in a lot more ways."

Wait a minute, I thought. *What do you mean, "That's great"? How can anything good come out of something so terrible?* That didn't register with me for a long time.

So it was that I came to Fresh Start to help others. As I sat there, I started soaking it all in. I told myself, *Tom, you're not even close. You need to be here for you.* I began to process all I had been through. I had never come to terms with a lot of it. And by the way, that was three years after my divorce!

Putting down my pride long enough to get the help I needed was another major step in my recovery. That step is especially difficult for men thanks to the "macho" image our society keeps promoting. Men aren't supposed to have needs. They just get back in the saddle and ride into the sunset, muttering, "Women, who needs 'em?" But that's stupid. Men and women alike need to take the courageous risk of reaching out for emotional help.

Go Slow

So that's a proper risk. What about a proper caution? Here it is: don't expect to make your reentry overnight. Go slow. That will be frustrating, but be patient. Research shows that it takes three to five years to learn to trust again, to fully reenter society. (I talked about a two-year period before. That's how long you can expect to be recovering from the grief of divorce, attaining a level of acceptance. But it's usually another year or more before you can really turn your attention outward again, restoring relationships and overcoming vulnerability. It's a long, slow road.)

In a way it's like a lingering illness. You lie in bed and think, 'This is stupid. I don't want to be sick. I should go to work. Why am I not better? It's been long enough. I should be better. You get angry at the sickness. It just doesn't make sense. But it's there, and you're still sick. You just have to let it run its course.

Divorce recovery happens over a long period. That doesn't mean you're totally incapacitated. You can still have fun with others and be learning new things about yourself and them and relationships. But all the while, you're still vulnerable. Any little thing can set you back. Don't be surprised when that happens. Don't be disappointed. Be glad for the progress you *are* making, and don't expect too much too soon.

MAKE IT YOUR OWN

➤ What have you done so far to seek help for your divorce recovery?
- ❑ Talked with friends
- ❑ Become involved with a church group
- ❑ Sought counseling from a minister
- ❑ Sought counseling from a psychologist/psychiatrist
- ❑ Attended a recovery seminar
- ❑ Read books on the subject
- ❑ Other _____

_____

➤ If you haven't sought help, why not? _____

_____

➤ What specific thing could you do in the next month to reach out for help? _____

_____

➤ How would you describe your expectations for recovery?

❑ I'll be all better in the next few months.

❑ I'm getting better each day, with some relapses.

❑ It will be another year or two before I'm at full strength emotionally.

❑ I can't imagine myself ever getting over this.

❑ Other _____

_____

ON THE REBOUND

About three years after my divorce, I started dating a woman I met in the singles group at church. I still wasn't heavily involved in the group yet, but it was somewhere to go, and it seemed safe. I also hit it off with this woman.

She was a very giving person. She was Italian—I don't know if that had anything to do with it—but any time I went to her house, the first thing she'd say was, "Can I make you something to eat?" It wouldn't matter what time of day it was—"Can I make you something to eat?"

It would be ten o'clock at night, and I'd say, "Well, yeah, a little something."

"How about veal cutlets? I'll just whip them up."

Here was this person who wanted to meet my needs, and I had a lot of needs, so I was attracted to that. Psychologist Larry Crabb describes it as being like a tick on a dog. The relationship was based entirely on need meeting.

About three months into the relationship, the woman said, "You know, I'm wondering where this relationship is going."

My answer was, unfortunately, typical: "Hey, why ruin a good thing? I'm having a good time, you're having a good time. Let's not ruin it by getting serious."

Six months into the relationship, eight months, the comment kept coming: "You know, I really care about you, but I don't want to get hurt. I just need to know some idea of where this relationship is going."

"Hey, don't worry about it," I'd say. "Let's just have a good time. We enjoy each other. Let's not talk about anything serious."

What was going on? Obviously, I was afraid to make any kind of commitment. I didn't want to trust this person. I wasn't trying to take advantage of her, but somehow my heart wasn't functioning right. I knew that in a way, but I couldn't describe what was going on. All I knew was that I was having a good time. It was nice to have somebody who cared for me. I was taking far more than I was giving, and I knew I wasn't ready for commitment.

Well, after about a year—you can probably guess how it turned out—she said, "Look, if you can't tell me where we're going, I don't know that I can continue this relationship."

And of course I responded, "Hey, I don't need that kind of pressure. If you can't just enjoy the relationship, I'm outta here."

That hurt both of us, but I learned something. Even though it was three years after my divorce, I obviously wasn't healed. I had *thought* I was. Yet when I tried to use my heart again, I found it still didn't work right.

You may be learning the same lesson the hard way. You're in a relationship based on need, but your heart isn't healed. Sometimes we think those relationships will do the healing for us, but it seldom works that way.

You're still wounded. You're a different person from the one you'll be in two or five or ten years. Right now, your emotions, your priorities, and your needs are all twisted. You're moving toward health, but you're not there yet.

At the moment, then, you're attracted to anybody who strokes your damaged areas. And there are lots of damaged areas. You probably feel rejected, and it's glorious to be accepted by someone, to be wanted. You may feel rejected sexually—you're afraid you're too ugly or not sexy enough. And when someone comes by who finds you sexy, that seems to be just what the doctor ordered. For the moment, it may be satisfying, just like my veal cutlets. But the danger is that the damaged area gets too much attention, so your relationship is tilted unhealthily in that direction.

Seek Honest Friendships

I've been talking about proper risks to take and proper cautions to avoid. Here's a pair that go hand in hand: you need to take the risk of finding true friends; you also need to avoid rebound romances.

You need people who love you for who you are and who accept you. Your most-basic emotional needs are not romance and sexual fulfillment, as the talk shows keep telling us, but security and significance. You need relationships in which you know you're accepted; that's security. And you need friends who care about you, whose lives you can touch; that's significance. The safest place to find security and significance is in honest, nonromantic friendships.

In order to develop friendships, you must take a risk. Your heart is still vulnerable. It's not easy to open up to others, to let them care for you, and to care for them in return. You've been hurt. There's lots of fear in you.

But the risk is worthwhile. Solid friendships are the most-important boost toward wholeness.

Avoid romance, however. You may not like to read that, but romance is fraught with pitfalls for a person recovering from divorce. Romance is tempting because it promises to massage your wounded areas. But it will probably wound you again.

One of the pitfalls of having a poor self-image is that when someone starts paying attention to you, it's hard to keep it in perspective. Either you run and hide or—voila!—"I've found the love of my life!"

I went through that myself. If a woman paid any attention to me at all, I got heart palpitations and began fantasizing about what a great relationship we'd have. I may not have even spoken with her yet, but already in my mind we'd be marching down the aisle.

Remember the analogy of the broken arm? My heart was still broken; my whole identity was broken. And I needed to immobilize my romantic inclinations, to put them in a cast. If you don't immobilize a broken arm, it's liable to heal crooked. The same is true with your heart.

A lot of people these days are walking around with crooked hearts. They've been shattered by divorce, but they think, *What I need is to get back in action.* And so they get shattered all over again.

The temptation is magnified by society, which keeps forcing romance on you. Sometimes it's your own family. I often hear people say, "My parents are always trying to set me up. They invite me over for dinner with the guy next door, the guy from the office, or someone they think is so nice from the church group." They're convinced you're only half a person until you marry again, so they want to set you up with somebody right away. They don't understand that the emptiness in your life is far deeper than one person can fill, no matter how wonderful that person is. You need to rediscover *yourself.* You need to bandage your heart. You need to learn how to love again.

I had people at work saying, "Oh, you're young, and you've got a full life ahead of you. There are plenty of fish in the sea. Just go out and find someone else."

Somewhere inside of me, however, I was saying. *That's the last thing in the world I need. I need to get myself together.*

I've heard dozens of horror stories about rebound romances. One woman told me, "I've been in a dozen relationships in five years, and they all seem to go the same way. At first I figured there were just a lot of horrible men out there. But now I'm beginning to think, *Maybe there's something in me that's not working right.* Do you think that could be?"

I asked her to tell me more. "Well, about two months after my original divorce, I got involved with this guy, and that didn't last. Two months after that, I got involved with another, and, well, I've never gone more than six months without somebody. I've always needed somebody in my life. What do I do about it?"

"Go back to your original divorce," I said, "and work though those issues. If you don't, you're just going to take the same issues into the next relationship and the next. You've got to stop, put your heart in a cast, and go back and work on the original issues. Don't rely on a romance to fix you up. You have to fix yourself."

As long as you're counting on a romantic relationship to make you whole, you won't be whole. As long as you feel you *need* to be remarried, you're not ready for remarriage. Only when you know you're able to live a full, healthy life on your own will you be able to enter a marriage as a giver and taker, as a full partner.

> *Move forward* slowly *in the reentry process. Learn to be comfortable with yourself, and don't look to other relationships to make you whole again.*

MAKE IT YOUR OWN

➤ What qualities do you want in a friend? _____

_____

_____

➤ What people do you know who could provide the friendship you need to get back to wholeness? _____

_____

➤ How will you go about communicating your need to these people?

_____

_____

➤ Have you been involved in a "rebound romance"? _____

➤ If so, what dangers do you see? Do you find that the relationship is primarily a need-meeting one? _____

_____

_____

➤ If you're in a rebound romance now, picture yourself five years from now in a state of emotional health. How will that relationship be different then from the way it is now? _____

_____

_____

➤ What could you do to make this relationship more honest and less need oriented? _____

_____

_____

START WITH YOUR STRENGTHS

Often those who have been divorced begin to think of themselves as losers. They wear "defeat glasses," seeing their entire lives in terms of their weaknesses. They know only what they've done wrong. They foresee only uncertainty and confusion.

In rebuilding your life and reprocessing the real you, you need to take a good look at your strengths. Open your eyes to what you *can* do. Ask yourself, *What kind of person do I now want to be?*

Accept where you are. You're divorced. You didn't want to be, but you are. You're hurting. You didn't want to be, but you are. Close your eyes to all that, and look forward. *From this point,* what do you want to become? What kind of person will you be? Once you have your act together, what will you do? Who will you be?

After months in hiding, this can be a risky venture. Once you start to dream, you might be disappointed. But this is one of those proper risks you need to take. Careful planning can result in some therapeutic involvement.

Identify Your Assets

First, you need to figure out what your strengths are. Friends can help you; they're usually more objective than you. You may not even realize you're uncommonly caring, especially energetic, or good at organizing things. Your friends can tell you.

Maybe there are things you're very interested in, though you're not sure how good you are. That's fine. Commit yourself to learn all you can about such things. Your enthusiasm counts for something.

➤ Identify your strengths. List three to five things you're good at. Include personality traits, talents, or strong interests. _____

_____

_____

_____

_____

Hang Out with the Right People

Next, you need to find people who are doing what you want to do. Look for those who exhibit the traits you want to exhibit. Search for those involved in the areas you're interested in.

Then, *associate with them.* Become a part of their lives.

For instance, what if you said, *I want to be a bar hound, one of those people who goes to bars all the time and hangs around, drinks too much, and is always telling the same old, sad stories?* If that's what you want, go to those bars and hang out with those people. You'll become just like them.

Of course, you might have higher aspirations. (I hope!) But the same principle applies. If you want to be like the people you see at church, go to church. If you admire the people who build houses for the poor with Habitat for Humanity, join up with that group. If you want to be an actor, get involved with a community theater. If you like organizing things, volunteer your services to some community service organization. They're usually more than happy to welcome a new volunteer.

My friend Tom Jones tells of how, three years after his divorce, a friend invited him to sing with the St. Louis Bach Society Chorale. He hadn't sung classical music in twenty years, but he was interested in it, and the experience turned out to be extremely therapeutic. He was doing something productive, enjoying the company of others, but not sitting around waiting for a new wife to show up.

I know a lady whose husband left her for a younger model, and she was hurting. But she had taken ballet lessons before she was married, and a friend suggested she get back into it. She signed up for some lessons and found she could still dance. Now that lady is teaching ballet. She has a whole new joy in life because she refused to sit around moping over her divorce.

I know another woman, devastated by a divorce, who was extremely compassionate. That was her strength. I suggested she get involved with some ladies who wrapped bandages. She didn't want to. "Listen," I said, "people are hurting, and somebody needs to wrap those bandages. Why don't you try it?"

I saw her again a few months later, and I asked, "Did you ever go and wrap those bandages?"

She gave me a look that said somewhat grudgingly, "I actually liked it. There are some neat people there, and they loved having me involved. They acted as if I was the greatest thing since safety pins."

It seems like such a little thing, but she began to find a new purpose in life. She was important to people. She had something important to do. Maybe that's what you need, too. (Remember redirection into the lives of people from chap. 1.)

MAKE IT YOUR OWN

➤ Where can you go to find people who are (a) doing what you want to do; (b) being the kind of people you want to be; or (c) involved in activities you want to be involved in? (Consider charities, community organizations, church groups, night school, theaters, sports organizations, and singles groups.) _____

_____

_____

➤ What could you do to associate with these people? _____

_____

➤ What's the first necessary step? When will you take it? _____

_____

_____

TAKE RESPONSIBILITY FOR YOURSELF

There's a "Peanuts" cartoon I love in which Charlie Brown and Lucy are leaning on a fence and talking. Lucy asks, "Why do you think God put us here in this world?"

Charlie says, "God put us in this world to make other people happy."

Lucy thinks about it for a minute, and then she screams at the top of her voice, "SOMEBODY IS NOT DOING HIS JOB!"

Maybe you feel that way, too. Whoever is responsible for your happiness is failing.

But I've got news for you. Nobody else in the world can make you happy. That's your job. If you don't decide to take responsibility for yourself, happiness will always elude you. You'll always be upset at somebody else. You'll always be blaming someone else for where you are. You'll always be complaining and bitter on the inside.

But the person who says "This is my life; I'm going to be responsible for myself" is going to grow. He is going to put his life back together. She is going to turn things around.

You may have been waiting years for your ex-spouse to come back and make everything better. He or she got you into this mess, and he or she will have to get you out. You have been convinced that your ex would see the error in his or her ways. But it hasn't happened. You've been waiting for the other person to fix things, and you've been disappointed.

Sooner or later you must realize that nobody can fix you but you.

If you're a Christian, you may be saying, "God can fix me." Yes, that's true. I wholeheartedly believe it. God can turn people around, He can fill you with power and work wonders in your heart. But God rarely (if ever) does that to anyone who is not ready to accept responsibility for her life.

My own healing didn't start until I decided, *I'm going to stop lying in bed feeling sorry for myself. I'm going to stop waiting for someone to come along and heal me, and I'm going to begin to move on with my life.* Yes, God was doing the healing, but it's a lot easier to steer a moving car than one that's standing still. I had to accept the responsibility for my life and decide to move forward.

When you do move forward, let me suggest you move in the direction of love. Not romantic love; we've discussed those dangers. I'm talking about friendship, giving, sharing, and serving. Don't rush it. It will be difficult to trust others, even your closest friends. But move slowly in that direction.

> *Your healing is your own responsibility. Don't wait for a person or anything else to come along to fulfill you or even heal you. You need to make the tough choices now for your own recovery.*

This, too, is risky. You're putting yourself on the line. You can't blame anyone else—it's just you now, and you might fail. But this is another of those proper risks you need to take.

MAKE IT YOUR OWN

▶ Which of the following statements are true of you?

❑ My divorce has messed up my life.

❑ I still hope my ex will come back to me.

❑ I'd like to be happy, but bad things keep happening.

❑ I'm upset with God because He has not brought me happiness.

❑ I feel pretty stagnant right now. My life isn't going anywhere.

❑ It's high time I took responsibility for my life.

❑ I've recently begun to move forward in my recovery.

❑ Life is still tough, but I'm heading toward happiness.

▶ Finish this sentence: My life would be a lot happier if only _____

_____

▶ In what way can you take responsibility for your life? What specific action can you take? _____

_____

_____

▶ When will you take this action? _____

_____

▶ In what way can you begin to show love to others? _____

_____

_____

Action Point: You have just written a specific goal for how you'll begin to take responsibility for your own growth and healing. Write that goal on page 287, where we're recording these action points for future reference.

LEARN HOW TO LOVE AGAIN

The last step you'll take in your recovery is learning how to trust again, commit again—all the necessary ingredients for learning how to truly love others. We've already talked about developing healthy friendships and learning how to be self-sacrificial, but this kind of love goes beyond that. Now we're talking about *agape* love, an unconditional love.

After what you've been through, it's understandable that you're going to have a hard time in trusting, committed relationships. So if you're cringing at the mere thought, that's okay, because as we've said before, that's all part of the self-protection that's so necessary for a while. But you don't want to stay there. For complete healing, you need to reach a point where you can start to love others unconditionally.

For many of us, this ability will be all new, because we may never have experienced it. Unconditional love is actually impossible for people to give regularly, but we need to strive constantly for it. It's the way God loves us, as only He can. It's demonstrated in the fact that He loves us just as much on the worst day of our lives as He does on our best. His love is undiminished whether we're in the midst of an adulterous affair or sitting in church.

Let me illustrate by telling you about my two weddings. At my first ceremony, I was young, but I had all the answers. (Just like you at age twenty, right?) People would say to me, "Aren't you nervous? Are you sure you know what you're doing?"

I would always answer with a very confident, "Yes, I know exactly what I'm doing, and I'm not nervous at all."

I was telling the truth. I wasn't nervous, and I really thought I knew what I was doing, because I was going to trust in God, and He would always take care of me.

When I said my marriage vows at my first wedding, I said with confidence that I would love my wife no matter what happened, I would always be there for her no matter what the circumstances, and I would put her needs before my own. Do you remember saying those things? But did we really have any idea what we were saying?

If you were like me, what you were thinking while you were saying those vows was more like, *Look at all I'm getting—a fine-looking wife who's going to help me get through school, be there for me, and . . .* My focus was generally on what I was getting, not what I was giving. Now please understand that I knew I had responsibilities. But isn't it true that we tend to focus on our own needs more often?

Now contrast that with my more-recent marriage. After being single again for about eight years and learning to be very content that way, I was faced with the decision to commit myself to another person, to trust again, and to love unconditionally. That was scary! And well it should be. As I thought about taking those vows, I now was contemplating the awesome responsibility I was about to take on.

I was going to promise to love even when I was treated poorly; to communicate even when I didn't feel like talking; and to put my wife's needs before my own. Is there anyone who believes he or she can do that regularly? If there is, I'd like to meet you.

I was nervous about getting married again, not because I loved my new wife less, and not because I didn't trust her or God, but because I knew I was setting myself up for a lot of hard work and failure. I knew there would be times when I would come home from a difficult day and my first thought would be, *Oh, good. I'm home. Now I can relax and just do what I want to do.* But inevitably, as I would walk in the door, my wife would say, "Oh, good. I'm glad you're home. I need you to ..." At that moment, would I be able and willing to love unconditionally?

It's a difficult task, but I believe that with God's help we can love others that way. Not all the time. Yes, we'll fail. But that's where the work comes in—as we constantly recommit ourselves to the task of loving others.

MAKE IT YOUR OWN

➤ Look at the following list of self-oriented versus love-oriented characteristics. On a continuum between the two, where would you rate yourself? Put an X where you think you would fall.

Self-oriented person:	**Love-oriented person:**
a) Sees only his needs	a) Sees her responsibility to others.
b) Expects others to fulfill her.	b) Knows fulfillment is his own responsibility and is available through God.
c) Wants pleasure without commitment.	c) Knows that satisfying relationships require commitment.
d) Cannot be fulfilled, can't commit, and can't truly love.	d) Is fulfilled through serving God and helping others.

As many of you have filled this out, you may have had this fleeting thought: *Boy, if I ever get married again, I want to find someone who is love oriented.* The point of this whole exercise is for you to come to the place where you say instead, "Lord, help *me* to *become* a love-oriented person."

CHAPTER 4

BEGINNING AGAIN: BIBLICAL INSIGHTS FOR THE DIVORCED*

A few years ago, I faced a test of personal maturity. It was my son's birthday, and he wanted a bicycle. *No problem!* I thought to myself. And off I went to one of the local toy superstores to find the right bike.

After looking over the fifty or so models available, I selected one that I particularly liked. It was a shiny black bike with only one gear (none of that fancy stuff!) and two brakes, a hand brake and a foot brake.

I took a slip of paper from the display; I was to use it to purchase the bike. At the register, the clerk told me to wait a moment for someone to bring my bike out. I expected to have the fancy, new two-wheeler wheeled out to me. Instead, a young man brought out a cardboard box.

At that moment, I noticed a sign hanging near the bicycle display: "Let us assemble your bike—only $15."

For a moment I thought, *Wouldn't that be easy?* Then I regained my masculine sanity. *No way,* I said to myself. *I'm not going to let some runny-nosed kid with a ratchet set rip me off for $15! I'll put it together myself!*

---

*This chapter provides a general understanding of the topic and is not meant to be a technical study. For a more-detailed review of the topic, see Appendix C: The Fresh Start Position Paper on Marriage and Divorce. That appendix also includes titles of numerous books of a technical nature.

That evening I began to assemble the bike. And what would take some runny-nosed kid about fifteen minutes went on for two, three, and even more hours! As a typical American male, I had taken one look at the directions that came with the bike and said to myself, *No problem! This looks easy enough.* Then I put the directions down and went at it by myself.

The finished product did look something like a bike. However, I never got the hand brake attached. And it wasn't until he was riding it that my son discovered I had put the handlebars on backward! It would have been so much easier to read the instructions.

SOCIETY'S PERSPECTIVE

Unfortunately, most people enter marriage today with the same type of attitude I had about that bike. *No problem,* they think. *Marriage is natural. He loves me, and I love him. Everything will work out.*

To make matters worse, it's easier to get a marriage license than it is to get a driver's license. I once had a person at a Fresh Start Seminar tell me, "You know, if we made it as difficult to get into marriage as it is to get a divorce, there would probably be a lot more people asking questions ahead of time."

Marriage as a Convenience

I don't mean to suggest that people in our society take marriage lightly. Most are very serious about their commitment when they "take the plunge." However, behind the decision to marry lies a disturbing attitude that dominates our culture. That attitude can be summarized in one word: convenience. Marriage is a convenience, a way for me to get my needs met and be fulfilled as a person.

There's nothing wrong with becoming a fulfilled person or having your needs met. If those are the primary motivations for marriage, however, then the opposite is also true: if I'm not fulfilled or my needs are not being met, this marriage must not be for me.

What we often find, then, are people who are considering divorce because marriage is no longer convenient. It no longer fulfills their expectations.

I was visiting a friend a short while ago. The day was beautiful, and we were chatting on the front lawn. As a side comment, my friend said, "See that house across the street? Those folks have only been married for a year, but now they're getting a divorce."

"Why?" I asked.

"Oh, he says he just doesn't like the pressures of his marriage. His wife never seems to be happy, and he's tired of the negative atmosphere."

Not every divorce is so simplistic! But his comment illustrates how much of a convenience marriage has become. And when it doesn't accomplish its implied goals, we often withdraw the emotional investment made in it.

Evaluating Marriage Quality

In the process of making the divorce decision, three broad standards are used to evaluate the quality of one's marriage. The first is *whether or not you feel happy in your marriage*. That depends, of course, on how you define happiness, which is a very personal matter. One might define happiness as the provision of creature comforts: "My husband gives me everything I need" or "My wife is a lousy cook." Others might define happiness in terms of emotion: "My wife understands me" or "My husband lacks all passion."

The second standard is *whether or not you have a better, more-desirable alternative*. Here one might look back longingly at the freedom he had as a single adult. He thinks to himself, *You know, it sure was easier not having all these hassles*. And he considers whether a return to the single life would be better for him.

Another better alternative could be a more-desirable partner. Perhaps a woman develops a friendship with a man at the office. He seems so much more sensitive than her husband. He looks better. Or he has so much more drive and ambition. Before too long, she starts fantasizing about living with him. She is pondering whether he might make a better alternative.

The third standard for marital evaluation is *whether or not there's social pressure to prevent you from getting a divorce*. This standard depends on the social context of your culture: whether it reinforces marriage or is lax about divorce.

We tend to consider our American culture liberal in the area of marriage and divorce. With "no fault," "shared custody," and other laws on the books, one wouldn't think of our country as a place that demands marital stability.

But subcultures in our society place a great deal of pressure on their members not to divorce. I remember talking to one woman who actually feared for her life because she was divorcing her husband. "Everyone in the family knows that he runs around with other women and beats me up," she said. "But that doesn't matter. You just don't get a divorce in our community."

Many sociologists would say that if one of the three criteria I've mentioned is negative in your marriage, there's a good possibility you might have a divorce. If two of the criteria are negative, you have a high probability for divorce. And if all three of them exist in your marriage—well, apart from the grace of God, we'll see you in domestic court!

"Divorce is Natural"

Because marriage is viewed as a convenience, many people have come to believe that divorce is normal and natural. It's not unusual to read social scientists who describe divorce as a regular step in the developmental phases of adult life. Just as a person grows from childhood into adolescence, then from adolescence into adulthood, so adults move developmentally from one marriage into another. So say these "experts."

"After all," they would argue, "you can't expect that the wife of your twenties will necessarily meet your needs when you're in your forties." With that kind of logic, they say a typical person could expect to have two, three, or more partners in his adult life.

> **The prevalent view of our society is that marriage is a convenience whose primary purpose is the fulfillment of the individual.**

Where's the Church?

You might expect the church to counter those arguments. But that's not necessarily the case. Some parts of the church only affirm what society is saying. One major denomination has even changed its book of worship to provide an alternative reading in the marriage service. Instead of vowing "until death do us part," you may now substitute "until love ends."

MAKE IT YOUR OWN

➤ As you listen to what society is saying about marriage, which of the following messages do you receive?

❑ Marriage is a beautiful thing—when it works.

❑ Marriages should last forever.

❑ Sometimes it's tough to be married, but you should work hard to keep the marriage together.

- ❏ When you're growing up, marriage is a dream; after you're married, it's a nightmare.
- ❏ In today's society, it's normal for husbands and wives to cheat on each other.
- ❏ If you make it through ten years of marriage, you're a pretty noble person.
- ❏ People change. If you grow and your spouse doesn't, go ahead and leave the marriage.
- ❏ If you don't have kids, there's really no reason to stay together if you're having trouble in your marriage.
- ❏ Once you stop being in love with each other, your marriage is a farce and might as well be ended.
- ❏ Marriage relationships can grow through good times and bad.
- ❏ It really doesn't make sense to stay together for the kids' sake.
- ❏ Marriage is not a word, it's a sentence.

➤ Where do you hear messages like this?
- ❏ "The Oprah Winfrey Show"
- ❏ *Newsweek*
- ❏ PTA
- ❏ *National Enquirer*
- ❏ Church
- ❏ Dear Abby
- ❏ On the phone
- ❏ "General Hospital"
- ❏ CNN
- ❏ *Wall Street Journal*
- ❏ Aerobic Center
- ❏ "L.A. Law"
- ❏ At work
- ❏ *Good Housekeeping*
- ❏ From your kids
- ❏ Other _____

_____

➤ When was the last time you picked up some message from society about divorce or marriage? What was the message? _____

_____

_____

➤ I mentioned that some subcultures, especially religious groups, can be dead set against divorce. Are you in such a subculture? _____ Do you feel a tension between this subculture and the world at large? Explain. _____

_____

_____

➤ As you look at the three common criteria—unhappy in the marriage; better alternative; lack of society support for marriage—how many of them applied to your marriage? _____

_____

➤ Which of the following apply to your church?
- ❑ Helped hold my marriage together as long as it could.
- ❑ Supported me following the divorce.
- ❑ Added pressure to my marriage that contributed to the divorce.
- ❑ Didn't understand what I was going through.
- ❑ Made clear to me the Bible's teaching on marriage and divorce.
- ❑ Seemed unsure of what the Bible teaches about divorce.
- ❑ I really have not been involved in a church.

➤ How did you feel about your church's response to you during this time? _____

_____

_____

THE BIBLE'S PERSPECTIVE

Because much of the church holds the same view of marriage and divorce as our culture, you might assume the Bible reflects a similar view. However, that's not the case. The Bible does *not* consider marriage a convenience. Rather, it defines marriage as a *covenant*.

What Is a Covenant?

For most of us, the word *covenant* sounds stuffy and old-fashioned. But it's actually quite simple to understand. A covenant is a contract. We all use contracts. When you buy a car, rent an apartment, go to a movie, or ride a train, you use a contract. With a contract, you agree to pay a price and receive goods or service.

A covenant is a relationship contract, an agreement between two or more people. It's not designed to exchange goods and services. Rather, it formally establishes or maintains a relationship.

When I was a boy, I enjoyed playing cowboys and Indians. And one childhood ceremony I performed with my friends was becoming "blood brothers." You may remember how it went. Both you and your partner pricked your fingers. Then you pressed them together so that the blood would (theoretically) mingle. You shared each other's blood. You were bonded together. That bonded relationship is a covenant.

In ancient days, covenants were legally binding. When two kings agreed to peace, they formed a covenant. When two friends were particularly close, they would make a covenant. And when two families agreed to marriage, it was established by a covenant.

Every contract consists of at least three things: obligations, blessings, and curses. For example, say I buy a car. My obligation is to make payments. The dealership is obligated to make delivery on my car. Then I receive the "blessing" of driving the car. However, if I stop making payments, the "curses" of the contract are enforced. A "repo man" comes (probably in the night) and takes away my car.

Marriage as a Covenant

As I said above, God describes marriage as a covenant. When a couple are married, they receive all the blessings of the relationship. However, there are also obligations. To put them in terms of the traditional marriage vow, they are "to have and to hold, for better or for worse, in sickness and in health, as long as we both shall live." God expects marriage to be a lifelong covenant.

God says that when a man and woman are married, they are bonded together. The Bible describes this as "becoming one flesh" (see Gen. 2:24). And we know what happens when that one flesh is torn apart: you go through the stages of grief! That's one of the "curses" that comes when one or both parties are not faithful to their covenant.

Since God views marriage as a lifelong covenant, divorce of any kind must be understood as a deviation from His original plan. God did not design marriages to end before death. However, that doesn't mean God doesn't recognize the reality of divorce. When He gave His laws to the nation of Israel, He included the proper legal procedures for a divorce (see Deut. 24). Again, that doesn't imply that God condoned divorce. He just knew divorces were going to occur. So He outlined the proper methodology for the courts to follow.

God understands that divorce is the end of a marriage. When the covenant is terminated, the man and woman are no longer husband and wife. That's a legal fact. However, just because a divorce is legal in God's estimation doesn't necessarily mean it's valid. God declares that some divorces are for valid reasons and some are not. In the Bible He allows for divorce on specific (valid) grounds. Divorces that occur for other reasons, while legal and binding, are not valid and should not have taken place.

> **The Bible describes marriage as a covenant commitment that's intended to be lifelong.**

MAKE IT YOUR OWN

➤ Besides marriage, what modern examples of covenants can you think of? _____

_____

➤ As you see it, what are the *obligations* of a marriage covenant? _____

_____

_____

➤ As you see it, are those obligations still binding on you? Why or why not? _____

_____

➤ What are the *blessings* of a marriage covenant kept? _____

_____

_____

➤ Have you experienced those? Explain. _____

_____

➤ What are the curses of not keeping a marriage covenant? _____

_____

_____

➤ Have you experienced those? Explain. _____

_____

GROUNDS FOR DIVORCE

The first place where the Bible offers a valid reason for divorce is Matthew 19. In that chapter, Jesus debates with some religious leaders. And in verse 9, He says that divorce is invalid except when there has been continuing marital unfaithfulness.

The Greek word for that unfaithfulness is *porneia*, which is best translated "sexual immorality." Taken in context, Jesus says that ongoing, unrepentant sexual deviancy of any kind is a valid ground for divorce. Why should that be so?

The reason is that the sexual relationship in marriage is to be a demonstration of the whole-person commitment that two people have with one another. It's meant to express their covenant. As my Fresh Start partner Tom Jones says in his book *Sex and Love When You're Single Again* (pp. 32–33):

> The meaning God has given to sexual intercourse is that of the marriage union. Sexual intercourse is symbolic of the whole-life sharing that God requires of spouses. God invented it to be such a symbol and, in fact, a seal of that union. It was not given to mankind merely for physical pleasure; rather, it was given to indicate in an outward way what has happened and is happening in the souls of the two people who so unite.

What's happening, then, when one partner is continually going outside the marriage and giving himself physically to other persons or things? What does that say about the condition of his soul and his covenant commitment? What does it express concerning the bondedness of that person to his spouse? It indicates a real brokenness in that covenant relationship. And that brokenness ought to be acknowledged and repaired. Jesus says, however, that if a partner is not willing to change and build his one-flesh covenant relationship—if there's a long-term, aggravated problem in this area—the other spouse has a basis for a valid divorce.

Later in the New Testament, in a book written to the Christians in the city of Corinth, the apostle Paul responds to some serious questions about marriage (see 1 Cor. 7:10ff). Apparently those questions came in response to a previous teaching of Paul. He had explained that a follower of Jesus Christ ought not to marry a person who was not committed to following Christ. It just doesn't make sense for two people with different priorities and life's purposes to try and work together.

"Well," they might have responded, "what happens if a Christian is already married to someone who isn't committed to Christ? Should that person get a divorce?"

It's interesting that in his response, Paul first restates what Jesus taught in Matthew 19. He explains that Christians ought not to divorce; but if they do, they ought to be reconciled. Covenant faithfulness was the standard Jesus taught throughout His ministry, and Paul affirms it. It can be safely assumed that Paul (and his readers) understood the one exception Jesus had given to this general rule. Then Paul goes on to address the issue of mixed marriages.

In his response, Paul explains that when a partner who is not a follower of Christ wants to leave the marriage, the believer is to let him leave. It cannot be inferred that the Christian is kicking his spouse out of the house (and she is thus "leaving"). No, Paul taught that the believing spouse ought to remain in the marriage if his partner wants it. Instead, Paul refers to the situation in which an unbelieving spouse has made a conscious decision to abandon the marriage. In that case the apostle says, "A [Christian] brother or a sister is not under bondage" (1 Cor. 7:15).

That phrase "not under bondage" is very important. It was used when a slave was freed from his bondage. Paul says the believer is no longer enslaved in the covenant relationship when his unbelieving spouse abandons the marriage.

Believers Abandoning Believers

I find it interesting that Paul's teaching on mixed marriages is different from his teaching to couples who claim to be disciples of Christ. Why does he say the Christians ought to be reconciled?

The reason is found in Matthew 18, one chapter prior to Jesus' teaching on divorce. In that passage Jesus said that when two Christians have a dispute with one another, they ought to work it out together. When they can't resolve it, they need to go to a member of the church who will act as a mediator and help them solve their conflict.

However, if that effort doesn't work, Jesus taught that the matter ought to be taken "to the church"—that is, the authority of the church—where the elders should bring the problem to closure (see vv. 15-17).

What happens when one of these believers still refuses to remain married? In Matthew 18:17, Jesus taught that a member who refuses to submit to the intervention of the church is to be treated as an unbeliever.

Note that the church cannot say, "You aren't a Christian." Only God can say that! But the church must say, "You're acting as though you aren't a Christian, and therefore we must treat you like an unbeliever."

In cases that terminate in excommunication, the believing spouse is considered abandoned by an unbeliever and is no longer bound in the marriage.

This process of restorative discipline takes hard work. It's one of the most-taxing responsibilities of the church. However, it is vital care for those who turn to their church for help in times of marital crisis. (For more about this, see pp. 168-72 of *Through the Whirlwind*.)

What Is Abandonment?

The church is responsible to provide emotional and spiritual support for members who are struggling in their marriages. Further, it needs to stand alongside members who are forced to make tough decisions in the midst of a destructive marital environment.

One of those tough decisions comes in the area of defining abandonment. Traditionally, abandonment has been understood as one spouse irrevocably leaving the household. In our day, however, it has been suggested that other ongoing, problematic situations be defined as abandonment.

For example, what about physical abuse? Shouldn't a situation where husband or wife beats up a spouse over a long period, refusing to change, be considered abandonment? Or what about two persons who live in the same house but maintain totally separate lives? Are they maintaining the covenant relationship of marriage?

Many who hear such questions respond by saying, "Wait a minute. When you think like that, a person could rationalize any problem as abandonment!" That's true. Therefore, we must ask if the Bible gives any criteria for abandonment other than physical desertion.

The answer is both no and yes! No, the Bible does not specifically address circumstances such as abuse and neglect. Yes, however, the Bible does give guidelines to interpret such problems.

The first guideline is our *definition of marriage*. If marriage is a covenant commitment, abandonment should be defined in terms of abandoning the covenant commitment rather than simple physical desertion. So, for example, the Bible teaches that a husband ought to love his wife as he loves his own body (see Eph. 5:28). If a man is continually beating up his wife, he may be abandoning his covenant commitment to her.

A second guideline is the *attitude of the offender*. Is she repentant about the problem? Or does she refuse to face the destructive nature of the situation? Perhaps even worse, does she seem repentant (desiring to stop the behavior and be responsible) yet act no differently? Matthew 18 implies that discipline ought to be used in cases where a party is unrepentant and refuses to change.

A third guideline is the *objective perspective of the church leadership*. There's nothing more difficult for a person in an emotionally destructive situation than to make a reasonable, rational decision. The elders of the church ought to be available to a member in this situation to provide wise, godly counsel. Furthermore, in Hebrews 13:17 we read, "Obey your leaders and submit to their authority. They keep watch over you as men who must give an account. Obey them so that their work will be a joy, not a burden, for that would be of no advantage to you" (NIV).

Here we read that a believer is responsible to submit his circumstances to the leaders for understanding and direction. And the leaders, who are accountable for their members, must respond. For a situation of marital difficulty to qualify as abandonment, elders must confirm that the actions of the unrepentant spouse have the same extreme effect as someone's physical abandonment.

Using those criteria, a Christian ought not to be able to define abandonment simplistically to provide an easy solution (divorce) to a complex situation.

Recently a study committee of one evangelical denomination seriously grappled with the question of abandonment. You may find a few excerpts from their conclusions helpful:

> Are there other forms of "separation" today that may be considered equivalent to this leaving of the marriage of which Paul speaks? We must be careful not to open the floodgate of excuses. On the other hand, we need to recognize the reality of the "separation." We should allow [leaders] the liberty to discern with much prayer what would be the proper response in a particular circumstance.
>
> Several considerations incline us to agree . . . that desertion can occur as well by the imposition of intolerable conditions as by departure itself. . . . It seems to us that sins which are tantamount in extremity and consequence to actual desertion should be understood to produce similar eventualities. . . . We are quick to add, however, that the list of sins tantamount to desertion cannot be very long.
>
> We are not unaware of the danger which lurks behind such a position in the temptation it may pose to some to spin out a vast array of marital sins equivalent to desertion. This danger, however, we conclude is best met in other ways than by an effort to forge a barrier to divorce sturdier than the Bible's own. In many more ways than this, the church's health and integrity depends upon her elders' ability and willingness to provide godly, wise, merciful and severe, and scrupulously Scriptural

application of Biblical norms to human situations. (Ad Interim Committee on Marriage, Divorce, and Remarriage to the Nineteenth General Assembly of the Presbyterian Church in America, p. 2345)

What About Invalid Divorces?

If you've gone through a divorce that would not be considered valid according to the Bible, you should understand a number of points.

First, *God still empathizes with the pain that brought about your situation.* Jeremiah 3:8 states that God Himself went through a divorce. He understands what you've been through and what you're facing now.

Second, *divorce is not the unforgivable sin in God's eyes.* I made a point of reading through every list of heinous sins recorded in the New Testament, and divorce isn't even mentioned! My point is this: God can forgive you of your sin of seeking a divorce for invalid reasons. First John 1:9 states, "If we confess our sins, He is faithful and just to forgive us our sins and to cleanse us from all unrighteousness." To understand that forgiveness, please read carefully the next chapter.

Third, if it's possible, *God expects you to work for reconciliation.* As I stated above, if you and your former spouse are disciples of Christ, there is no just reason for divorce outside of ongoing sexual immorality. While you're divorced, you ought to be married.

Or if your former spouse is not a follower of Jesus but still desires a marriage, you ought not to have left her. You should seek to be reconciled.

If your former spouse has remarried, however, or is not interested in reconciliation, there's nothing more you can do about it. You are forgiven and no longer bound.

MAKE IT YOUR OWN

➤ Based on what you've read here, along with your personal study or your church's teaching, what do you feel are valid grounds for seeking divorce? Circle any of the following reasons that qualify:

1. Spouse has an affair.
2. Spouse has repeated affairs.
3. Spouse moves out.
4. Spouse abuses you physically.
5. Spouse abuses the kids.
6. Spouse abuses you emotionally.
7. Spouse is addicted to drugs or alcohol and will not seek treatment.
8. Love is gone from the marriage.

9. You two have grown apart.
10. Spouse does not communicate with you.
11. Spouse does not care for your needs.
12. You become a Christian, and spouse doesn't.
13. Spouse insists you stop going to church.
14. Spouse insists you give up Christianity.
15. You find someone else who fulfills your needs.

Discussion

I don't presume to be the final arbiter on these things, but you might be interested in my views, and those of my Fresh Start colleagues, on the situations listed above. I urge you to seek counsel from your own church leaders wherever possible.

1–2. An affair, especially if it's ongoing and the spouse is unrepentant, certainly qualifies as *porneia* in the biblical sense. Yet even here, repentance and restoration are the most-desirable options. *Repeated* affairs indicate there's a deeper problem and a lack of repentance. (Even if your spouse claims to be sorry after each one, true repentance requires behavior change, or at least a concerted effort to deal with the offending actions.) That could certainly be seen as abandonment.

3. This is abandonment, pure and simple. However, the Bible stipulates abandonment by a nonbeliever is valid grounds for divorce. If abandonment is by a believer, you need to get the church involved.

4–5. Physical abuse can certainly be seen as a violation of the marriage covenant. It is no sin to escape a dangerous situation. Try to deal with the problem, but if it persists, you may have grounds for staying separated and perhaps divorce. Again, seek counsel from church leaders for a neutral opinion.

6. Emotional abuse is hard to define. Severe cases could be considered valid grounds for staying separated and perhaps divorce, but be careful not to draw your definitions too broadly. It is important to seek help from your church in coming to these conclusions.

7. "Will not seek treatment" is a key phrase here. Spouses can help each other overcome addictions. But obstinate denial of a problem is impossible to deal with. This may qualify as abandonment. Get the church involved.

8–11. No way. Society may accept those explanations, but God does not.

12–14. The Bible is clear that a Christian should stay with a non-Christian spouse unless the non-Christian instigates the breakup. If the unbelieving spouse demands that you stop going to church, you have a conflict of commitments. If it cannot be resolved, you must ultimately obey

God's orders to assemble with other believers. Certainly, if your spouse insists you give up your faith, you can't do that. Your spouse may, as a result, seek divorce, and in such cases you should let him go.

15. No.

➤ How do you think God feels about the circumstances of your divorce? Check all the following that apply:

❏ He knows I did what I had to do.

❏ I was an innocent victim. He sympathizes.

❏ I made wrong choices. He has forgiven me.

❏ There is distance between God and me because of my sin.

❏ I blame Him for my problems. I don't care what He thinks.

WHAT ABOUT REMARRIAGE?

The topic of remarriage is so important that we devote an entire session to it in our Fresh Start alumni seminar entitled Second Wind. In this chapter I'm going to limit myself to commenting on what the Bible teaches concerning remarriage and then point out some general guidelines.

The Bible's teaching on this subject has been hotly debated for generations. Numerous (and sometimes complicated) answers are given to the question of when remarriage is okay. However, the biblical basis for remarriage can be boiled down to a very simple principle: if you had biblically valid grounds for divorce, you have biblically valid grounds for remarriage. And (as I stated above) if you didn't have biblically valid grounds for divorce, you ought to seek reconciliation when it's possible.

However, as I said in the last chapter, you need to be very careful before you go running into a new relationship. Just because you have the biblical right to remarry doesn't necessarily mean it's right for you!

When I talk to someone about remarriage, I always want to cover a number of questions prior to encouraging the person in that direction. Let me review those questions with you.

1. Have you worked through the implications of your divorce?

As I said in the last chapter, you need to work through your own healing and recovery before you commit yourself again in a lifelong covenant relationship. Remember the illustration I used about the broken arm? When people rush back into marriage, they apply pressure on themselves that they're not prepared to handle.

What implications of your divorce am I talking about? The first is *forgiveness.* Are you still carrying around the negative emotions of your past relationship, or have you come to closure with the pain? In the next chapter I will explore this in more detail. But if you haven't forgiven yourself and the significant others of your past, you'll be carrying unhealthy, destructive baggage into your new marriage.

The second implication is *restoration of relationship with your former spouse.* Are you able to work together with your former spouse, particularly in the area of coparenting? Restoration implies the ability to respect one another and communicate with each other as responsible persons. You don't have to be friends. You don't even have to like each other. You do need to be able to work together in a sane manner without consistent tension and blowups.

Restoration of relationships may never happen with your former spouse. However, as much as is possible from your side, have you honestly made attempts to do it?

The third implication of your divorce is *reconciliation.* Of course, this is often not possible. (If you skipped over the chapter on separation and reconciliation, however, you may want to work through it at this point just to review the issues involved.) But you need to remember that from God's perspective, reconciliation is always the first preference. Often, when we're in the pain of separation and divorce, we don't even want to think about reconciliation. Yet God wants us to review this step in our own minds and hearts before we consider the possibilities of marriage to someone else.

2. What are the reasons you want to remarry?

There are many wrong reasons to remarry: for example, escaping from singleness, seeking financial security, and finding sexual relief. Remember that rebound marriages have a higher percentage of divorce than first marriages. Why? Because people on the rebound are looking for someone to make them whole and healed. But no one else is going to make you into a whole person. Two whole persons make a healthy marriage. Trying to find another person to solve your problems and make you whole is simply another way of defining codependency.

I have found over the years that the person who would like to remarry but doesn't *need* to be married is best prepared for remarriage. When you feel you're a whole person who can live life fully without a mate, you may be ready to commit again.

> *The right to remarry doesn't necessarily mean it's right for you to remarry.*

➤ Do you currently have a desire to remarry? Check mark the answer that best expresses your feeling.

❑ Strongly

❑ Mildly

❑ Maybe someday

❑ Are you crazy? I just got *out* of a marriage!

➤ When do you think you'll be ready to remarry?

❑ Right now

❑ I have no idea

❑ I'll know when the right person comes along

❑ Give me another year or two

❑ Five years

❑ Does "hell freezing over" mean anything to you?

➤ Do you believe you may remarry *validly*? Why? _____

_____

_____

➤ Have you dealt with the necessary issues from your previous marriage?

a. Have you forgiven your former spouse (and sought forgiveness where necessary)?

b. Have you restored a working relationship with your former spouse (if that's possible)?

c. Have you done all you can to reconcile that marriage on healthy terms? (In other words, was it a valid divorce from your perspective?)

What does this statement mean to you: "You are ready to remarry when you don't need to be married"? _____

_____

_____

_____

_____

Getting On Course

I have a number of friends who work for airlines, and I've learned from them that if a pilot sets his instruments even slightly wrong, when the plane is supposed to land, it won't be close to its proper destination. In a similar way, if we set an improper course for marriage, the final result can be disastrous.

Our society has set its course by defining marriage as a convenience. The results can be seen all around in broken marriages, children without stable homes, and people who haven't learned how to maintain commitments.

The Bible sets a different course. I would not be so simplistic as to say that viewing marriage as a lifelong covenant commitment would resolve our society's problems. However, living the biblical norm could go a long way toward stabilizing our social condition.

Fortunately, when planes are off course, they can make a mid-course correction. And the same is true for us. We can make the responsible decisions to define marriage biblically and to order our lives according to it.

Now, if I could only find those directions for my son's bike, I could get that hand brake connected....

CHAPTER **5**

SEXUALITY*

I am supposed to be a mature man at about half a century in age. The general presumption is that people my age know all about sex and sexuality. But generally, I don't think we do. Even though we're living in a time thought to be awakened and free in regard to sexuality, I find that I'm not alone in feeling my education in sexual matters has been everything but complete and correct.

GROWING UP

I can't remember exactly when sexuality became interesting to me, but I know it was early. I was only ten years old when a girl in my class at school sent tremors of fascination and desire all through me. I didn't think much about the nature of that state of trembling back then. I just enjoyed it. But what was beginning to happen to me then has continued to influence my life ever since.

Certainly the kids of my generation had a head start on their parents in understanding sexuality, but we still lived in ignorance. Nobody really talked about sexuality when we were growing up. Oh, sure, there was a sprinkling of "sex talk" in almost every conversation, but it never really got serious. Nobody ever sat down with us and explained everything sexual in a

---

*This chapter was written primarily by Tom Jones, vice president of Fresh Start. The topic is covered more fully in his book *The Single-Again Handbook*.

meaningful and helpful way. We were pretty much left at the mercy of the literature on the rest-room walls and the library books on anatomy.

There was "health class," of course, but that was a course in biology. It was good to find at least one place where we could look at the subject of sex and feel it was legitimate. The facts about sexual anatomy, the reproductive system, and venereal diseases were important, but you had the feeling there were other facts you should know. If anyone knew those other facts, however, they weren't talking.

Then along came Hugh Hefner and his magazine. He began to publish *Playboy* when I was fourteen, but he didn't help much either. He did draw a lot of attention. Even while we boys were going out of our minds "reading" *Playboy*, somehow I think most of us knew we weren't getting a fair shake from Hefner. The morals of our homes and the general negativism of the church were too strong for us to simply accept his philosophy without question. Then there were the real girls we knew.

Real girls were so different from the pinups. The pinups just stood there without their clothes and smiled at you. Real girls kept their clothes on and didn't always smile (at least, not at me). Real girls could talk, too, and they never talked about sex. When we started dating, sex just wasn't discussed. Certainly it was on our minds. (I assume it was on the girls' minds, too.) But instead of talking, what you did was act real knowing and grope around in the dark.

Whoever dared to say right out loud, "I really need some help understanding sexuality. Do you understand sexuality?" No one dared.

Even when we got married, most of us didn't talk about sexuality. We had sexual intercourse, and we enjoyed that, but there was still a cloud of confusion covering so many things. Most distressing of all, we still didn't know where to turn for help. The doctors talked only about biological facts, the social organizations talked about diseases and unwanted pregnancies, and the church just didn't talk. Any thinking you did concerning sexuality you did *all alone*.

Finally, however, we had the sexual revolution of the 1960s. Society rebelled against the old traditions, and people threw off their clothes. Suddenly, everything was being talked about. The shock was almost too much for us, especially those of us who were Christians. What should we think? What should we do? Most of us probably felt some inner gladness that finally it was okay to talk about sex in public, but it was scary. It seemed as if society was going too far. Mere nakedness and sexual conversation were not enough in themselves. If this new sexual revolution didn't produce helpful insight into the meaning and nature of sexuality, we might be worse off than before.

The new openness produced a flood of literature on the subject of sexuality in general. There are even books *without pictures.* The church is finally talking, too. What a relief to finally be able to read and discuss this side of our lives!

But do you understand sexuality? You may be very much like me—still stumbling along, trying to put a number of undefined questions into meaningful form, still listening hard to everything that's said in the hope that answers really do exist.

MAKE IT YOUR OWN

➤ How does your experience match up to the author's? Consider the following statements. Check all responses that apply.

As I grew up, my family:

❏ talked freely about sexuality.

❏ joked about sexual matters.

❏ spoke very seriously about sexual matters.

❏ never talked about sexuality.

❏ Other: _____

_____

➤ I learned most about sex from:

❏ my parents.

❏ health class.

❏ friends.

❏ experimentation.

❏ graffiti.

❏ Other: _____

➤ As I look back, I think I:

❏ knew too much about sex too soon.

❏ knew a lot about sex, but I'm glad.

❏ didn't know much about sex, but that was okay.

❏ didn't know as much as I should have known about sex.

❏ Other: _____

➤ My attitude toward sexual matters now is:

❏ I think about sex all the time.

❑ I am generally embarrassed about the whole subject.

❑ I talk pretty freely about the subject.

❑ It's a private thing, so I only talk about sex when it's appropriate.

❑ It rarely enters my mind.

❑ Other: _____

_____

➤ Is there something you wish you had known about sexuality when you were younger? If so, what is it? _____

_____

_____

DEFINING SEXUALITY

It may seem a bit bold of me, having just admitted I'm still seeking the truth, to now burst into print on the subject of sexuality. So allow me to say emphatically that I don't think of myself as an authority. I'm a learner, like you.

Some things, however, are becoming increasingly clear in my thinking on the subject, and I want to share them with you because I know how difficult it can be to get a proper perspective. I'll begin by giving a definition of sexuality. And let's look first at some things sexuality is *not*.

Sexuality Is Not a Substitute for God

Sexuality is *not* a substitute for God. You may think that's a strange thing for me to say. "Who in the world ever thought it was?" you might ask. It is indeed doubtful that anyone ever consciously formed the concept that sexuality was God. (There have been cultures, however, in which sexual activity was thought of as a method of communion with God, and in which sexual intercourse was part of the worship ceremony.)

Still, many people have turned sex into a kind of idol. Ours is a sex-obsessed society. Our books, movies, music, clothes, and a tremendous amount of advertising consistently beat a sexual rhythm into our brains. Underneath it all is a powerful statement of the place of sexual things in our view of human life. We're being told that life aims largely, if not entirely, at sexual fulfillment. The assumption seems to be that if we aim for it and seek it with all our hearts (not to mention our time and money), we shall soon achieve the atomic sexual experience, and presumably we will be fulfilled and complete. That attitude, I submit, is idolatrous.

When anyone tells you that anything other than God Himself can make you fulfilled and happy, that person is encouraging you toward idolatry. Idolatry, after all, is nothing more or less than placing something other than God in first place in your life. No matter what it is, if you give something first priority in your life, that thing has become a god to you, and you have become involved in a form of false worship.

Two significant things occur whenever people turn to idolatry, no matter what the false god is. First, *they expect the false god to do for them what only the true and living God can*—they expect it to complete and fulfill them. They assume they will achieve the greatest happiness by seeking and serving the false god. The result, of course, is disappointment and emptiness. This has obviously happened with sexuality in our society. Millions of people have swallowed the *Playboy* philosophy, only to end up burned out and disillusioned.

Second, *people lose the meaning and significance of that thing they have chosen as their idol*. When the idolater gives first place in his life to his idol, he has removed it from its proper place. Now it can't even provide the good it was designed to provide when God created it.

All things were created by God with good purposes inherent in them, and that includes sexuality. God designed it for our blessing. However, that good can be obtained only by those who keep the proper perspective. When we lose the right perspective, we also lose God's blessing.

> **Sexuality must not be put in God's place. If it is, it will lose its power to bless and will always disappoint us.**

Sexuality, like all other aspects of human nature, is only part of our createdness, and it must be subordinated to God like everything else. However, while sexuality is not God and cannot provide our ultimate happiness, it is a marvelous part of the way God made us. It is His gift to us, and when it's properly understood and enjoyed, it provides us with much good.

MAKE IT YOUR OWN

➤ In what ways do people make sex an idol? _____

_____

_____

➤ Have you done this in your life? If so, how? _____

_____

_____

➤ In what ways (if any) has your worship of sex hurt your worship of God? _____

_____

_____

➤ In what ways (if any) has your worship of sex diminished the true value of sex in your life? _____

_____

_____

SEXUALITY IS NOT LOVE

Here's a second negative definition: sexuality is not the same thing as love. Sexuality, as God intends it, certainly has something to do with love; it cannot be correctly understood apart from love. However, we can choose to express our sexuality in ways that aren't loving.

An obvious example is rape. Clearly, rape is sexual, but it's not love. Prostitution is also sexual, but only a confused person would think of it as love. In addition, there are numerous selfish and, therefore, unloving ways in which even married people sometimes use sexuality.

Many people have found themselves in great confusion and pain because they have mistakenly supposed that sexuality was identical to love. Many a young woman has yielded to a young man's sexual demands, all the while assuming his sexual desire for her meant he loved her. How wrong we are to make "lovemaking" synonymous with sexual intercourse! Intercourse can be a wonderful way to express love, but it may also express many unloving things. We had better learn the difference between sexuality and love.

It would be wrong for me to assume that someone loves me just because she has a sexual interest in me. To reverse the emphasis, it would be wrong for me to assume I necessarily love a woman just because I sexually desire her. The inability to discern this difference caused many problems for me when I was growing up. If I became sexually attracted to a young woman, I found it easy to think I was in love. What I loved, however, was not the girl but the surge of sexual need and desire within myself. In many cases, I didn't even know the girl.

It's simple to determine if I have sexual urges in the direction of a woman, but it's much more complicated to find out whether I love her. To know that, I'll have to ask myself many questions other than whether I desire her body's pleasures. I must concern myself with her whole being—her whole personality, her mind's peculiar way of thinking, her varying moods, her attitudes, and her interests.

Beyond that, if I love her, I must be willing to make some commitments to her not only for the moment, but also for the future. Recall the familiar concepts of the marriage vows: "for better or for worse," "in sickness and in health," "for richer or for poorer." Such thoughts go beyond sexuality to the whole of life.

There are also other kinds of love that don't include sexual expressions. One may love his parents, for example, or his brothers and sisters, children, and friends.

One last distinction may prove helpful here. Love relationships normally include expressions of affection—warm handshakes, hugs, and kisses. However, such expressions aren't necessarily sexual in nature. Physical touch is legitimate in its own right and plays an important part in all love relationships.

This last distinction is important for a variety of reasons. Many people carry around a tremendous burden of false guilt because they're affectionate and enjoy touch. In our society, such people are sometimes viewed as necessarily sexually motivated. Therefore, if I affectionately touch a woman, I may be seen as sending her a sexual overture. Or, worse, if I affectionately touch another man, I may be viewed as having homosexual tendencies. A person may accept such views and wrongly interpret his own desire for affectionate expression as proof of sexual overeagerness. This has had particularly damaging effect on men in our society, many of whom have grown wary of touching anyone, especially other men.

MAKE IT YOUR OWN

➤ Do you like the term "making love" as it is used by our society? How would you define it? _____

_____

_____

➤ What are the dangers of equating physical sexuality with love? _____

_____

_____

_____

➤ List ten expressions of love that are not sexual.

1. _____   6. _____
2. _____   7. _____
3. _____   8. _____
4. _____   9. _____
5. _____   10. _____

➤ Have you tended to equate sexuality with love in your relationships? Why? _____

_____

➤ Describe the experience of another person who equated sexual desire and love. _____

_____

_____

What Sexuality Is Not:
a substitute for God
the same thing as love
merely a biological function

MORE THAN BIOLOGY

A third thing we often confuse with sexuality is biological sex, or sexual intercourse itself. Biological sex is sexual. But there's much more to our sexuality than mere physical contact. Yet our society does a lot of talking about sex without saying anything at all about sexuality.

Most of the books on sex today are entirely on the subject of biological sex. They tell us how to have sexual intercourse—what to move; how, when and where to touch. The purpose, by and large, is to produce that atomic orgasm I spoke of earlier. The assumption seems to be that sex has only one purpose, physical pleasure.

Such a view says almost nothing about sexuality as I understand it. Sexuality is not merely physical, biological, or genital. Neither is sexuality *primarily* physical. *Sexuality is spiritual and personal.*

Sexuality Is Spiritual

If you've had any degree of sexual experience, I probably don't have to prove to you that mere biological sex can be extremely frustrating and empty. It's quite possible to have intercourse, even to the point of explosive physical climax, without having much personal satisfaction. Many married people experience a lot of negative feeling about their sexual relationship, and I believe the reason is often that the spiritual aspect of sexuality is being ignored. The mental, emotional, and spiritual dimensions must be recognized, along with the physical, if there is to be any genuine fulfillment and satisfaction.

Woody Allen, in his movie *Annie Hall*, makes this point forcefully. In one scene, Woody and Diane Keaton are in bed together having sexual intercourse. Then a strange thing happens. Suddenly, while they continue to have intercourse, a second Diane appears, a rather ghostly one. She gets out of the bed, steps across the room, sits in a chair, and stares at Woody and Diane in bed. The look on her face shows clearly that she's bored.

Then Woody looks over at the Diane in the chair and says something like, "That's what gets me about you, you never put yourself into this." The ghostly Diane responds that he should be happy because he's got all he really wants there in the bed. He has her body.

It's an amusing scene, but it's only funny on the surface. Deep down inside, we all know from experience the loneliness, hurt, and anger that often accompany sexual intercourse. A man and woman can unite sexually and still feel very far from each other in personal ways.

Look more closely at what Woody and Diane are saying. Diane is hurt and angry because she believes that all Woody wants from her is the use of her body to satisfy his physical desires. Woody, however, is hurt and angry because all Diane will give him is her body. Diane wants more than Woody's body, and she wants him to want more than her body. Woody wants more than Diane's body, and he wants her to give him more than her body. Both Woody and Diane know that sexuality is not mere genital contact.

That illustration provides a great help in moving now to a definition of sexuality. *Sexuality is the human potential for the sharing of one's whole life with another.* It is the ability and need imprinted upon our nature by the Creator to give ourselves completely to another human being. It's also the ability and need to receive another person into our own life completely. The romantic expression "body and soul" perhaps says it best. I have the ability and need to give myself, all of myself, the body and soul of myself, to another person. I have the ability and need to receive another, all of another, the body and soul of another, into my life.

The Meaning of Sexual Intercourse

This understanding of sexuality helps us to gain a correct understanding of sexual intercourse. It's the symbol, or emblem, of that total life sharing that God requires of those who marry. In sexual intercourse, one person actually enters into the body of another, an outward expression of what exists between the souls of two people who are totally committed to each other. Understood this way, intercourse is lifted out of the merely physical realm. This spiritual aspect is what makes human sex unique in all of God's creation.

> *Sexuality is our God-given potential to share our whole selves—body, soul, and spirit—with another person. Sexual intercourse is the symbol of that sharing and lifelong commitment.*

MAKE IT YOUR OWN

It has been said that a relationship should develop in the following order:

* Social

* Mental

* Spiritual

* Emotional

* Physical

➤ Why is that a good order of progression? _____

_____

_____

Answer the next two questions only if you have experienced what they're talking about.

➤ How does it feel to have sex *without* spiritual commitment? _____

_____

➤ How does it feel to have sex *with* spiritual commitment? _____

_____

➤ What does the following quotation from Lewis Smedes mean to you: "Sex without interpersonal intimacy is like a diploma without an education"? _____

_____

_____

SEXUAL MORALITY

This understanding of sexuality as a whole-life sharing—and sexual intercourse as an outward expression of that total union of husband and wife—helps explain Christian morality. It provides an important part of the rationale for viewing sexual intercourse between unmarried persons as sin.

Because extramarital sex violates the true meaning of sexuality, it therefore violates the very humanity of the two persons who commit the act. People who decide to have intercourse without also having mutual commitment to whole-life and lifelong sharing are, in effect, deciding against their own wholeness and happiness.

You just can't separate sexuality into parts without causing pain. When people seek the physical pleasures of sexuality without the spiritual pleasures, they will find the experience becomes empty and hurtful.

What do I mean by the "spiritual pleasures" of sexuality? I mean the knowledge that I am loved honestly and certainly; the assurance that my sexual partner is devoted to me alone; the confidence that my sexual partner loves me as a whole person and not merely for my body's attractiveness. The spiritual pleasures also include the joy of knowing I'm loved regardless of how well I perform in physical sex on a particular day, as well as knowing I am loved on the days when there's no intercourse. Underpinning all such assurance and comfort is the certain knowledge that my sexual partner is committed to loving me in all the variety of life's experience *through my whole life*. Only the marriage promise can provide that assurance and pleasure.

The Importance of Commitment

In our day, many will argue against the need for the marriage commitment. Two people can certainly enjoy the pleasures of sexuality without marriage, they'll say. They will support that contention with two arguments.

First, they'll insist that it *is* possible to separate the two aspects of sexuality and enjoy physical sex without the spiritual and personal assurances.

Of course sex can be enjoyed physically apart from the spiritual assurances. But where those spiritual and personal commitments do not exist, our sexuality cannot possibly be fully satisfied. Beyond that, those who have extramarital intercourse guarantee they will experience inward spiritual pain.

That pain includes fear, guilt, and loneliness. All of those grow directly out of the absence of the mutual commitment to whole-life sharing and support. The woman (or man) who wonders, "Will he/she respect me in the morning?" is fearing that she/he is not loved honestly and certainly.

The guilt of uncommitted sex has little to do with our social or religious views. Its deeper and more-real cause is our own soul's awareness that *love, to be real, must be committed love,* and that we have not given it. We have not committed our whole selves to the other person, and we know instinctively that we should.

Those who manage to avoid the fears and guilt (and I sincerely doubt that anyone can completely avoid them) will never escape the loneliness that accompanies unmarried intercourse. The more a person insists on physical pleasure without the undergirding of committed love, the more that person builds a wall around himself that no one can penetrate and he cannot escape.

Yes, the physical pleasures can be enjoyed apart from the spiritual, but not without denying some very basic needs in our own humanity. Every person needs the joy and satisfaction of committed love, and the longer a person goes on telling himself he doesn't, the more guilt, fear, and loneliness he will create for himself.

The second way people try to argue against the marriage commitment is by making certain personal commitments *short of marriage* that provide a kind of safeguard around their intercourse. The common practice of living together is the prime example of this approach. Of course, such arrangements don't prove commitment is unnecessary. In fact, they do quite the opposite! The couple who live together are saying by their decision that a certain kind of commitment does, indeed, exist. While they don't take the final step of formal marriage, they're demonstrating that they know sexuality is more than merely a physical pleasure. All they lack is the willingness to make a public commitment that would bind them together legally in a marriage recognized and honored in society.

In the final analysis, however, lovers who live together are failing to give each other the ultimate assurance of committed love. At any time, one or the other could simply move out. Nothing binds them permanently.

"Will you still respect me in the morning?" has merely become "Will you still respect me in six months or a year?"

Marriage alone is able to provide the solid foundation and necessary framework for the full expression of sexuality. Let me emphasize that I am speaking of marriage in the historic Christian sense of a *permanent*, whole-life commitment between two people.

That's right—"till death do us part!" Nothing but that absolute promise will do. Any other view of marriage is susceptible to the same weaknesses as living together. If we say marriage is only binding until one party decides to leave, we do not have what our sexuality cries for most deeply. We do not have committed love.

Some people will argue against marriage precisely on the ground I've just given. How can anyone possibly know himself or his spouse-to-be well enough to make a lifelong commitment like that? No one knows how things will be a few years down the road. People change: feelings change.

My answer is that *you cannot know for sure unless you decide to commit for sure.* Marriage can't possibly be safe for anyone if it's based on things that change. That's why the vow of commitment is so important. To be safe, marriage must be based on unconditional promises of love. The marriage vow says, "I will love you even if you change," and further, "I will love you even if I change." Only people who are willing to make that kind of commitment to each other, to become that vulnerable to each other, have the right to the delights of sexual intercourse.

MAKE IT YOUR OWN

▶ According to this chapter, why should sexual intercourse be restricted to marriage relationships? _____
_____
_____

▶ Do you agree or disagree with this reasoning? Why? _____
_____
_____

▶ What pain can result from sex without commitment? _____
_____
_____

▶ Do you think divorced people are more or less tempted to engage in extramarital sex than the never-married? Why? _____

_____

_____

➤ How do you respond to the following statements?

  a. You really can't know if you'll be good marriage partners unless you live together first. _____

  _____

  b. As long as you're not a virgin anymore, it doesn't matter if you have sex. _____

  _____

  c. Sex is just for fun. Why get so hung up about commitment? _____

  _____

  d. Why bother with all this fancy reasoning? God's Word says "No sex outside of marriage," and that's enough for me. _____

  _____

  e. We can experience the fullness of sexual intercourse only when it's expressed within the spiritual commitment of marriage. _____

  _____

  f. The prevalence of divorce proves that marriage is an outdated institution. To reserve sex for marriage is archaic. _____

  _____

For your assistance, I'll add some thoughts on each of those statements. Mine are not definitive answers, but they may help you weigh the issues.

  a. The permanence of marriage is a unique factor that no live-in arrangement can test. You must commit by faith. Certainly people should enter marriage with their eyes wide open, knowing a great deal about their prospective spouses. But sexual intercourse should still be reserved for that relationship of permanent spiritual bonding.

  b. Some religious subcultures have made a big deal about virginity, which is fine except for this backlash. Nonvirgins sometimes feel they can no longer be sexually pure, so why not live it up? Obviously, this applies to many divorced people. You saved yourself for marriage, the marriage broke up, so what's there to save yourself for anymore? But God's mercies are new every morning, and so is your purity—and your responsibility. Each day you make new moral decisions. The past doesn't matter if you're in Christ; today's choices do.

c. As I've said, to divide the spiritual aspect of sex from the physical is to vandalize one of our most-precious gifts. Sex without commitment can be fun, sure, but it's not what it's supposed to be, and it's ultimately dangerous.

d. Yes, God says it, I believe it, and that settles it. But God says things that make sense. He has given us minds to understand His commands. Especially in a world that increasingly thinks Christian morality is crazy, it helps to figure out the sense of it. As we're bombarded by temptation, our minds can help us to obey God rather than lead us astray.

e. That's what I've been saying.

f. Old isn't necessarily bad. The prevalence of divorce proves nothing. It may be that the modern factors contributing to a high divorce rate—no-fault divorce, our sex-crazy age, materialism, and so on— are the problem. Marriage is a God-given, time-honored institution. Maybe things would be better for all of us if we honored it more.

Sex without commitment brings spiritual and personal pain.

SINGLE (AGAIN) SEXUALITY

For the person who has been divorced, this study of sexuality may seem like an exercise in utter frustration. What possible sexual fulfillment or wholeness can I now expect? Apart from remarriage, and there may be many reasons remarriage simply is not in the picture for me, I'm condemned to a life of sexual emptiness.

No, not necessarily. While the road to sexual fulfillment and wholeness is treacherous for the person who is single again, it's possible to travel that road successfully by God's grace and with His guidance. I am writing to you as a person who has traveled that road. I've stumbled and fallen into many of the pitfalls myself. I've learned hard lessons about my own weakness and emptiness. I've also found that there is sexual fullness and wholeness for the single person who will commit himself to the pattern God has given us. Let me offer some suggestions for your guidance.

Develop a Positive Attitude Toward Your Sexuality

The first thing we need is to feel good about our sexuality. We can begin to accomplish this by recognizing that our sexuality is God-given and that God designed us as sexual beings for the furtherance and strengthening of our lives.

If you go back and study the definition of sexuality I've given, you will recognize that your sexuality has to do with your whole being. You were created with the God-given ability to seek and find wholeness in others. You are able to give yourself to others and to receive others into yourself.

Don't permit yourself to be tripped up by guilt or fear in regard to your sexuality. Perhaps you've made a lot of serious sexual mistakes. Perhaps others have abused you sexually. Undoubtedly you have experienced pain and disillusionment. Still, your sexuality is God's good gift to you, and if you'll take the time to learn well how to understand your sexuality, it can lead into wholeness.

Set the Goal of Self-Sharing for Your Life

Sexuality demands self-sharing, not just body sharing. We were created capable of giving more than our bodies to others. That's the fundamental truth about sexuality, but perhaps you haven't yet learned it.

Here, then, is a good starting place for becoming fulfilled and whole persons. We need to learn how to share ourselves—our real, personal selves—if we're to become what we ought to be as sexual beings.

At this point, however, one of the sexual pitfalls lies in wait. How is it possible to develop personal intimacy without sexual involvement? Good question, and there are good answers.

In the first place, make clear in your mind the distinction between personal intimacy and sexual intimacy. It is possible—indeed, it's essential—to learn to become an intimate person in ways that don't involve sexual touch. For many people, the very word *intimacy* means being close to another in a sexual way. But there are many ways of being close that don't involve sexual touching. I am being intimate any time I reveal my true self to you and trust you with that knowledge.

The best road to intimacy is *talk*. If I'm to develop as a self-sharing person, I must learn to talk about my true self. I must therefore learn to be very honest. I must recognize what I truly am like and develop the courage to disclose the truth about me to others.

A necessary corollary to self-revealing talk is *trust*. To be a self-sharing person, I will have to learn to trust. The lack of trust causes me to be cautious and self-protecting. We all fear that if we honestly revealed ourselves and others saw us as we truly are, we might be rejected. But if I don't develop the trust necessary to reveal myself, when I reveal only a false self to others, no one will have the opportunity to love the real me.

For the person who has been deeply injured in a love relationship, this step of trust will be extremely difficult. But it's absolutely necessary if he is going to move toward wholeness. Let me add that trust is also the only pathway of escape from loneliness. If I do not trust anyone, if I never reveal my true self to anyone, no one will ever be able to be my friend. I may have many superficial relationships, but I will have no honest ones.

Loneliness is one of the greatest causes of our sexual distress and sorrow. Far more than mere physical desire, loneliness drives single strangers into bed with each other. Here again, we must see that the spiritual side of sexuality comes into play. As sexual beings, we long for fulfillment in another. We long to share ourselves with another. However, because most of us have learned far too little about self-sharing, we're tempted to move quickly past the spiritual side of sexuality and plunge headlong toward the physical sharing of our bodies.

An important caution is therefore necessary. The person who is recently single again may find herself stricken with terrible loneliness. And it's very easy to misinterpret that longing for intimacy with another as a merely physical sexual need. This confusion is one of the greatest reasons so many divorced people so quickly land in bed with someone they hardly know. An even greater danger is that a rebound relationship that includes intercourse may produce an even greater mistrust and unwillingness to share oneself, which in turn will only deepen the loneliness.

I would suggest, then, that a person who is single again go very slowly and cautiously in developing his ability to trust others and reveal himself. At first it is probably best for women to seek other women and for men to seek other men for self-sharing friendships. Gradually, those who are learning to share again will develop the strength to reveal themselves to others of the opposite sex without great vulnerability to sexual temptation.

As we learn to reveal ourselves to others in deep, personal ways, other healthy characteristics will develop in us. First, *we will be learning to understand ourselves.* Talking honestly with others requires us to think about what we really want and what things are motivating us. It will also allow us to ask questions we might never have asked ourselves while alone. One of the healthiest things a person can do is to discover there are attitudes and behavior patterns in his life that he has never honestly analyzed and, therefore, never understood.

This matter of learning to understand ourselves has a lot of bearing on our sexual behavior. Many people play sexual games without ever realizing they're doing it. One of the reasons for such games is the simple fact that those people have not examined their thoughts and motives honestly.

A man may, for example, put on a great show of tenderness and understanding for a woman that is entirely a superficial veneer. His true motive may be pure sexual desire. So often in such cases, the tragedy is that the man is very lonely, aching to love and be loved, but simply does not know how to understand his personal needs in any terms but physical, sexual ones. And the greater tragedy may be that the poor fellow doesn't even know it. He hasn't learned to know himself honestly. He needs talk far more than he needs sexual intercourse.

A second healthy characteristic that develops when we reveal ourselves to others is that *we learn how to let others reveal themselves to us.* The process is reciprocal. When I take the time to reveal myself honestly, I'm going to learn about the process of self-revealing. That will, in turn, help me to understand what's happening when others honestly share themselves with me. It will also help me to see the truth when others are being only superficial and manipulative with me.

A third thing that happens is that *we will begin to develop greater control over our actions.* We will find that we know much better than before who we really are and what we really want. We will have become much-stronger persons who know how to say yes and no seriously. Perhaps no quality of life has greater value to us morally than the ability to say those words with strength. What a devastating thing it is to discover that, no matter what I think I want, and no matter what I say, I cannot honor my own principles and keep my word! Self-sharing helps us to develop into people who can honor their own words. This, obviously, will be a great help in keeping ourselves free from the control of others, but more importantly, it will keep us full of inner peace. I'll find that I am becoming much happier with myself because I'm making decisions that I'm also sticking with. More deeply than that, I'll be growing in true self-knowledge.

Perhaps this last thought is so obvious that it doesn't seem to need mentioning, but let me underscore one more thing—a fourth result of self-sharing. As we learn to share ourselves, we will be learning how to do the one thing most important to sexual fulfillment. We'll be growing into people who have *the ability to commit ourselves to others.* Remember again my definition of sexuality and the importance of personal commitment in order to find sexual fulfillment. Many people never find that because they've never learned to give themselves. They've given only their bodies. We can learn to give our whole selves.

MAKE IT YOUR OWN

➤ How positive is your attitude toward your own sexuality? Check all that apply.

- ❏ It gets me in trouble all the time.
- ❏ I am regularly frustrated by it.

❏ I enjoy my sexuality, within limits.

❏ I don't feel like a sexual being at all right now.

❏ Other: _____

_____

➤ On a scale of 1 to 10 (10 being best), how good are you at sharing yourself with others through *talk*? _____

➤ On a scale of 1 to 10, how good are you at trusting others? _____

➤ What effect did your divorce have on your ability to trust others?

_____

➤ Which of the following best describes you?

❏ I share myself deeply in conversations with others.

❏ I tend to rush right past talking and get sexually involved with others.

❏ I'd like to talk with people more, but I'm never sure what to say.

❏ I talk with people, but I don't trust them enough to reveal much of myself.

❏ I'm afraid to reveal myself to others.

❏ Other: _____

_____

Sexuality demands self-sharing, not just body sharing.

LEARN SELF-CONTROL WITHOUT SELF-CONDEMNATION

In the previous section, I emphasized that as a person grows in self-knowledge, she will also grow in the ability to control herself. As she learns better who she is and what she honestly desires for her life, she will grow in her ability to say yes and no. The ability to control oneself is an extremely important part of healthy single sexuality.

The importance of developing into a self-sharing person in no way alters the fact that sexual intercourse is absolutely out of the picture for the single Christian. Biblical morality simply forbids sex outside of marriage. A serious Christian single must willingly accept that truth as a binding principle for his life. And he must do so because he understands the true nature of human sexuality as a whole-life (and lifelong) sharing of two persons. Unless he reaches the point of being willing to share himself with someone who shares that same commitment, he will never possess the right to physical sexual union with another.

The single Christian must, therefore, practice self-control of his sexual desires. Of course, that's easier said than done. There are many temptations to sin along this part of the Christian's journey, but it's possible for the sincere Christian to control himself if he honestly wants to.

Let me mention something here that gets at a tremendous problem in contemporary society. I don't believe the satisfaction of the sexual appetite is a basic life need. That may surprise you if you've seen many movies or read many sex books recently. The attitude of much of society seems to be that our sexual appetite *must be satisfied*. We're told that normal, healthy life requires it. We have to eat, drink, and have intercourse to live. But that's simple falsehood. It *is* possible to live a fully normal, healthy, and happy life without sexual intercourse. You'll die if you don't eat and drink, but you won't die if you abstain from sex. It's the failure (perhaps I should say *refusal*) to recognize this fact that makes it impossible for many people to honestly consider self-control in regard to their sexual life. Self-control is not only possible, but it's also required of the Christian single. It's God's rule of life for us, and we must seek it if we mean to walk with Him.

Let me suggest some things that will help in the struggle for self-control.

First, self-control is simply impossible for the person who refuses to make a commitment to it. Self-control begins with a hard and clear decision to be a certain kind of person. The single person who toys around with his commitment is simply guaranteeing his failure, but the person who honestly determines that he will refrain from sexual intercourse is going to have success.

I want to emphasize the *certainty of success* for those who make a personal commitment to refrain from intercourse. A real commitment made by a person who knows himself well will bring success. I'm talking of a life-and-death determination.

For example, for the person who feels that given the "right" circumstances, she couldn't be expected to control herself, let's put the situation in a different light. Suppose you're with the one you love, the mood is right, and things are moving along physically to a point where you're about to have intercourse. Many would say that at that moment, self-control goes out the window. But now suppose your partner announces, "Oh, by the way, have I told you I have AIDS?" Now let me ask you again; do you have self-control at that moment? Why the difference? Probably because now you see it as a matter of life and death. Suddenly your determination is raised to a satisfactory level.

This kind of determined commitment includes a number of ingredients. It includes *full honesty with yourself*. The person who is committed to not having intercourse, for example, will not lie to herself about her relative strength and weakness. She will be honest, admitting to herself when she's being tempted. She will also admit to herself that she's still weak enough to yield to that temptation. One wonders how many sexual tragedies might have been avoided if people had only known how to be honest with themselves.

The person who is thus honest with herself will, therefore, *avoid tempting situations*. Anything and everything that in itself is a temptation, or that tends to lead toward a greater vulnerability to temptation, must be avoided.

A number of examples are obvious. A person working on self-control needs to have the good sense to turn off the myriad influences that draw people toward sexual activity. Certain types of music are powerful sexual stimulants. The same is true of TV programs, movies, magazines, and books. The person should also stay out of the kinds of social gatherings that are designed to be sexually supercharged. Singles bars and other such places are not suitable places to learn self-control.

Another obviously tempting situation is *privacy with persons of the opposite sex*. I suggest strongly that recently divorced people ought not to date at all until they have good reason to believe they're strong in self-control. There's really no substitute for good sense. Even the strong person needs to watch his step in this matter of privacy. I doubt if any of my readers will need proof of what I'm saying. What you may need, however, is help.

The last suggestion I'll make, then, is that you seek *the support of others*. You need the kind of friends with whom you can (and will) be honest about your weakness and who will, in turn, encourage and support you in your commitment to self-control. In my own life following divorce, I found that I began to grow in self-control precisely at the time that I began honestly to share my struggle with a close friend. The mere fact that he knew the nature of my struggle was a constant help to me. In addition, he was able to pray for me and encourage me regularly.

No Condemnation

The heading for this section included the words "without self-condemnation." By that I mean simply that we must always remember that our sexuality is God's gift and that its purpose is for our development as whole and fulfilled persons. Therefore, I must not permit myself to fall into patterns of guilt and self-condemnation as I think about my sexuality. I may be weak and I may be struggling for self-mastery, but that's no reason to feel guilt, and I should seek the cleansing and strength God offers me in Christ.

Furthermore, I would then be wrong to approach my sexual nature as if it were an evil part of myself that deserves condemnation. The struggle for sexual self-control ought to be viewed in the same way that we view any other kind of personal growth and development. It's positive and healthy and right to learn and grow. The process of sexual self-control is one kind of personal growth. The more we set the right goals for ourselves and honestly strive for self-control, the more we will become the strong, fulfilled persons God wants us to be. It's also true that the more in control of ourselves we become, the better we'll feel about ourselves, and the more we'll know we're becoming the kind of persons who have the ability to commit ourselves to others. Commitment requires self-control.

Place Marriage in the Hands of God

It's not always God's purpose for us to marry. Every single Christian must consider that fact. It's especially important for the divorced person to recognize you might not marry again.

A serious mistake made by many single people is that they make marriage an unqualified personal goal. Such people may have great difficulty in learning what they need to learn about themselves and, in particular, in coming to a healthy understanding of their sexuality.

The person who makes marriage his only goal may easily short-circuit the lessons about self-sharing I described earlier. The reason is that those things may get in his way. Suppose, for example, that you get involved with someone romantically, and after six weeks, that person suggests marriage. If you've made marriage your primary goal, you may say yes without giving serious consideration to what you're doing. There are many good reasons some people ought not to marry, and you may be ignoring some that apply to you.

For example, have you become a person who is able and willing to share yourself on a whole-life basis? Have you learned how to reveal yourself honestly and trust others with the knowledge of who you are? Does your new love interest really know you well enough to make a whole-life commitment to you? These are questions many people simply will not ask themselves if they're committed to marriage as an unqualified goal.

Unexamined motives often exist within people that drive them toward marriage. A person may desire it merely to solve his problem of loneliness.

Another may marry because she needs help with raising children. Some people get married to solve financial problems. And, of course, some marry just to satisfy the genital urge. All of those are entirely selfish and, therefore, unacceptable reasons for marriage.

No one should even consider marriage who does not have ample reason to believe he has learned how to share himself honestly, trust another fully, and make and keep promises. In the end, the happiness and wholeness of every marriage depends on the ability of the spouses to make and keep a vow of personal commitment.

The single Christian must accept a responsibility to grow into the kind of person who is able to share herself deeply with others. As she does so, she will be developing the very aspects of her nature that make possible a balanced and whole sexuality.

An interesting thing will happen to the person who accepts the possibility that he may not marry and who also determines to grow as a self-sharing person. He will gradually learn that he doesn't have to get married to be a happy and fulfilled person! Instead of concentrating on marriage as a goal, he will be emphasizing his growth as a person who give himself to others and who receives others into his own life. He'll also be growing in the ability to know himself honestly and to give and keep his word to others. Further, he'll be growing in self-control. The result will be that he has a strong positive attitude toward his sexuality. He will also see his sexuality as a gift from God, and he'll willingly submit it to God. Finally, he will be content to follow the guidance of God in the matter of whether it's right for him to marry.

Sexual Fulfillment

As a final note, it should be said again that the only people who ought to consider marriage are those who have become happy and fulfilled without it. Perhaps the worst thing two people can do to each other is to get married in order to be fulfilled. If you enter marriage as an unfulfilled person, you're very likely to remain unfulfilled. Marriage requires a great amount of giving and sharing. It therefore requires a great amount of mature personal strength. Only those who have learned to share on deep levels and who have the maturity and strength to give themselves unconditionally to others should consider marriage.

It is primarily because of the potential destructiveness two unfulfilled persons can bring upon a marriage that I say it ought not to be an unqualified goal for anyone. Marriage ought to be considered only if God leads two people to the point of honest life sharing and personal commitment.

One final word ought to be given about sexual fulfillment. This section on single sexuality began with a statement that singles can find fulfillment if they follow God's rules. What did I mean by that?

Obviously, I didn't mean a single Christian will be able to have everything his sexuality desires and promises. He won't have the privilege of sexual intercourse while he remains single. But that won't keep him from fulfillment as a sexual being. Because he understands his sexuality as a spiritual as well as physical dimension of his life, he will emphasize his growth in responsible self-sharing and self-control. Within boundaries, he will discover a tremendous potential for fulfillment and satisfaction as a sexual being.

In conclusion, let me summarize the characteristics of the sexually fulfilled person. As I understand sexuality, no single person is ready for marriage with these qualities, nor can any marriage work without them.

The sexually fulfilled person does not deny but rather affirms the basic goodness and beauty of her sexuality. She sets a goal of self-sharing for her life and works toward that goal with a whole heart. She accepts her responsibility for sexual self-control and honors God's guidelines in the choices she makes regarding her sexual relationships. She sees marriage as a possibility only if God leads her and a potential mate to the place of whole-life commitment. She is fulfilled in life because she has learned what and who she is as a sexual creature, and because more and more she is becoming the whole person she wants to be.

The satisfaction of your sexual appetite is not a basic life need. If you're single again, the need for fulfilling relationships needs to be your focus.

MAKE IT YOUR OWN

➤ On a scale of 1 to 10 (10 being best), how good are you at sexual self-control? _____

➤ How did you decide on that number? _____

_____

➤ Some suggestions were presented in this section. Check those you think can help you.

❏ Make a commitment to self-control.

❏ Be confident of success.

❏ Be honest with yourself.

❏ Avoid tempting situations.

❏ Avoid privacy with people of the opposite sex.

❏ Get support from others.

➤ What tempting situations do you especially need to avoid? Be specific.

_____

_____

➤ How will you avoid them? _____

_____

_____

➤ What other people could you get support from? _____

_____

Consider the following quotation:

"You grow by learning how to endure (resist, not repress) sexual tension without transforming it immediately into pleasure. The more you learn to stand up under tension, the more energy you set free in order to be mature" (Walter and Ingrid Trobisch, *My Beautiful Feeling* [Downers Grove: IVP, 1976], p. 33).

➤ Do you agree or disagree? Why? _____

_____

_____

In their book *The Divorce Experience*, Morton and Bernice Hunt make a rather shocking indictment of those who would take a position of moral and sexual purity. They state:

> In a society that has become increasingly tolerant of premarital sex, and in a "formerly-married" subculture that is thoroughly tolerant of post-marital sex, those formerly-married who abstain on the grounds of belief usually have some underlying emotions or sexual problem that makes them shun sexual activity.... Most, though not all, of the others who ascribe their celibacy to moral convictions seem to have similarly pathological inhibitions for which their beliefs serve as a disguise. (pp. 136,138)

➤ What do you think about that? How would you respond? _____
_____
_____

Compare the Hunts' statement with the following quotation from the Bible.

It is God's will that you should be sanctified: that you should avoid sexual immorality; that each of you should learn to control his own body in a way that is holy and honorable, not in passionate lust like the heathen, who do not know God; and that in this matter no one should wrong his brother or take advantage of him. The Lord will punish men for all such sins, as we have already told you and warned you. For God did not call us to be impure, but to live a holy life. (1 Thess. 4:3-7, NIV).

➤ What differences do you note between the Hunts' perspective on sex among singles and that of the apostle Paul? _____
_____
_____

➤ Why do you think Paul would so closely tie together the sexual use of one's body with holiness? _____
_____

Action Point: After reading this section, what is one thing you'll do differently? _____
_____

Use the space below to write a prayer or statement of commitment, declaring the sexual principles by which you will live your life. Also write your commitment on page 287 (appendix A) for future reference. _____
_____
_____
_____
_____

A final word: God accepts us where we are in order to take us where He wants us to be. Perhaps you've made some sexual errors in the past. God will forgive you if you ask. Perhaps the standards I've set forth seem far away from you—unattainable. God will give you power to live by them. In 1 John 1:9, God promises to forgive and heal the past, as well as to restore us for a life of wholeness: "If we confess our sins, He is faithful and just to forgive us our sins and to cleanse us from all unrighteousness."

CHAPTER 6

COMMUNICATION AND CONFLICT

What are the two biggest problems in marriages today?

The textbook answer is "Sex and money." That's what I learned in school.

But the more I talk to people whose marriages have broken up, the more I find a different answer: lack of communication. Even where sex and money seem to be the culprits, the problem usually is that the people are not *talking* properly about sex and money.

Think about it. Suppose one or the other partner is dissatisfied sexually—but they never talk about it. The frustration builds until it affects other parts of the marriage, or perhaps the one partner seeks satisfaction in someone else's arms. Or suppose they fight over money. Why? Because they've never come to terms with how to make mutual spending decisions.

How can we learn to talk and listen to each other?

"Too late now," you may be muttering. "Maybe communication principles could have saved my marriage, but that's dead and gone." I'm right there with you. I look back to the years before my divorce, and I realize how little I knew about communication. I made some mistakes, and it's too late to undo them.

But there are many other relationships in our lives. All of them need good communication. Children. Relatives. Friends. A new spouse. Even your ex. It's never too late to learn to have healthy communication with the people all around you. You can't undo the past, but you can thrive in the future.

LEVELS OF COMMUNICATION

Let's start by considering various levels on which we communicate. Obviously, there are times and places for all these, but we'll never deepen our relationships unless we move our communication to deeper levels.

✳ *Nonpersonal conversation.* You engage in this every day. "I'll have a Big Mac and a Coke, please." You're not divulging anything beyond simple, nonthreatening facts.

"My name is..."

"It's raining outside."

"The Dodgers lost again last night."

I had a friend visiting from Europe a few years ago. He came out of a store once, all smiles. "What are you so happy about?" I asked.

"What a nice country you have!" he answered. "The clerk just told me, 'Have a nice day.' She was actually interested in my life!"

I had to assure him that she probably had no interest in his life, that it's just a phrase we use. He was getting his levels of communication mixed up.

✳ *Facts about others.* You probably know people who *live* on this level. "Did you hear about Joe and Fran? Well, their niece is marrying some guy from Boston, and they never invited Aunt Helen, because they thought she was going to Bermuda on that senior citizens' cruise thing, you know?"

This level can get very involved, but it's really not personal. It's all about others. You don't have to divulge anything about yourself.

✳ *Self-judgments, ideas, opinions.* At this level, you discuss your opinions about external matters.

"I support the independence movement of Slovenia."

"My favorite author is Walker Percy."

"I'm pulling for the Braves to win the pennant."

Suddenly you're expressing your*self*, what you feel and think. But it's still focused on outside issues. For those who feel insecure about their own opinions, moving into this level can be a big risk. If an insensitive listener says, "That's the dumbest thing I've ever heard," it will chase them back to level two.

Those who are confident in their intellectual ability, however, can "hide out" at this level. They think they're opening up to others, but they're just revealing their thoughts. Their deeper feelings remain hidden.

✳ *Feelings and emotions.* This can be difficult. At this level we expose our true selves, not what we think but how we're feeling.

"I'm very concerned now about my health."

"Seeing Ted again brought up some painful feelings. I cried all night."

"I feel very happy whenever I see you."

"I know this sounds crazy, but I get a bit depressed whenever the Phillies lose. Bear with me."

Our emotions are closer to the core of our being. That can make this a threatening level for some. Often, when negative feelings are expressed, a listener will say, "Oh, there's no need to feel that way. Don't feel sad. Don't be concerned. Don't cry." And the person who has just expressed his emotions feels embarrassed. *Oh, he figures, I guess it's not right to feel that way. I shouldn't have said anything.* And once again, communication regresses to a safer level.

Emotions need to be accepted, reinforced, and nurtured at this level. And—here's a generalization for you—men tend to have a harder time expressing emotions. We tend to get stuck at level three. For some reason, in our culture women are allowed to have emotions, and men aren't. In order to progress to deeper levels of communication, a couple will have to overcome that tendency.

But it's not just a gender-based problem. Much of it depends on the patterns you learned while growing up. How did your parents communicate? What patterns did you pick up at school or church? Some families are very emotional. Others are more intellectual. Some share freely. Others are more guarded. Some cultures are more open about emotions. In my church background, there was great emphasis on the supremacy of facts over feelings. I still believe Christian faith is based more on the facts of Christ's death and resurrection than on our feelings about them, but somehow this seeped into the rest of my life as well. Feelings, I assumed, could not be trusted, and therefore they should not be talked about. I've had to work at overcoming this on the road to more-intimate communication.

✳ *Intimate communion.* This is that feeling of oneness often felt in a marriage or in an extremely close friendship. It involves emotional, spiritual, and sometimes physical intimacy. Communication is open and honest in all those areas.

Interestingly, this level of communication often results from some sort of conflict. You have to work things out. Perhaps you've experienced this—a sharp disagreement that results in a greater understanding. You want to hug the person you were fighting with just moments earlier.

It takes work to stay at this level. It involves regular sharing, regular giving, regular talking. A marriage relationship, or even a good friendship, can bounce through various levels in a short time. Researchers have found that most marriages spend most of their time at levels one to three. You must be vigilant to stay at the more-intimate levels four and five.

MAKE IT YOUR OWN

➤ How do you feel about this workbook right now? _____
_____

➤ Looking back at your marriage, about what percentage of time did you spend in each of the five levels of communication?

_____% Level One (non-personal)

_____% Level Two (facts about others)

_____% Level Three (ideas, opinions)

_____% Level Four (feelings, emotions)

_____% Level Five (intimate communion)

➤ Often one partner will try to pull the other toward deeper levels of communication. In your marriage, who was the puller, you, your ex-spouse, or neither? _____

➤ As you grew up, which level of communication was practiced most in your home? _____

➤ Which of the following statements are true of you? Check all that apply.

❑ I feel hesitant to express my opinions.

❑ I'm good at talking with others on nonpersonal levels.

❑ I've been hurt by people criticizing my opinions.

❑ I find it hard to express my true feelings.

❑ I spend more time talking about others than about myself.

❑ I feel more secure in my ideas than in my emotions.

❑ I think I have experienced a level 5 intimacy.

❑ I've been hurt by people making fun of how I felt.

❑ In my relationships, I usually pull the other person toward deeper levels of communication.

➤ Look back at the first question in this section, "How do you feel about this workbook right now?" Did your answer express what you *thought* or how you *felt*? _____

➤ Your response can help you learn something about yourself. If you answered more about how you *thought*, it may indicate that you tend to stay around level three and resist efforts to move to level four. Is this true of you? _____

➤ Think of one of your closest relationships right now—a friend, a child, a sibling, a new romantic interest. About what percentage of time do you spend in each level of communication?

_____% Level One (non-personal)

_____% Level Two (facts about others)

_____% Level Three (ideas, opinions)

_____% Level Four (feelings, emotions)

_____% Level Five (intimate communion)

(You may want to monitor this relationship for a few days and come back to this question.)

➤ What could you do to deepen this relationship? _____

CONFLICT

Conflict can make or break your communication patterns. Consider the following examples:

✸ *Couple #1* fights a lot. They express their feelings quickly and heatedly, but they make up rather quickly, too.

✸ *Couple #2* never fights. They have disagreements, but they never talk about them. They're afraid of conflict, so they try to keep the peace by shoving their problems under the rug.

✸ *Couple #3* fights a lot. They always seem to be disagreeing, nagging, proving a point. They don't listen to each other, and they never back down. This marriage is in trouble.

✸ *Couple #4* fights sometimes, but not often. Occasional disagreements are voiced, discussed, and dealt with. They keep the peace by talking through their problems.

Recognize anyone you know? Most couples would fall into one of those patterns. To a great extent, the strength of a marriage is based on how the partners deal with conflict. As you might guess, couples one and four have the healthiest relationships.

We must understand a few basics about conflict.

Conflict is natural and unavoidable. Life is full of conflict. Driving on the expressway, waiting in a bank line, lobbying for a promotion at your job—you can't live in this world without experiencing some level of conflict. The best you could do would be to shut yourself off as some sort of hermit, but what kind of life is that?

This leads us to a second fact: *Conflict creates an opportunity for increased communication and, therefore, learning and growth.* I desperately needed to learn that lesson in the years following my divorce. I had had my fill of conflict. I never wanted to see any more conflict for the rest of my life. That's why I isolated myself. I didn't want to be with people. I certainly didn't want to communicate with people beyond that "Have a nice day" level.

What I didn't know was that in saying I didn't want any more conflict, I was indirectly saying, "I don't want to learn. I don't want to grow."

Everything we learn in life is indirectly a result of conflict. In first grade, when we don't know how to read, the teacher writes a word on the board, and that creates conflict in our minds. *What does that mean? I don't understand. I want to know what those symbols mean!* The conflict motivates me to figure out what those letters mean.

It's the same way with relationships. *Why does she always seem cold to me just before I go off on a business trip?* There's a conflict. Talking about it, however, you can learn that she has a deep-seated fear of rejection, which is triggered by your departure, so she "rejects" you first.

To shut out all conflict is to shut out all learning, all growth. What we really want is an optimal amount of conflict—just enough to keep growing, but without causing undue stress.

Obviously, however, it's not just the conflict that causes growth, it's what we do with it. That pre-business-trip coldness could go on for years. It's not until you talk about it that you learn those new things about each other.

This leads us to another truth: *Unresolved conflicts interfere with growth and destroy relationships.* Let's go back to that first grader seeing the words on the board. Unless he resolves his mental conflict by beginning to learn what the words mean, he will be frustrated and stagnated in his mental development. That may be what happened to you with calculus. The teacher starts writing odd symbols on the board, and you experience conflict: *I don't understand this.* But for some reason, you may have let the conflict go unresolved: *I don't want to understand this.* Your mental growth stagnated, your relationship with mathematics was destroyed, and that's why you're not a rocket scientist today.

My apologies if you're an engineer or computer scientist, but many of us gave up on math at that moment. Essentially, we said one of two things: (1) My relationship with mathematics is not worth the resolving of this conflict. (2) It's just too hard to learn this stuff.

The same goes for relationships with people, even spouses. If the commitment to the relationship is strong, it's "worth it" to resolve the conflict. If the circumstances are against you or the other party is obstinate, however, you may decide it's "too hard" to resolve the conflict. In such cases, the relationship stops growing, stagnates, and often moves toward dissolution.

So conflict gives us that classic fork in the road. We can seek to resolve it and gain greater closeness, or we can ignore it and move apart.

> *While we tend to want to avoid all conflict (particularly after a divorce), we need to view it as a natural and necessary part of life. What we need to work on is using improved communication skills to resolve our conflicts in a healthier way.*

MAKE IT YOUR OWN

➤ In your relationships, when has conflict led to greater intimacy? _____
_____
_____

➤ What unresolved conflicts led to your divorce? _____
_____
_____

➤ Do you tend to deal with conflicts or ignore them? Why? _____
_____
_____

➤ Of the four couples presented at the start of this step, which did your marriage most resemble? _____
_____
_____

ATTITUDES—LOVING MYSELF

We need to learn how to resolve conflict in positive ways. That requires communication skills. As we develop those skills, we can grow in our relationships, feel better about ourselves, and feel better about others. This takes work. We need to be aware of our communication habits. If we let them slip, our relationships will slip, too.

Good communication starts with our most-basic attitudes. And the first attitude we should examine is our attitude toward ourselves.

As I've already implied, one of the greatest hindrances to intimate communication is insecurity. If I'm afraid that what I'm feeling is stupid or inappropriate, I won't share my feelings. If I think my opinions will be laughed at, I won't talk about them.

You can be the most-tender, loving person in the world, hanging onto every word your partner utters, but unless you take the risk of sharing *yourself* in a relationship, you won't find true intimacy. Many relationships are lopsided in this way. One partner does all the thinking and feeling for both. That's not healthy.

Getting a better attitude toward yourself isn't easy, especially if there are forces around you putting you down. For some, it's the spouse or ex-spouse who subtly (or overtly) discounts what you say. For others, it may stem from your upbringing. Others' self-attitudes may have been formed in adolescence. That can be a cruel time. And, unfortunately, even the church can sometimes send the wrong message. An emphasis on Christian love urges us to put others first, and that's great. But sometimes that can be carried to the extreme of total self-abasement. The fact is, Jesus affirmed the commandment: "Love your neighbor *as yourself.*" An evenness of attitude needs to underlie our relationships. Yes, I should put the other person first and even love in a sacrificial way. But if I deny the value of my own God-given personality, what do I have to give? Make no mistake: to appreciate yourself is not pride but gratitude to the God who made you. To deny your own value is not humility but blasphemy.

If you have a bad attitude toward yourself, you need to work on improving it. Get up every morning and tell yourself that you're a unique individual, made in God's image, and that you have a lot to offer. Even if no one else is telling you that, tell it to yourself. This world is not known for its encouragement. Encourage yourself. Even if you don't really *feel* very unique or valuable, keep telling yourself you're important. Soon you'll begin to believe it. (See article 1 at the end of the workbook for more help in developing a positive self-image.)

➤ How would you describe your attitude toward yourself?

_____ I am God's gift to humanity.

_____ I like myself a lot. I'm glad God made me like this.

_____ Some days I enjoy myself. Other days I hate myself.

_____ There are a lot of things I want to change about myself. Once all that is taken care of, I'll like myself just fine.

_____ I really wonder why God made me this way. I can't stand myself.

_____ Other: _____

_____

➤ How much affirmation do you get from those around you?

❏ A great deal

❏ A fair amount

❏ Very little

❏ None at all

❏ Instead of getting affirmation, I get torn down.

➤ Who affirms you the most? _____

_____

➤ How can you spend more time with this person? _____

_____

➤ Who tears you down the most? _____

_____

➤ How can you spend less time with this person? _____

_____

➤ In this space, write a statement thanking God that He has made you the way you are. _____

_____

_____

_____

_____

ATTITUDES—LOVING OTHERS

The flip side is true, too. We need to *love others* as we love ourselves. Some people fail on this point. They love to hear themselves talk. They're totally sold on their own opinions, and they don't care about anyone else's. They must get their own way. They tend to see everything from their own narrow perspective. They're quick to judge, quick to take offense, and slow to give in.

You have probably known people like that. But we all move into this behavior from time to time. And just as a lack of appreciation for myself results in lopsided, ineffective communication, so does a lack of appreciation for others.

We need to develop a *nonjudgmental* attitude toward the other person. That doesn't mean you can't sort through and analyze your thoughts and feelings. But underlying all that must be an appreciation for who that person is and where those thoughts and feelings are coming from. You can say, "The Astros win the pennant? How stupid can you get?" Or you can say, "Well, you've been right before, but I just don't see that happening." You can tear down or build up. If you adopt an accepting, nonjudgmental attitude, you can disagree (even on more-important issues than baseball) and still build up the other person. That's an expression of love.

Intimacy also requires a *forgiving* attitude. "You always hurt the one you love"—so goes the song. And it's true. The closer you get to someone, the greater the chance for pain. I deal with major issues of forgiveness in another chapter, but the fact is that close friends or marriage partners can hurt or disappoint each other in a lot of little ways. If one of them holds a grudge, it will automatically hinder their communication. I won't share myself with you if I think you're mad at me. You won't listen to me if you're thinking about how I've hurt you. Good communicators offer forgiveness and understanding.

Intimate communication can be reached by those with *humble* attitudes. Suppose you have a simple disagreement—say, over what color to paint the living room. Your roommate says cream; you say blue. And maybe you put it off for a while, but you come back to it and you're still disagreeing. "I don't see how anyone could like cream. It's just so dull!" And before long you're not arguing about colors anymore but about yourselves. It's not blue or cream, it's *who's going to win.*

I know you've been through that, because it's the most natural thing in the world. It's hard to give in. But that's what love demands. Take a look at the Bible's famous love chapter, 1 Corinthians 13. "Love...does not behave rudely, does not seek its own, is not provoked [easily angered], thinks no evil" (v.5). Jesus told His disciples that the way of the world was to seek first place, but that they should seek to be servants (see Matt. 20:25-28). That kind of attitude freely expresses a disagreement but willingly gives in, in deference to the other person. And if the other person is giving in, too, so much the better. Then the conversation can get back to what color to paint the walls, and maybe a suitable compromise will be reached.

> **We need to have proper attitudes about ourselves and others in order to be effective communicators.**

MAKE IT YOUR OWN

➤ On a scale of 1 to 10 (10 being best), how good are you at putting others first? _____

➤ When have you found it most difficult to act with love toward others?

_____

_____

➤ As you seek to develop an attitude that is nonjudgmental, forgiving, and humble, which of those would you say is most difficult for you? Why?

_____

_____

➤ What person has been the most loving toward you? What did you appreciate most about this person's attitude? _____

_____

_____

ACTIVE LISTENING

Have you ever had a friend you just enjoyed talking to? You walk away from a conversation feeling very satisfied. You said everything you wanted to say. You got to know the other person better, and he or she got to know you.

Chances are, that person practiced active listening. Active listening is simply a way of practicing love in conversation, a way of caring for the other person by paying attention, by interacting, by supporting.

Many of us think we practice active listening when we don't. For example: Mary comes home for a day of teaching school. She says, "I had an awful day. The kids were bouncing off the walls, and the principal came to observe..."

John says, "What's for dinner?"

Is John practicing active listening? Of course not. He's not listening at all. He doesn't care about her. He only cares for himself.

Now suppose Mary comes home and says the same thing. John says, "Yeah, that's rough. I know what you mean. I got stuck in traffic and was late for an appointment, and then I..." And he goes on talking about his own day. Is John practicing active listening?

You might think so. John probably thinks so. After all, he interacted with her. He heard about her rough day and told about his own. But notice how he turned the conversation toward himself. Instead of drawing her out and learning more about her feelings, he wanted to hear himself talk.

In my job, I practice active listening all day. I'm amazed, however, at the number of people I talk to who say, "I feel as if you're my best friend. You're about the closest person to me. I can tell you anything." Why do they say that? They don't know a thing about me! But active listening is such an act of giving that those people feel *loved*. Perhaps if there were more friends practicing active listening, we'd need fewer counselors.

The skills are simple. You merely need to put yourself in the other person's place. Imagine the feelings that he or she may have felt, and then get the person to talk on that level. "What did you think about that? How did you feel?" Be interested in what's inside the other person, and let your questions flow.

MAKE IT YOUR OWN

➤ Have you ever practiced active listening? If so, when? _____
_____

➤ Has anyone actively listened to you? Who? When? _____
_____

➤ How have you felt when someone else was actively listening to you?
_____
_____

➤ How have you felt when you were actively listening to someone else?
_____

➤ What do you think is the hardest thing about active listening? _____

SELF-DISCLOSURE

Self-disclosure is the flip side of active listening. If all I do is listen, that's not a true friendship forming—it's more like a counseling relationship. I need to self-disclose, to reveal what's going on inside me. If a friend hurts me in some way, I need to let him know he has hurt me—and do it in a loving way. That's how our friendship will grow.

Self-disclosure isn't always easy. There are many good listeners out there who are terrified to self-disclose. That makes them vulnerable, open to judgment and analysis. Maybe the other person won't like how they think or feel. But for an intimate friendship to grow, they must take that risk.

Many other people self-disclose in negative ways. They feel no hesitation to tell you exactly how they feel at any given moment. Some of them self-disclose through *nagging*. "You didn't do this. You made me feel awful. If you were really a friend, you'd do that." And when you complain about their nagging, they say, "Hey, I was just being honest about my feelings. Can't we be honest with each other?" Yes, but the Bible talks about "speaking the truth *in love*" (Eph. 4:15, emphasis added). We need to self-disclose in loving ways.

Other people self-disclose only *in self-defense*. That is, if they're criticized (by someone else's self-disclosure), they shoot back a list of ways the other person has hurt them. "Well, what about the time you did this and this and this...?" That's self-disclosure; those things probably need to be said; but the timing's bad.

We need to self-disclose when the relationship is at its best. That's tough to do, because it may ruin the mood. But the time to bring up negative points for fixing is when things are going well. "I appreciate you very much, but when you said such-and-such the other day, it really bothered me. I felt as if you were putting me down." At the right moment, in the right spirit, that problem can be dealt with positively, and the relationship will be strengthened.

If you don't take advantage of those good moments for healthy self-disclosure, the problems will squeeze out in unhealthy moments. You need to make it a point to self-disclose regularly to be honest about how you're feeling at all times in the relationship.

➤ On a scale of 1 to 10 (10 being best), how good are you at self-disclosure? _____

➤ When was the last time you made a significant statement of self-disclosure to a loved one? What was it? _____
_____
_____

➤ About what percentage of your self-disclosure statements are said in the wrong way or at the wrong time? _____

➤ How could you decrease this percentage (move toward the positive side)?
_____
_____

➤ Are you better at active listening or self-disclosure? What could you do to become better in your weaker area? _____
_____
_____

➤ Is there a statement of self-disclosure you need to make to someone soon? What is it? Write it out by completing the following sentences.

I feel _____

when you _____.

➤ And here's what I'd like us to do about it: _____
_____

PATTERNS OF CONFLICT

Often in our relationships, we experience the same conflicts again and again. Maybe the subject matter changes, but the patterns remain the same. One partner gets hurt but doesn't say anything. Instead, he carries it inside and adds to it until six months later, when he blows up. And the other partner doesn't take it seriously because at the time it seems so trivial.

Or maybe one partner stonewalls the other and just grows cold. The other goes crazy trying to please the cold partner, bending over backward until he snaps and starts yelling, which breaks down the wall but makes the yeller feel guilty.

We all have our crazy patterns. We need to be avoiding the bad ones and finding the good ones. We need to break our bad patterns at opportune moments and develop new habits that will improve our relationships.

I tend to be like that first pattern. I let things build until I blow up. I've been trying to learn (with some success) how to let off steam earlier so I never reach that boiling point.

I've appreciated one research report based on a study of couples that got along well and other couples that were breaking up. The researchers found three common patterns of conflict; agenda building, arguing, and negotiating. Both the happily married and the unhappily married went through those stages. But the unhappy couples spent most of their time agenda building and arguing, while the happy couples majored in negotiating. (This is further evidence that healthy relationships aren't devoid of conflict, but the partners *work through* their conflicts.)

Interestingly, the report showed that the happy couples had one partner (usually the wife) who took responsibility to stop the arguing before it got out of hand. She would blow the whistle and move into negotiation. Take note of that. It takes *one partner* to stop the arguing and start the problem solving. Of course, the other partner has to be somewhat cooperative and committed to the relationship. But it takes two to keep a fight going and only one to stop it.

As I read that report, I kept thinking about a similar report issued about three thousand years earlier. It's in the book of Proverbs: "A soft answer turns away wrath" (15:1). Do you want to stop the pattern of building your own agenda (figuring out how to get your own way) and then fighting about it? Just give a soft answer and start negotiating.

"Let's calm down and talk about this honestly."

"You're right. I was wrong. I'm sorry."

"I care about you too much to argue like this. Let's start over."

Soft answers like those can defuse arguments and get you headed toward good patterns of problem solving.

Now you tell me! Is that what you're thinking? Now that you're divorced, it's hard to apply my advice to your marriage. But you're probably developing new relationships now, not necessarily dating relationships (though that day may come), but new friendships. Be on the lookout for people with whom you can develop good patterns of problem solving. Listen for those soft answers.

MAKE IT YOUR OWN

➤ How would you describe your pattern of conflict? _____

_____

➤ In the space below, draw a picture of your normal pattern of conflict.

➤ When you are in conflict in your closest relationship, what percentage of your time would you say you spend in the following areas?

_____% Agenda building

_____% Arguing

_____% Negotiating

➤ What can you do to break your negative patterns and establish good patterns? _____

_____

_____

➤ In the space below, draw a picture of how you would like your pattern of conflict to be.

➤ Is there one person in your closest relationship who usually defuses the argument? Who is it? _____

_____

➤ Have you ever been in an argument when a soft answer defused it? When? What happened? _____

_____

_____

Action Point: When you think about the way you communicated in your marriage, what are some of the areas you now see you need to improve before you get into another serious relationship?

➤ Write here and on page 287 (appendix A) the skills you need to work on most in order to be an effective communicator. _____

_____

CHAPTER 7

WORKING THROUGH BITTERNESS AND LEARNING TO FORGIVE*

You probably know the cartoon character Ziggy. He's the one who can never seem to do anything right. One Ziggy cartoon really tickles me. A psychiatrist is talking to Zig, and he says, "Sir, you have a low self-esteem. It is very common among losers."

How does it feel to be a loser? My favorite Ziggy cartoon has Zig standing at a street corner on a perfectly sunny day. However, there's a cloud over Ziggy, and it's raining on him. It's not raining anywhere else. There he stands with an expression on his face that says, "Why me?" We laugh because we've all had experiences like that.

UNDERSTANDING BITTERNESS

Everyone's life contains some bitterness. Life can cheat and hurt us. I heard one radio commentator put it succinctly: "One big step toward maturity is learning that life just isn't fair."

As a divorced person, you have probably felt that your life has been

---

*This chapter has been supplemented with material adapted from *The Adult Child of Divorce*, by Bob Burns and Michael J. Brissett (Nashville: Oliver-Nelson, 1991).

shattered, perhaps beyond repair. I know I felt that way. The anger, disappointment, and pain of divorce remain long after the experience. Bitterness can actually shape your personality so that you approach life with a hardened, negative attitude. Anger that won't let go—that's bitterness.

A friend named Jack told me the following story: "I remember my father and mother having some struggles when I was about twenty-five years old. I had been married a couple of years. I was a young, idealistic Christian. My mom had asked my dad for a divorce. Eventually, my mother stayed with my dad, and they're still together. But I remember Dad going through real pain over it. I can recall Dad saying to me one day, when he was rather tearful and really struggling. 'Son, I hope you will never have to face anything like this.'

"With all the pride and arrogance of a zealous young Christian, I said, 'Father, there isn't any possibility of that happening to me, because our marriage is based on the Lord.'

"I meant what I said to my dad. I believed it. Divorce was simply not possible. A few years later, my marriage broke up. I lost my wife, my kids, and my way of life. And because I have a big mouth, my words tasted worse than crow. All my confidence has been shaken. Sometimes I don't know who I am. I feel like an oddball. I just don't fit."

Many things happen to those of us who have been divorced. Probably one of the worst is that we see our own failure. No matter who was at fault, we look back and see failure.

Our Attitude Is Our Choice

What happens to us when we feel the sense of failure? We can change the *experience* of failure into an *attitude* of failure. And it's this attitude that sours into bitterness. It is one thing to go through a bitter experience; it's another to become a bitter person.

If our divorce experience causes us to become bitter, it is because we've *chosen* to take a certain approach to life. Bitter people actually make choices to become bitter. Yet the bitter person never accepts responsibility for the kind of person he has become. He always says somebody else did it to him. But that's never true. Some of the most-beautiful people I know have gone through deeply disappointing experiences. But they became better people as a result.

What causes a person to become bitter? When anger toward past experiences and resentment toward current problems begin to solidify into a bitter attitude, a number of things take place inside us. First is the fear—or even the prophecy—of future failure. That fear is exhibited in comments like:

"Oh, why should I go there? I wouldn't enjoy it anyway."

"And why should I try that? I probably wouldn't be any good at it."

"That's the way things go. Everything turns out wrong."

The more we develop this attitude, the more we expect failure and define the future in terms of it.

The second thing that happens is that we can become extremely distrustful. It's one thing to have our trust broken; it's another to become a distrustful person. We begin to expect the worst of people. We begin to overlook the positive, helpful things others do. At the same time, we magnify the mistakes they make.

A third thing that happens is that we develop an attitude of cynicism. Cynicism is an approach to life that says, "Nothing is really what it's cracked up to be. Everything is really disguised evil." Cynicism is an attitude that never believes. There's no faith with regard to anything.

One of the most-beautiful passages found in the Bible is in the book of Lamentations, written by the prophet Jeremiah while sitting in the ruins of Jerusalem. Known as the "weeping prophet" because of the despair, heartbreak, and constant unhappiness he experienced, Jeremiah said:

> I remember my affliction and my wandering,
>   the bitterness and the gall.
> I well remember them,
>   and my soul is downcast within me.
> Yet this I call to mind
>   and therefore I have hope:
> Because of the Lord's great love we are not
>   consumed,
>   for his compassions never fail.
> They are new every morning;
>   great is your faithfulness
>
> (Lam. 3:19-23 NIV).

You might be thinking, *Jeremiah must have been some kind of nut.* No, Jeremiah was not a nut. He didn't deny his bitterness. He was very realistic. He said, "Look, I feel terrible. I'm downcast and depressed. I'm disillusioned and angry. But when I remember the Lord's mercy, I have hope. Because I know God—what he's like and how He works—the whole picture isn't bleak. My bitterness is not the whole picture; it's only part of the picture."

The problem with the bitter person is that he's looking at all of life through the framework of that bitter experience. On the other hand, Jeremiah shows us that bitter experiences can be put within the framework of God's love and compassion. He says that God's mercy is always real and is new every morning.

I have a poster at my house that says, "When life gives you lemons, make lemonade." That little line holds some wise, homemade philosophy, and it can help us understand how to deal with bitterness. It has to do with our attitude. We all go through some tough moments. And the way we choose to go through them will affect the rest of our lives. So the idea of this poster is that when you have the sour experiences in life, mix them with some sweet stuff, and turn them into something that's better. Then, in terms of human experience, some of the best things we ever learn come through hardship and difficulty.

MAKE IT YOUR OWN

➤ How would you define bitterness? _____

_____

➤ How bitter are you right now?
- ❏ Very bitter. I'm constantly snapping at others and putting them down.
- ❏ Somewhat bitter. Some days I feel that the universe is stacked against me, but other times I'm okay.
- ❏ A little bitter. Occasionally those feelings will poke through.
- ❏ Not bitter at all. I have forgiven everyone involved, and I've put it all behind me.

➤ When was the last time that bitterness affected something you said or did? What happened? _____

_____

_____

➤ As you see it, have you chosen to be bitter (or not bitter)? How do you know? _____

_____

_____

➤ What do you think would happen if you decided you would not let the negative events of your life give you a negative attitude? If you lived that way tomorrow—having a positive attitude in spite of everything—how would that change your day? _____

_____

_____

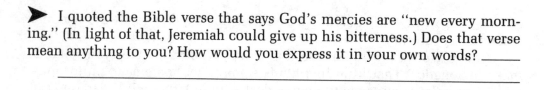 I quoted the Bible verse that says God's mercies are "new every morning." (In light of that, Jeremiah could give up his bitterness.) Does that verse mean anything to you? How would you express it in your own words? _____

_____

_____

Key Definition: Bitterness is anger that won't let go.

> **You may not be able to choose the things that happen to you, but you can choose how to respond to them. Your attitude is up to you.**

HANDLING BITTERNESS

We can handle bitterness in many ways. But the worst possible way is to decide it isn't there. The best possible way is to look at it for what it is—to recognize it, identify it, and decide we're going to deal with it in terms of reality.

Then, following the recognition of bitterness, we must get rid of it. You say, "Great! How do I do that?" As you might guess, I'm going to find some clues in the Bible. In Paul's letter to the Ephesians, we find some "sweet stuff" to turn the lemons to lemonade. "Let all bitterness, wrath, anger, clamor, and evil speaking be put away from you with all malice. And be kind to one another, tenderhearted, forgiving one another, just as God in Christ forgave you" (Eph. 4:31-32).

First, this passage says to put away, or get rid of, all bitterness. The little phrase "put away" was used in ancient Greek documents to refer to taking out the trash. Once I went on vacation for two weeks in the hot summer. When I came home, I put the key in the lock, opened the front door, and was almost knocked out by the stench coming from my house! I had failed to take out the trash before leaving, and after two humid summer weeks, it had stunk up the whole place.

That's what happens when we don't clean out our bitterness. It stinks up our lives. So the apostle Paul said, "Take out the trash." Then in the next verse he explained how to do it: through the process of forgiveness. Forgiveness can turn bitterness into lemonade.

Silverware and Sacrifice

We can learn a few things about forgiveness with a brief foray into the world of literature. Consider the ancient Greek tragedies. Play after play depicted the ongoing rivalries of the ruling families. This king killed that king, so that king's son had to kill this king, whose son had to kill the other guy's brother...You get the idea. It's the law of vengeance. As you read those stories, you keep wanting someone to stand up and say, "Stop the violence! I forgive you!"

A couple of thousand years later, we find that very thing happening in Victor Hugo's classic novel *Les Miserables*. (Perhaps you've seen the recent stage musical.) The hero, Jean Valjean, gets out of prison after several years. He had stolen bread to feed his starving niece. Under strict parole requirements, he must carry papers that identify him as an ex-con, but that keeps employers from hiring him. It's a crazy Catch 22 situation. He has supposedly paid his debt to society, but apparently the society still harbors bitterness against him. No one wants to trust a man who has been in jail. After being rejected in town after town, he lands at the home of a local bishop, who puts him up for the night.

He eats his dinner from the bishop's silver plates. He begins to think how this silverware could launch him into a new life. Desperate, he sneaks away, early in the morning, with a sack full of the bishop's silver. He doesn't get far. The police find him fleeing with his loot and haul him back to the bishop's home. "Sorry to awaken you, Father," they say, "but we caught this crook with your silverware. He has this crazy story that you gave it to him as a gift."

Under normal circumstances, Jean Valjean would be tossed into prison. By refusing to forgive him for his original crime, society forced him into another crime. And if he ever got out again, the whole cycle would continue.

But here's where the surprise occurs. The bishop was moved with pity for Valjean and said, "That's right. I gave the silver to this man. But my friend, you forgot to take these candlesticks." After the police left, the bishop urged Valjean to use the goods to start a new, righteous life for himself. Valjean does so. In a simple act of mercy and forgiveness, the wise bishop stopped the downward spiral of bitterness and mistrust.

The story goes on. Valjean builds a new life, becoming a respected citizen and business leader. But the old police captain has been hunting him down, seeking to arrest him for parole violations. The captain, Javert, is so intent on enforcing the letter of the law that he is blind to its spirit. Valjean must be punished, he figures, no matter what he has become. Javert knows nothing of forgiveness. He hounds Valjean throughout his life. Finally, Valjean has an opportunity to kill Javert. He has gun in hand; Javert is helpless; Valjean can do away with his persecutor forever. But he lets him live.

Forgiveness wins out again. Valjean lives his whole life as one who has been forgiven. How can he fail to forgive others? Ironically, Javert does himself in. Unable to deal with the forgiveness he has just received, clinging to the importance of a letter-of-the-law justice, he kills himself. Valjean goes on to spread his mercy to others.

As we deal with our bitterness, each of us has a choice. We can be like Javerts, nitpicking at technicalities, driven by the need for retribution. "This is the third time this month she's been late picking up the kids. How can I get back at her?" And maybe it's not so trifling: "His affair with that woman has messed up my life. I'm going to make both their lives a living hell!"

Or we can be like Jean Valjean, who realized every moment that he was a forgiven person and so had to forgive others. That attitude keeps us from piling up grievances and frees us to build a new and productive life.

> *If you choose to let go of your bitterness, you're the one who benefits. If you don't let go of it, you can suffer a lifetime of consequences.*

MAKE IT YOUR OWN

➤ If you're bitter, why are you? List the person(s) you are bitter at and as many reasons for your bitterness as you can think of. (Perhaps you will need several more sheets of paper.) _____

_____

_____

_____

➤ Look back over your list of reasons. Are they valid? Do you have legitimate reasons to be upset? Have you been wronged? About what percentage of your bitterness is valid? _____ Cross out any reasons that don't make much sense.

➤ Now look at the reasons that remain. How many of those do you think the person would like to be forgiven for? Circle them. If the person has apologized, asked forgiveness, or would ask forgiveness if given the chance, circle that reason. Now, what's keeping you from offering forgiveness? _____

_____

➤ How would you go about forgiving the person for those wrongs? Do you need to do so in person, or can you just do so in your head? _____

_____

(There may still be uncircled reasons on your list above. We'll deal with those later.)

FORGIVENESS: A STRATEGY FOR LIVING

Every so often, you'll see a story in the news about major U.S. banks "forgiving" the debt of a Third World country. As you know, some of those nations are hopelessly deep in debt. With the flick of a pen, a bank can wipe the slate clean. Billions of dollars of debt can be erased in an instant.

You might applaud the generosity of those banks, and maybe there's a germ of kindness somewhere. But don't kid yourself. The banks write off that debt because they feel it's to their advantage. It doesn't do any good to keep it on the books anymore. The debt will never be paid anyway, and in the interweaving fortunes of the world economy, the bank benefits more by giving the poor nation a break.

I'm no monetary expert; my checkbook will attest to that. But we can learn a lesson here: forgiveness is good for you. Sure, it's moral and godly and the right thing to do. But it also helps you put the past behind you and move into the future. For your own sake, if nothing else, let your grudges go!

Forgiven and Forgiving

Amazingly, as you watch the thrilling musical of *Les Miserables*, it comes as no great surprise when Jean Valjean restrains himself from shooting Javert. That's because Jean—and we viewers—can never forget who he is, a man who has been forgiven a great crime. Forgiven, he must forgive.

Remember that line in the Lord's Prayer, "Forgive us our trespasses [or debts] as we forgive those who trespass against us"? There's a great truth expressed there, and it works on both a human and a divine level.

If you've ever ridden on a crowded bus or subway, you've had a sense of "trespassing." As the vehicle starts and stops, the passengers sway and jostle one another. There are two attitudes you could have in such a situation. You could be very bothered every time someone jabs an elbow into your personal space (or your personal stomach). Or you could recognize that you're jostling others as well, and they're forgiving you for that, so you must forgive them. On public transportation, there *is* no personal space.

Life is like a crowded subway. We all trespass. We all invade each other's space. We jab each other. And if everyone takes offense at every jab, we wind up with a Greek tragedy. You have probably been in moods like that, though, where you tally up the wrongs everyone has done you. Your ex bounces a check, the checkout clerk is slow, and a careless driver cuts you off. When you get steamed at every little thing, who gets hurt? You.

But look at it another way. Each of us is forgiven a dozen times each day by people we unwittingly offend. If we have the humility to realize that, we'll be more ready to forgive others.

The Best Revenge

Did you ever see that snooty ad that boasted, "Living well is the best revenge"? That line may be going through your mind in the wake of your divorce. You dream of the day when you will rise above it all and your ex-spouse will rue the day he or she rejected you.

Here's a new wrinkle on the old adage: Forgiveness is the best revenge.

Think about it. Normally, revenge ties you up in knots. If you're bitter toward your ex-spouse, he or she is still controlling your emotions. Bitterness hurts you far more than it hurts the other person. It keeps you from living a happy, productive life. It hardly touches the other person.

But I have more biblical wisdom to share with you, this from Proverbs. "If your enemy is hungry, give him bread to eat; and if he is thirsty, give him water to drink, for so you will heap coals of fire on his head" (Proverbs 25:21-22). When the apostle Paul quoted that in the New Testament, he added the postlude "Do not be overcome by evil, but overcome evil with good" (Rom. 12:21).

Bitterness is an evil response to evil things. You probably have good reason to be bitter. Evil things have been done to you. But a bitter attitude doesn't help. It just allows you to be "overcome by evil." Forgiveness allows you to regain control of your emotions. It helps you to win, to overcome. That is, by far, the best revenge.

MAKE IT YOUR OWN

➤ In what ways has bitterness hurt you? Check all that apply:

❑ Bad attitude/never happy

❑ Anxiety-ridden

❑ Bad health
❑ Hurt relationships
❑ Other: _____

_____

➤ As you think over the last month or two, what have other people forgiven you for? _____

_____

➤ How does it feel to be forgiven? _____

_____

➤ What good things could you do toward the main object of your bitterness to overcome evil with good? _____

_____

_____

> **Bitterness is bad for you. It can hurt your health, your relationships, your work, and many other things. Get rid of it.**

A DIVINE PERSPECTIVE

I would be remiss if I left our discussion of forgiveness on a merely human level. It's true that "forgiveness is the best revenge" and that we all forgive each other for a million little things. But those reasons seem flat compared with the most-powerful reason of all—God forgives us.

If you're a Christian, you're well aware of that fact. If you're not, I still urge you to pay close attention to the next few pages. We're going to look closely at the nature of God's forgiveness and how we can apply that to our own relationships. This God talk may be unfamiliar to you, but you may find some revolutionary concepts that can lift you out of the pit of bitterness.

Understanding God's Forgiveness

When we talk about forgiveness, we have to be careful. I've read numerous books about it. I have also listened to lectures and sermons on the topic. And I've been disturbed by the superficial approaches often presented.

Some teachers encourage the offended to absorb their pain and release the offender. Others urge those who are hurt to simply turn to God and confess it. Then, they are assured, God will resolve the pain, and everything will be fine. A third approach is to tell those unable to forgive to examine their own lives. They should see what mistakes they've made—even if the mistake is carrying pain from those who harmed them—and seek forgiveness from the ones they can't seem to forgive.

There's a problem with those approaches (and many others like them): they all contain certain elements of healthy forgiveness, but they present only part of the forgiveness process. They leave out basic steps that must take place for forgiveness to be authentic and complete.

As we look at forgiveness, I am reminded of my friend Kathy. A crucial issue for her was this matter of forgiveness. As she realized that she herself had been forgiven by God, she was more able to put aside her bitterness. "As a result of the forgiveness and love I experienced from God," she says, "I had the power and security to make necessary changes in my life. Part of this was taking the difficult experience of my divorce and utilizing it to help others who were going through separation and divorce. Another part was learning how to forgive others the way I was now forgiven by God."

Kathy's experience reminds us of Ephesians 4:32. This is how we "take out the trash" of bitterness—"forgiving one another, just as God in Christ also forgave you." God has made forgiveness available through Jesus Christ. And the way God forgives us forms a pattern for the way we're to forgive others.

The Bible teaches that just as a coin has two sides, heads and tails, so the forgiveness of God has two sides. One side can be called the *legal* side of God's forgiveness; the other can be called the *relational* side.

The Legal Side of Forgiveness

Ask anyone who has been caught in a speed trap: if you break a law, you must legally pay a penalty. Or if a spouse is delinquent in child-care payments, he is supposed to be penalized. In the same way, the Bible teaches that God, who is holy and righteous, can legally accept only perfect people. However, we can't live perfect lives! Since we have broken His law, a penalty must be paid.

The good news is that Jesus Christ lived a perfect life. He is the only person who ever deserved acceptance by God. Yet by His death, He paid the penalty for *our* failures. He offered His perfect life to be credited to our account. We can be considered legally perfect by God, since the penalty we deserved has been paid by Christ.

The Relational Side of Forgiveness

As I said before, just as there are two sides to a coin, so there are two sides to forgiveness. The flip side concerns the personal acceptance of forgiveness.

To help us understand this, let me ask you a question. If God's forgiveness is available to everyone, is everyone in the world forgiven? Unfortunately, the answer is no. Just because forgiveness is available doesn't mean it's always accepted.

For Christ's forgiveness to be real in our lives, we must receive it. That's exactly what happened to my friend Kathy. The relational side of forgiveness is what happens when we accept God's verdict and receive God's legal solution for our condition.

MAKE IT YOUR OWN

➤ Do you feel you have done things that God needs to forgive you for?

_____

➤ On what basis are you *legally* forgiven by God? _____

_____

➤ What would you have to do to claim *relational* forgiveness from God?

_____

➤ How do you think that might change your life? _____

_____

FORGIVING ONE ANOTHER, LEGALLY

How is an awareness of God's forgiveness supposed to help us learn how to forgive others? Our relationships with others bring us right back to the Bible passage we looked at earlier. Remember that Ephesians 4:32 says, "Forgiving one another, *just as God in Christ also forgave you*" (emphasis added). That tells us that God's forgiveness is a pattern we ought to copy. So if there are two sides to forgiveness between us and God, we can surmise that there are two sides to forgiveness between us and others.

The Legal Side of Forgiving One Another

In the Sermon on the Mount, Jesus taught that when two people are harboring hate and resentment toward each other, a violation of God's law is taking place.

> You have heard that it was said to the men of old, "You must not murder," and "Whoever murders will have to answer to the court." But I say to you: Everyone who harbors malice against his brother, will have to answer to the court, and whoever speaks contemptuously to his brother, will have to answer to the supreme court; and whoever says to his brother, "You cursed fool!" will have to pay the penalty in the pit of torture. (Matt. 5:21-22, Williams)

One of Jesus' disciples, John, was probably thinking about that teaching when he wrote, "Whoever hates his brother is a murderer, and you know that no murderer has eternal life abiding in him" (1 John 3:15).

Do you squirm a little while reading that verse? I know I do. Much of Jesus' purpose in the Sermon on the Mount was to show us that there's something terribly wrong with us. We usually don't think of ourselves as "too bad" or "too good" before God. And when we do recognize a failure in our lives, we acknowledge it.

But in His sermon, Jesus showed us that we fall desperately short of God's law. And one place where we fall short is in our handling of anger toward others, even when we quietly think but never verbalize our anger.

Regardless of what others might do to us, our improper attitude and expressions of anger reveal the real condition of our hearts. Jesus labeled it the way God sees it: we are murderers!

There might be some real justification for your feelings of anger toward your former spouse or others. People can do cruel and unjust things that understandably produce feelings of anger. But we are complicated creatures. Our anger feelings are never pure. Righteous anger becomes mixed with feelings of hatred, bitterness, revenge, and the like. That's why we must deal with both sides of forgiveness.

One of my favorite stories in the New Testament is the parable Jesus taught in Matthew 18:21-35. A servant owed his king the equivalent of several million dollars. When the king called in his note, the servant had no resources to pay the debt. Just when the king was about to throw the man and his family into debtors' prison, the servant cried out for mercy. The king took pity, canceled the debt, and let him go.

With the weight of his debt relieved, the servant walked out and spotted a fellow servant who owed him a few dollars. Immediately he grabbed the man, choked him, and demanded repayment.

When his fellow servant cried out for mercy, the man wouldn't listen. He had the fellow thrown into debtors' prison.

When the king learned that the man whose debt he had canceled acted that way, he called him back in. He harshly reprimanded the ungrateful servant and put him into jail.

At the end of his story, Jesus explained, "So My heavenly Father also will do to you if each of you, from his heart, does not forgive his brother his trespasses" (v. 35).

Now, before we assume we must immediately respond to Jesus' teaching by asking forgiveness from those we have hurt or offended, remember that we're looking at the legal side of forgiveness. If we have an attitude of anger or a lack of forgiveness toward others, God wants us to deal with the attitude before Him (the legal side) before we deal with the others (the relational side). Legally we have broken His law. We've got to resolve that with Him.

To help clarify this aspect of forgiveness, consider what Jesus said in Mark 11:25: "Whenever you stand praying, forgive, if you have anything against anyone; so that your Father also who is in heaven may forgive you your transgressions" (NASB).

Imagine you're praying. And while you're praying, God brings to mind your feelings toward your former spouse. You know that before God, you are much like that unforgiving servant in Matthew 18. Jesus died on the cross to forgive you, and yet you haven't been willing to forgive your former spouse. Remember, the unmerciful slave had forgotten about his own forgiven debt. He focused only on the debt owed to him. In the same way, when you get caught up in feelings of anger toward your former spouse, you forget your own condition before God and what it took for Him to forgive you.

According to Jesus' teaching in Mark 11:25, the first thing we must do is deal with our own attitude before God—the "murder" we have committed through our bitterness—which has become evident while praying. He says we must do business with God before we do anything else. We must remember the depth of forgiveness He has given us and consider the problem we have with another (in this case your former spouse) as a few dollars in comparison with the problem we had with God. We cannot be ready to deal with the relational side of forgiveness until we have come before God and worked through the legal side of it.

At this point, you may be wondering why the legal side must come before the relational. Well, have you ever had your former spouse confront you when he's angry and bitter at you? You know how you feel under these circumstances. He seems to be acting like the judge with a verdict already in hand. He doesn't really want to resolve the problem; he wants you to see what you've done wrong, to make you feel bad about it, and to make you grovel a bit. No respect here—just condemnation.

How well can we work through our problem with someone while we have that kind of attitude? Do we even *want* to work through them? However, if we go before God and deal with our own attitudes and feelings, we are humbled before Him. The result is what the Bible calls a gentle spirit. And if in our relationships we exhibit a gentle spirit, our bitterness is diffused and we can focus on the real issues. We no longer have to win to feel good. Our bitterness has been resolved.

MAKE IT YOUR OWN

➤ Take another look at that story Jesus told of the unmerciful servant. Which character do you resemble most? _____
_____

➤ Why was it wrong for the first servant to demand payment from his fellow servant? _____
_____

➤ How do you think the second servant, the one who owed a few dollars, felt when payment was demanded from him? _____
_____

➤ Was there some way the first servant could have gently asked for payment of the few dollars? What *should* he have said to his fellow servant? ___
_____
_____

> ### As forgiven people, we must forgive.

RESTORING RELATIONS

In the legal side of forgiveness, we get our attitude right before God. But we still need to deal with our relationship with that other person.

It's really hard to talk to someone with whom we have a problem. Few of us enjoy conflict. But that doesn't mean we can use denial to resolve our problems. As long as we avoid the issues, we will feel relational pain and anger.

If God offers forgiveness by extending His good news to those who are out of relationship with Him, and if we're to forgive just as He has, we must offer forgiveness to those with whom we are out of relationship.

However, that doesn't mean we just forgive and act as if nothing has ever happened. A breakdown in a relationship demands an honest dealing with the facts and feelings involved. Jesus addressed this in Luke 17:3 when He said, "If your brother sins against you, rebuke him; and if he repents, forgive him."

Let's look at that verse piece by piece. First Jesus said, "If your brother sins against you." That assumes there is brokenness in a relationship. Jesus is speaking to the one who has been sinned against. In those cases, He said, the one who has been violated in a relationship is responsible to go and rebuke the one who has sinned.

That can be hard. When we hear the word *rebuke*, we assume it means we are to sharply reprimand or criticize the person. To put it simply, we think we should chew him out.

However, that's not what Jesus meant. The word for "rebuke" actually means to go to a person, share your side of the problem, and seek clarification of your understanding. You may not know for sure that the rebuke is deserved until you hear the response of the other person. So you gently reveal the facts you do know. You must be willing to hear any new evidence and also give this "brother" the benefit of any doubt. Your motive is to help him both recognize the problem that exists and do something about it.

This happened to me once when I was in college. I was working as a youth volunteer in a church, and I would occasionally sneak into a pastor's office to have a quiet place to study. Once when I did that, I jostled things around on the desk. When I was about to leave, I noticed that I had pulled some pages of his good Bible out from its binding.

Later, when the pastor returned to his office, I went to him and said, "I accidentally pulled the pages out of your Bible. I hope this isn't a problem and that it's okay."

The pastor looked at me and said, "No, it's not okay."

What that pastor said was a rebuke. He didn't say it with anger or bitterness. He was showing me that something was wrong and we shouldn't just pass it off. We needed to talk about it. His rebuke helped me understand the seriousness of the situation.

Jesus said, "If your brother sins against you, rebuke him." That is, if there's brokenness in a relationship, be honest about it. Go and reveal it to the other person. Allow it to be seen for what it is. Don't live in denial. Don't act as though everything is okay when it isn't. Rebuke him. That is, reveal it to him.

Then Jesus said, "If he repents, forgive him." Here Jesus challenged our stereotyped idea of forgiveness. He put a condition on forgiveness. He said that if the person repents, forgive him. That means the opposite is also true: if he does not repent, you're not to forgive him.

Does that surprise you? After all, we already read in Mark 11:25 that if we have something against a person, we're to forgive him. Did Jesus contradict Himself? No.

Remember there are two sides to forgiveness. On the legal side, I have to deal with my attitude before God. I have to face my anger, my bitterness, and my frustration. By the time I go to the one who has hurt me, I have worked through my attitude. When I approach the relational side of forgiveness, I go to reveal and discuss the problems in our relationship with humility and gentleness, not condemnation.

Now, suppose the person I go to refuses to recognize there's a problem. Or even worse, suppose he sees what he has done but won't accept his responsibility for our broken relationship. What am I to do, smile and say, "That's all right! I've worked everything out with God, and our relationship is fine whether you like it or not"?

No, that wouldn't be honest. At best it would be playing the old denial game: close your eyes and act as if the problems aren't there; maybe they'll go away. But you know they don't go away.

We must recognize the relationship is still broken. It's unresolved, and there is still pain. And in such a case, no relational forgiveness has taken place.

Remember, God has extended forgiveness to the whole world. In a real sense, He has "rebuked" the world by showing how it is out of relationship with Him. When a person refuses to acknowledge the truth and accept His offer, there is no forgiveness. In the same way, Jesus says, if we go and show a person the problem in our relationship, and if he doesn't repent, the relationship is still broken. We shouldn't play a game and act as though the problem doesn't exist.

However, when the other person recognizes the problem and genuinely asks forgiveness—that is, he repents—we are to genuinely forgive him. His repentance and our forgiveness bring closure to the problem and newness to the relationship.

Working Forgiveness

A number of follow-up questions come to mind about this process of working forgiveness. For example, you may wonder, *What happens if I go through this whole process and the other person won't listen to me, laughs it off, or gets angry with me?*

When that happens, we will still feel the pain that comes when the offer of forgiveness is rejected. But before God we'll be able to live with the fact that we have done everything possible to resolve the problem. We will also feel relief and freedom in choosing to speak the truth instead of saying only what we think will please others. Furthermore, we can come to closure over our own responsibility in the relationship.

"And what happens," you ask, "if this person comes back later, accepts his responsibility for the problem, and asks forgiveness?"

The model of God's forgiveness answers that. God's offer of forgiveness is always available for the asking. Our forgiveness must be available as well.

Working On Ourselves

Finally, you may wonder, *What if my relationship with this person remains broken indefinitely? What do I do in the meantime?*

Many people attempt to rush forgiveness to avoid the painful work of dealing honestly with others and themselves. They think forgiveness is a shortcut to feeling better. But that's just not the case. When we work both sides of forgiveness and a relationship remains broken, we must work on ourselves. And if we want to be healthy, growing people, we need to do that anyway.

I love to tell the story about my friend Grace. I met her when she was in her mid seventies, and she was so crippled with arthritis that she couldn't move any of the major joints of her body. She could just barely move her arms, her knees were locked in position, her ankles wouldn't move, and her toes were frozen. Attendants had to move her about, and she was in terrible pain most of the time.

When I first visited her, she was facing the other wall. Her daughter introduced me, and this lady, with a bright, cheery, little voice said, "Well, come around here where I can get a look at you."

I walked around, and her eyes were just as bright as could be. She looked up at me and said, "Well, you're not half as bad looking as they said you were."

I thought, *There's somebody special living here.*

And she was. I went to see her many times, and she was always an encouragement to me. Eventually she was put in a nursing home. There the head nurse said, "If we ever get a crab in here, we put her in the room with Grace, because Grace will cheer her up."

I'd go to the home to see her, and I would often think, *Well, what can I say that will brighten up Grace's day?* But Grace never seemed to have a dull day. I never, ever heard her complain. She never said, "How long must this last?" or "Why has God done this to me?"

Grace knew God. And by knowing God, she found something you and I fail to find, because all we look at is the pain and injustice in our lives. We don't look at the opportunity that has been given us to grow.

As a matter of fact, sometimes pain is the greatest opportunity to make lemonade. For the most part, we never learn the great lessons of life until we learn how to deal with pain. I don't learn very much of spiritual value when everything is going well. I learn it when I'm hurting. That's when I ask about the real meaning in life. That's when I ask who I ought to be. And that's when I grow.

Chuck Swindoll tells the story about the violinist Paganini who, while playing a concert, had a string break on his violin. (*Strengthening Your Grip*, pp. 205-6). As the crowd went, "Ooh," he just kept playing. Then, "Bonk," another string broke. But he kept playing the music. Finally, a third string popped! But Paganini kept playing like mad.

Finally, the master finished the piece, and you can imagine the crowd's response. They went wild with enthusiasm. But Paganini wasn't done yet. He came out and played an encore on one string!

In life we break strings. For us, divorce has been one of the more-traumatic of those times. However, as Swindoll says, there is one string in life that can never be broken or taken away, and that string is the right and power to choose our own attitude. We will always have the choice of how we're going to approach life. And what we become does not depend so much on how many strings break as on what we do with the one string that remains.

In conclusion, I want to say something about my life. I still look back on what happened to me and hate it. I didn't want my divorce. And I'm sorry about the pain it brought into the lives of my family and others. I wish those things had not happened. *But I wouldn't go back to being the person I was before*—not for anything in the world. And I wouldn't trade anything for what I've learned in the process. I'm a wiser and better man today as a result of my divorce.

We have a choice to make. We can decide to feel sorry for ourselves. We can do nothing with our pain and anger and be bitter the rest of our lives. Or we can say, "I'm going to become fruitful in the land of my suffering. I'm going to learn the process of forgiveness. I'm going to play on that one string. I'm going to make some lemonade."

MAKE IT YOUR OWN

Go back to that list you made of the people you have bitter feelings for and the reasons why. You should have circled some of the easier problems. Those are cases where the person is sorry for wronging you.

➤ As you look over that list, find one of those circled things and choose, right now, to clear it up. In the next week, what specific thing can you do to resolve that matter and restore that relationship? _____

_____

_____

➤ Now look at the uncircled things, problems that the person seems unrepentant for. Relist one to three of those things here.

    1. _____

    2. _____

    3. _____

Have you "rebuked" the person(s) for those matters? (Remember that "rebuke" here means merely to present your case clearly.) Put a check mark beside the item if you have.

➤ If there are matters for which you have not confronted the person, where and when will you be able to do it? _____

_____

_____

If you *have* presented your case, and if the person doesn't want to clear up the matter with you, you need to put the matter aside. Don't dwell on it. Let it go. Your offer of forgiveness is on the table. The person refuses to restore the relationship on the proper terms. There's nothing else you can do.

Action Point: Is there some symbolic action you can take in the next few days to put this matter behind you? It could be as simple as throwing away a picture, donating to a charity, or taking yourself out to dinner. It merely needs to be your way of saying (to yourself, mostly), "I will not live in bitterness. I will move on from here."

➤ What is that symbolic action? _____

_____

➤ When will you take it? _____

_____

➤ Write your actions and strategies here and on page 287 for future reference. _____

_____

_____

_____

Key Definition: Rebuke: to go to a person, share your side of the problem, and seek clarification of your understanding. Gently reveal the facts as you see them. You must be willing to hear any new evidence and also give the other person the benefit of any doubt. Your motive is to help him both recognize the problem that exists and do something about it.

> *God's offer of forgiveness is always available for the asking. Our forgiveness must be available as well.*

CHAPTER 8

KIDS IN THE MIDDLE*

"I was five or six when I first remember my parents fighting a lot. I remember that Dad was working more and more, and that I missed him. There were times when Dad was gone for weeks at a time. When we asked my mom where Dad was, she would always say, "Away on a business trip." I now know that my dad and mom were separated. Whenever they tried to reconcile, my mom would say that Dad was home for a vacation. This went on for about two years. It didn't matter what my mom said anymore, my brother and I knew there was something wrong, and we knew we didn't like it. When Mom finally told us the truth, that she and Dad were getting a divorce, it was only because he was getting married to someone else and wanted my brother and me to be in the wedding.

"I wish my mom had told us the truth two years earlier. Then we could have started the grieving process and maybe been more accepting of our new stepmother and stepsister. That was really tough for us to swallow." (a fourteen-year-old boy)

BREAKING THE NEWS

Kids usually know "there is something going on" long before you think.

---

*The following chapter is largely excerpted from the book *Innocent Victims: Helping Children Through the Trauma of Divorce*, by Thomas Whiteman, Ph. D.

I don't know the specifics of your situation. I can't tell you exactly what to say to your children. Certainly the example at the beginning of this chapter is *not* the way to break the news, but you may have unique challenges. This chapter may sound like a cookbook of do's and don'ts. Keep in mind that I'm presenting a list of guidelines, some of which you can implement and some of which you can't.

Have you ever heard of the serenity prayer? "God, grant me the serenity to accept the things I cannot change, the courage to change the things I can, and the wisdom to know the difference." That could be renamed "The Single Parents' Prayer," since it so aptly describes the attitude you need to adopt while raising your children. Keep in mind that there are no secret formulas or even standard methods of operation. Your child is an individual, and you'll need to tailor the information to fit your situation and your child's.

How Do I Tell My Children?

In the book of Ephesians, the apostle Paul writes that we're to speak the truth in love (see 4:15). That's the best way I can describe the communication that should take place between all parties involved in a separation or divorce. It may be near to impossible at times, but it needs to be our goal.

If possible, both parents should sit down with the kids and together tell them about the separation or divorce, before one of the parents leaves. If the separation happens abruptly, the parent with the children will need to give them some preliminary information right away. But as soon as it can be arranged, both parents need to come together to tell the children what will happen to the family.

This method is important for several reasons. First, with both parents present, there's the greatest possibility of a balanced and honest presentation. Second, if the children have any questions, they need to address them to the parent who is best able to answer. And third, the united front makes it clear that both parents are in agreement on the decision. That helps to reduce the splitting of loyalties, the playing of one parent against the other, and the fantasy that "my parents will work this out." If one parent is missing, the children are likely to think, *Yeah, that's what Mom says, but I know that's not what Dad told me.*

If one parent is not present, it's even more important that the parent who tells the children remembers to speak the truth as lovingly as possible. Representing both sides of the issue is very difficult when you're so emotionally involved. Even though you're irate with the other parent, you want to let the children know it's an issue between the parents and that you both still love them.

If your child has questions about the other parent or his reasons for leaving, try to answer as honestly as possible. Don't attribute motives or make judgments about the other parent. Just state what you know to be true, as nicely as you can.

Don't say: "Your father left because he's irresponsible. He'll probably move in with his girlfriend and forget all about us."

Try this instead: "Your father loves you very much, but he doesn't seem to love me. Even though he doesn't want to live with me anymore, he wants to visit with you whenever he can."

By taking the "high road," you will end up better off, even if you have good reason to drag your spouse's reputation through the mud. Remember, the children will know the truth sooner or later, and it would be better for you if they remember you as the one who chose the most-loving course.

When Should I Tell Them?

It's important to tell the kids what's going on as soon as both of you know. If you're just having marital problems, you need to get help, but don't feel compelled to tell the children anything of a personal nature between you and your spouse. If the children are older, they will know something is not right and may even know you're seeing a counselor. If they ask, use the opportunity to demonstrate the proper way to handle problems. "Your mother and I are having some personal problems that we need to work out. Because we're committed to each other and to the family, we want to get help in resolving these problems as quickly as we can." If your children are too young to understand the problem, or if they don't ask, there is no need to share your personal conflicts with your kids at this stage.

Once the problem reaches a point where divorce or separation is imminent, it affects the whole family. The children need to be told as soon as it can be arranged. This should be delayed only if you need to work out some of the details or if it happens to fall on a day such as Christmas or one of the children's birthdays. It's reasonable to wait until some of the details are worked out, such as: Where will Mom live? Where will Dad live? Where will the kids stay? And how often will we see each parent? You need to present a scenario that is well thought through and reassuring to the children if possible. If these matters cannot be settled and it looks as if the children are going to find out, you may need to sit them down and tell them as much as you know.

Many parents tend to "protect" their children from the truth as long as possible. One study found that 80 percent of the preschoolers questioned had received no information about their parents' separation. But parents do a disservice to the child by withholding such information; that merely creates anxiety about the future and distrust toward the parent.

What Should I Tell Them?

When deciding how much you should tell the kids, you must consider the development level of your child. Get the key points across, and then allow for open discussion. If the child knows enough to ask the question, he or she is old enough to get an honest answer.

The key points to cover include:

▶ How did this happen? What are the reasons?

▶ Do you still love me? Does my mother/father still love me? Am I wanted?

▶ How will my life be changed? Where will I live, go to school, church, and so on?

▶ Am I part of the reason for the breakup? Could I have done something to avoid this separation or divorce?

It's vital to cover what will happen to the children. Reassure them of your love for them, and be prepared to back it up with actions. Give the children permission to love *both* parents. For preschoolers, reassure them that they will be cared for, and then explain the divorce in terms they can understand. For example:

"Mommy loves you very much, and Daddy loves you very much. You're going to live with me, and we'll stay in this house, where you will eat, sleep and play, just as you do now. Daddy is going to live in an apartment nearby so he can come and visit you every week. In fact, he will pick you up this Saturday and show you where he lives. You'll eat lunch there, and then he will bring you back home where I'll be looking forward to seeing you. We are separating because Daddy doesn't want to live with Mommy anymore. But Daddy still loves you and wants to spend time with you."

Children who are elementary age or older need more-specific information, particularly about where they will live and the visitation arrangements. They will also require more specifics about what went wrong. You need to be as honest as you can without discussing sexual problems overtly. (You may want to say something like, "Daddy is acting like he is married to someone else.") If possible, avoid placing blame, since it's true that divorce is rarely, if ever, all one person's fault.

Don't expect your children to understand your explanations or to ask all their questions the first time you talk about it. Be prepared to explain the situation and answer questions over and over again. Stress that separation or divorce is an adult decision. It wasn't their fault, not can they do anything to get the parents back together.

If the truth is particularly ugly or hard to talk about, you need to tell them in as loving a way as you can. The earlier they hear the truth, the sooner they can start to deal with the problem and begin the healing process. You need to use discretion in light of the age of the children and how much they really can understand. But once again, if they're old enough to ask the question, they're old enough to hear an honest answer. For example, if Dad is leaving because he has a girlfriend or he's a homosexual, you may not want to give them all that information in the first meeting. Soon thereafter, however, you need to tell them what is really going on. Eventually the kids hear the whispers and innuendos, so it's best that they hear the truth in a straightforward manner from their parents. If possible, the information should come from the one with "the problem." That way, they would know they were hearing firsthand information, which is usually more reliable. They would then have opportunity to discuss openly their questions and concerns.

If that parent isn't available or willing to talk with the children, it obviously falls to the other parent to present as balanced an explanation as possible. Then, if they have questions, you may want to offer to let them discuss the issue with someone more neutral. That might be an aunt or uncle they trust, a counselor at the school or church, or a relative on their father's side whom they might view as being more objective. Your children may not want to do that, but it's important that you at least offer, since it allows them the opportunity to seek a second opinion without feeling they're betraying you.

In cases where the child is actually abandoned by one of the parents, it's difficult to speak the truth in a loving way. This is not only because it's hard to be loving, but also because you rarely know what the truth is. I don't believe you can tell the child that "Daddy doesn't love you" or that "Daddy's not coming back," because there is much evidence to indicate otherwise. Many parents, both mothers and fathers, who apparently abandon their children will later try to contact them and reestablish a relationship. In addition, their leaving does not prove their lack of love. Studies have shown that many times the leaving parents feel so bad about themselves that they believe the most-loving thing to do is to get out of their families' lives.

Therefore, in cases of abandonment, the remaining parent needs to balance his or her comments so that the children don't have undue hope or despair. "I don't know if your father is coming back or not. We need to go on with our lives as if he will never be back, but you never know; he might realize what he's missing someday and decide to come back to see you."

Another critical reassurance needed is the child's lovability. "I don't know if your father loves you, but I do know you're a very lovable child. He is not thinking properly right now and has to work through some problems, but I know that if he ever works through them he'll realize what a wonderful child you are." Or, "I know your father loves you. He just is not able to express it or show it right now because he's trying to figure out his own life. That doesn't change the fact that you're a wonderful and lovable child. Your father's problems have nothing to do with you."

To summarize how to break the news about your divorce to your children, let me suggest the following guidelines:

✳ Be honest and open in the way you present the information. Give explanations, not defenses or opinions.

✳ Focus on what will happen to each child. Assure them of their continued well-being in spite of difficult transitions.

✳ Make sure the children understand they were not the cause of the divorce.

✳ Give clear and definite statements of mutual love and acceptance. Be prepared to back this up with actions such as hugs, interest in their world, and a listening ear.

✳ Let them know they can't get their parents back together. Encourage a realistic view of what life will be like after the divorce.

✳ Expect that you will have to reinforce this information by opening discussions with your children about the divorce at regular intervals throughout their lives.

> **When breaking the news of separation or divorce to your children, it's critical that you tell them the truth as lovingly as you can.**

MAKE IT YOUR OWN

Checklist for telling children about your divorce

❏ Both parents told the children together.

❏ The situation was presented fairly and charitably.

❑ The reasons for the breakup were presented in ways the children could understand.

❑ Your love for the children was emphasized.

❑ The children were told specifically how their lives would be affected.

❑ The children were assured that they were not the cause of the divorce.

❑ The children were prepared for the fact that their parents probably would not get back together.

If you have not yet talked thoroughly with your children about the breakup, use this space to practice what you'll say. _____

_____

_____

_____

_____

_____

➤ When and where will you talk with them about this? _____

_____

> **Your children probably know more about your divorce than you think.**

RESTRUCTURING YOUR FAMILY

"My whole world was turned upside-down when my parents broke up. My mom took my brother and me away from our home in order to live with our grandparents for a few months. After that, we moved into this lousy apartment with no furniture. I had to attend a school I used to make fun of. They were our rivals in sports, and the kids all seemed like druggies. Now I'm in this school, trying to make friends. It's like my worst nightmare come true.

"My parents are always arguing about stupid stuff, mostly money and when my brother and I are coming over to see Dad. I get tired of being in the middle of it. My mom tells me to ask Dad for the support check when I see him. Then my dad starts yelling at me about how he'd send the check if 'your mother would let me see you guys when she's supposed to.'

"I hate it when my parents talk to each other, because they always fight. But when they're not talking, I end up having to send messages back and forth." (a sixteen-year-old boy)

Restructuring a home and family is always difficult and stressful. When you add the grief and trauma of a divorce, you have the makings of an explosive situation. The purpose of this section is to provide guidelines for how to make those changes with the least turmoil and emotional harm to the participants. Granted, we can never eliminate all the negative consequences, or even our own mistakes. However, there is much that you as a parent can do to smooth the transition.

Here are some of the more-prevalent problem areas in the transition from married life to single parenting.

Custody and Visitation

Other than money issues, I'm sure there is no other issue more troublesome or emotionally charged than the custody and visitation rights of each parent. In this book, we won't discuss the different types of arrangements and which one would work best in your situation, because there are too many variables involved. For information on your options, talk with a lawyer or divorce mediation specialist. Each state has its own laws as well as trends, which vary according to the views of the judges who oversee such cases. You need to be advised by someone who is familiar with the system and the way it works in your specific area.

However, there's much I can say about the emotional side of the custody and visitation issue. Most of all, *don't make it a battle*. Remember, the more you can resolve amicably between yourselves, the more you will save in money, time, wear and tear on your nerves, and damaging effects on your children. I can't tell you how many times I've heard stories like this: "My husband and I fought over who would get the children for almost five years. It started out bad but only got worse with each new round of hearings. By the time we were done, we had used every possible devious tactic and called each other every name in the book. Of course, the children heard it all, and the only winners were the lawyers. Our legal fees were over $40,000, which was more than we had tried to split between us some five years earlier."

Whenever I have a divorcing parent tell me that he or she wants to fight the other parent in order to "come out on top," I feel compelled to say that *there are no winners in a divorce*. If you think you're going to fight your particular case until you finally "win," please rethink what you're doing. You are not going to win. You will merely run out of resources and energy, at which point you'll probably compromise to a position you probably could have obtained much earlier and at half the expense.

Now that I've made an absolute statement, let me give you the exception. In cases of abuse or extreme misconduct on the part of the other parent, you need to fight for the rights of your children. I encourage all parents to stand up for their own rights, but they're not worth battling the other parent for unless you or your children are in some type of physical or emotional danger. (Fortunately, that's the exception rather than the rule.)

Since you're not the most-objective person to judge whether your case falls into the extreme category, I encourage you to seek third-party objectivity from a counselor or spiritual adviser. Recognize that your friends and relatives are usually biased in your favor, and your lawyer may tend to advocate an adversarial position for obvious reasons.

Here are some other guidelines in regard to custody and visitation rights.

✳ Set up a good, workable visitation arrangement as soon as the separation occurs. That will help the child adjust to a new routine while assuring continuity with both parents. It also paves the way for a smoother settlement of the official agreement. Keep the visitation consistent so that children know what to expect and when they will see the other parent. When unscheduled changes occur, let your children know as soon as possible.

✳ With teenagers, flexibility is needed because of their busy schedules and outside activities. Both parents should respect the teens' wishes, but not at the expense of the relationship with the other parent. For example, if your teen is planning to work on weekends, it must be decided and arranged in consultation with both parents, since it tends to greatly affect the relationship with the noncustodial parent.

✳ Holidays need to be planned well in advance and then explained to the children. Don't wait until the week before Christmas to make arrangements with the other parent. That creates undue stress for the parents and children at a time when you need it the least. Older children and teens may be consulted about their wishes for the holidays, but once again, the final decision must be the parents'.

✳ Unless your children are preschoolers, you should consult with them about the visitation arrangement. This is particularly true of teenagers. Even though you ask them their opinion, however, make sure they understand that the final decision is up to the parents. Keep in mind your children's tendency to tell you what they think you want to hear. Therefore, expect that they will say one thing to you and something else to the other parent. Don't embarrass them or punish them for this. They desperately want the love and loyalty of both parents. Use their wishes as input into your final decision.

✳ If a court case becomes inevitable, try to keep the children out of it. If their testimony is crucial, see if it can be handled in the judge's chambers, through a court-appointed psychologist, or via video tape. Don't force a courtroom confrontation that will compel the child to testify for or against one of the parents.

✳ Keep the communication lines open between you and the other parent. Keep all discussions of changes in the arrangements and any money issues between the two of you. Don't pass messages through the children. Try to have those discussions over the phone when the kids are not around. That way, if they become unavoidably heated, your children won't be subjected to the disagreement. Don't wait until the other parent comes to pick up or drop off the children to say, 'Oh, by the way...'' As you know, that leads to disagreements the children can't help but witness. (If you have a particularly amicable relationship, however, you may have no problem with last-minute changes.)

✳ When the children are back with you, encourage them to talk about their time with the other parent unless you find you cannot listen without reacting. Don't pump them for specific information such as dating relationships or how "their mother" is spending her money. You know the motivation behind those questions, and you also know what that does to you. Ask, "Did you guys have fun with your father this weekend?," and then be prepared to bite your tongue when they talk about how much fun it was or even how nice his new girlfriend is. This is extremely difficult, but for the sake of your children, encourage their honest expression of that significant part of their lives.

If you find you cannot listen without reacting, be honest enough with your children to say, "It hurts me to hear this right now. I want you to have fun with your dad, and maybe someday we'll be able to talk all about it, but for right now maybe we shouldn't." Then find ways to work on your own adjustment so that you can later encourage your children to share all areas of their lives, especially their relationship with the other parent, and perhaps a stepparent.

✳ Both parents should set aside time alone with each child. That gives them opportunity to create special bonds and to talk on a deeper level than is possible when all children are constantly together. Such times have proved to be important in the building of a strong sense of security and a healthy self-image.

✳ Avoid being a "Disneyland Daddy" or a "Magic Mountain Mommy." Parents who don't normally live with the children tend to avoid the normal patterns of a realistic home environment. They want to make sure the children have a good time when they come to visit, so they may eat out frequently, do special things every visit, and fudge on the rules regarding bedtime, homework, and so on. To decrease the instability and competition between the parents, they should strive to provide the same stable and consistent discipline that is expected of the custodial parent. Although special events are nice, the majority of the time should be part of a daily routine, similar to what they do in the other home. Avoid presents or treats that seem like relationship bribes. Focus on building the relationship with your children through open communication and time spent doing everyday tasks.

✳ Each child needs to feel the continued love of both parents. The children should also feel they aren't betraying one parent by enjoying the company of the other. Ready access to the departed parent, by phone and in person, is necessary. You will benefit if you help your child accept and love the other parent, even when the other parent doesn't do the same.

Your Child and School

Mrs. Graham didn't want the school to find out her husband had left. She had her two children, Martha and Michael, in a private Christian school. She was afraid the school's conservative philosophy would prejudice the teachers and administrators against her children. If the teachers knew, they might watch her children too closely and almost look for trouble in her kids.

The problem with Mrs. Graham's cautious attitude is that her fears are unfounded and may be depriving the children of significant help. Teachers get harder on children when they start falling behind or missing assignments with no apparent reason. But they tend to be sensitive and compassionate when they became aware of students' struggles. But in the case of divorce, teachers would make allowances for the children's distractibility, academic regression, emotional withdrawal, or hostility.

Teachers have a variety of resources available for helping children. Books, tapes, videos, and counselors are usually at the disposal of your children as long as the school is aware of your need. The school might be holding support groups for children of divorce or at least know where they're being held in your community. The bottom line is that you won't know this unless you inform the school of what's going on at home.

If you have a teenage child, he or she probably has a variety of teachers and likely would not appreciate your contacting all of them. In that case, a call to the guidance counselor or adviser may be most helpful. If it's a large school, there is little the counselor will probably do unless the school has a special program, or unless your child comes in for help. Older children are more influenced by their peer group and therefore will tend to talk with friends far more than they will with teachers or a counselor. Encourage the peer interaction, especially with other children who have been through the same thing. They can become a tremendous help to each other. (This is a major premise of the "Kids in the Middle" programs we conduct: kids helping other kids.) However, you may need to correct distorted peer feedback from time to time, especially if your child's friends are immature or hostile. Try to be aware of the kinds of support your child is receiving from other kids.

MAKE IT YOUR OWN

➤ On a scale of 1 to 10 (1 being most peaceful), how much like a battle is your divorce? _____

➤ How does that affect your kids, positively or negatively? _____

_____

➤ If your situation is rather heated, how could you make peace with your ex-spouse, at least as far as arrangements with the kids are concerned?

_____

➤ Which of the following statements accurately present your feelings about custody arrangements? Check all that apply.

❑ I don't trust my ex-spouse with the kids.

❑ I'm afraid my kids will like my ex-spouse more than me.

❑ All the old feelings of love and anger come out when the kids tell me about visiting my ex.

❑ I don't get to see my kids as much as I'd like.

❑ I think my kids have a healthy love and respect for both parents.

❑ I like to give gifts to my kids to make up for the pain I've caused them.

❑ I think my ex-spouse is a pretty good parent.

❑ I wish I could talk more honestly with my kids about my feelings and theirs.

Other: _____

_____

➤ Outside of your home, where can your children find support? Are there resources at school or in the community that could help them? Are there other kids in similar situations who could help them? _____

_____

_____

CHANGES AT HOME

"When my family got a divorce, my whole world changed forever. We moved to a new home, a new school district, a new church, and all new friends. I don't know what hurt the most, missing my dad or missing my friends from my old neighborhood and school."

That statement from an eleven-year-old girl illustrates children's need for stability amid the turmoil. There will always be changes to face. Some of them may even be good, especially over the long term. Yet when separation or divorce first occurs, it's helpful if you can keep the changes to a minimum. If you have to move, try to stay in the same school district or the same social group. Your friendships will evolve toward more single people and fewer married couples, but try to make this transition gradual and smooth.

As parents get together in singles groups and social clubs, the children will inevitably socialize as well. The result can be positive new relationships with other kids who have been through similar changes. This reinforces the thought that *I am not alone* and gives children opportunity to talk to other kids about their concerns. Nevertheless, as a parent, you can't push those new friendships too quickly. Encourage children to continue their long-term friendships while allowing new ones to develop naturally.

Keep the household schedule, responsibilities, and discipline as consistent as possible. If you did not work before and now have to, your schedule will obviously change. Sit down with your children, explain the need for the changes, and let them know what they can expect for the future. Your children need to know that you want to be with them and care for them, but that the changes force everyone to take on more responsibilities. You might say, for example, "I have to go back to work to help pay the bills. That means I won't be here when you get home from school. I would love to be here for you, fix your snack, and hear all about your day. But unfortunately, you'll have to wait until I get home at 5:30. That means you'll have to fix your own snack, and you may even need to help set the table before I get home. What's important is that we work together and make our relationship even stronger than it was before."

Here are a few additional guidelines that should help you handle the changes at home.

✳ Although increased responsibilities are inevitable, don't allow your kids to become hyper-responsible, taking on burdens and chores they shouldn't shoulder. Let them remain children. No matter how maturely they act, don't fool yourself into believing they can take on adult responsibilities. Boys are particularly susceptible to thinking, *Now that I'm the man of the house, I need to be here for Mom.* One boy told me how he could not go away to college in the fall because his mom was going through a difficult time and would need a man around the house. Remember the "overburdened child syndrome"?

✳ Avoid confiding in your children as you would with other adults. Moms often talk to their daughters about "what a tough life it is out there." Dads tell their sons all about the women they're dating. Let your children remain children.

You want a close relationship with your kids, but there must be some boundaries in that relationship. If you have a problem with setting limits or grew up in a home where boundaries were confused, you may be unconsciously passing that on to your children. If that's the case, I encourage you to seek counseling for your own issues so you can create a healthier balance for your children.

✳ Don't force your children to make choices that will create loyalty conflicts for them. For example, don't ask your children, "Who do you want to spend your birthday with, your mom or your dad?" That creates a no-win situation for them. If they pick you, they hurt the other parent. And how can they tell you that they'd rather be with the other parent? It would be best to get their input by asking a neutral question like, "How would you like to spend the holiday?" If they neglect the other parent, you may want to suggest a compromise that includes both parents. This approach demonstrates you're sincere when you say you want your kids to have a good relationship with the other parent. It also discourages the children's tendency to tell you what they think you want to hear.

✳ Encourage your children to keep their fond memories of the other parent. Many times, upon separation, parents do a clean sweep of the house, throwing away all pictures or mementos that remind them of the other parent. While I understand the sentiment, try to save a photo album or two for your children that will remind them of good times together. A special picture or memento beside their beds or in their wallets should also be suggested. Remember your suggesting it gives children permission to love the other parent. If you don't suggest it, your kids may assume that "Mom would hit the roof if she saw a picture of *him* around."

➤ What things have changed in your children's lives since your divorce?

_____

_____

➤ What things have stayed the same? _____

_____

_____

➤ In what ways have you been able to keep changes at a minimum? In what ways could you do so? _____

_____

_____

➤ On a scale of 1 (not at all) to 5 (a great deal), to what extent do your children do each of the following?

  a. take on too much responsibility
     not at all   1 2 3 4 5   a great deal

  b. act as your personal counselors
     not at all   1 2 3 4 5   a great deal

  c. have to deal with conflicting loyalty
     not at all   1 2 3 4 5   a great deal

  d. feel pressure not to keep mementos of your ex-spouse
     not at all   1 2 3 4 5   a great deal

Your children need your permission to love the other parent. That may be difficult for you to give but it's essential for them.

NEW RELATIONSHIPS

When you're trying to restructure the family, adding a new "friend" or a stepparent to the system is like throwing a monkey wrench into the works. Such additions generally cause a whole new set of adjustments that take years to work through. If the change happens while children are still adjusting to the trauma of divorce, generally within the first two years, all the emotions can be intensified, and acceptance can be much further away. Therefore, many therapists recommend that newly divorced people not get involved in intimate relationships for at least two years following their divorce. That not only helps you to make your adjustment to the divorce, but it also helps your children.

This doesn't mean you should avoid new friendships or even relationships with the opposite sex. On the contrary, those friendships, assuming they're healthy, are vital to your recovery. What you need to avoid is *committed* relationships with the opposite sex and emotional entanglements that complicate the recovery process for you and your children. Rebound relationships rarely last, and most often they lead to more pain for everybody involved. The statistics on remarriage show that when people remarry within two years of their divorce, they have a greater than 80 percent chance of going through another divorce. Do you or your children need that? For those who wait the two years, however, the odds of "making it" increase to about 50 percent, which is the same percentage as for first-time marriages.

Having read that advice, your reaction may be, "That's fine for me, but try telling that to the other parent. He's already involved with someone else, and we're not even divorced yet!" Unfortunately, reality suggests your divorce was probably exacerbated by the involvement of another party in the life of at least one parent, and perhaps both. So now what do you do?

Many parents will use the existence of an illicit affair as an excuse to keep the children away from the other parent. While I don't condone such relationships, and I certainly understand the depth of your resentment and jealousy, once again I must defer to the greater good of your children. As one "kid in the middle" put it: "My dad left my mom to live with his girlfriend. When Dad asked if he could pick us up for a visit, my mom refused to let us go over, because she didn't agree with his lifestyle.

"We knew that what my dad had done was wrong, and in many ways we were really ticked at him. But he was still our father, and we still loved him. Mom not letting us go only created a bunch of mudslinging between my parents. I think I would have respected my mom a lot more if she had told us how she felt and then allowed us to see him. Now my dad is married to his girlfriend, and our relationship is still strained. I don't want to do it, but sometimes I blame my mom for the fact that I don't really have a relationship with my dad."

Unfortunately, dating relationships have a way of becoming an additional battleground in the postdivorce experience. Those and other pitfalls await your children as you move toward that "special relationship." Here are a few additional guidelines as you seek to include opposite-sex relationships in your restructured family.

✳ As the noncustodial parent, it would be best if you curtailed your dating on weekends when you have the children. Parenting needs to be your first priority. Particularly in the first few years of your restructured family, you need to give your children as much of your time as possible. Your dates will generally be viewed as an intrusion into your relationship with your kids. As one particular person becomes important, you'll want to introduce that person into your children's lives in a very gradual, nonthreatening way.

✳ It's usually much harder for the custodial parent to have a social life. Some potential dates may be scared off by your children, and then there's the problem of the time and energy it takes to maintain a social life. When the opportunity arises, however, you should not feel guilty about getting a baby-sitter and enjoying a night out. A balance is needed between your right to privacy and your need to be honest with the kids. Your children don't need to meet and approve of everyone you go out with, but you shouldn't hide the fact that you're dating. Your children's trust is built when you're honest with them, even though they may not like your going out without them. Expect some acting out and jealousy of your time and attention.

✳ Don't encourage your casual dates to get close to your children. A positive male role model is not a series of men you happen to date. That only confuses your children and reinforces the idea that relationships are not permanent, adding to their insecurity. While teens are more understanding of temporary relationships, they, too, are not helped by your pushing your new "friends" on them. Integrate your opposite-sex friends into your children's lives only as they become an important part of yours. Allow a relationship to develop at its own pace, never pushing your children into an artificial acceptance.

✳ Avoid the temptation to ask your children about the other parent's new friends. Such probing puts your children in the position of a spy and creates additional loyalty conflicts. If they volunteer the information, try to show little reaction. Encourage your children to treat your friends, and your ex-spouse's friends with respect. Don't allow the dating relationship to become a source of conflict.

✳ If your children ask you questions about your dating relationships, give them honest answers without personal details. For example, "Do you love Mr. So-and-So?" should be answered as honestly as you can without giving information about the depth of your relationship or your plans for the future. That should wait until you're ready to take definite steps.

If your child asks, "Do you and Mr. So-and-So kiss?" you should answer honestly without making a big deal out of it. Give no further details, however, about your physical relationship.

Once such a relationship progresses to a point where it looks as if a remarriage is imminent, you need to have a discussion with your children similar to the one suggested in the previous section, when you were contemplating separation or divorce. Out of courtesy to your former mate, you may want to forewarn him or her before you tell the kids. That way your ex-spouse can prepare emotionally. Let's face it, remarriage of either spouse is a difficult transition for both the children and the parents.

Psychologically, it's an especially big hurdle for the children. It (1) ends the fantasy that their parents might get back together, (2) triggers the fear that the new spouse will take away the parent's love for them, and (3) creates anxiety about whether they will get along with this intruder in their family. For the parent getting married, it finally closes one chapter in his or her life and opens the door of new challenges and opportunities. For the parent remaining single, there's the feeling of being left behind and the anxiety of wondering, *Will I ever be able to move on like that?*

As everyone makes the necessary adjustments, the anxiety that increasingly grips your children is the feeling, *Now that Dad has a new life, he will have even less love and less time for me.* The feeling can be especially threatening when the new marriage includes children. The blending of families is filled with so many complexities that it needs to be the subject of another book. For our purposes, a general overview is in order.

In the '90s, one-third of all children will spend at least some time with a stepparent before their eighteenth birthday. It's estimated that by the year 2000, the blended family will be the most-common type of family in this country. Yet researchers estimate that it takes an average of five years to successfully blend a family. For most of those who get remarried, the children will be out of the house before the necessary transitions are made.

I have two close friends who both had teenagers at home and were both in long-term relationships that were moving toward marriage. Rather than go through the difficulties of blending a family, both couples decided to wait until the children were out of the house before they got remarried. I'm not saying you should do the same; I merely want to point out that the blending process is more difficult than most people realize. One of my friends explained the decision this way:

"I know of over twenty remarried couples, all with teenagers in their blended families. I can't name one family who hasn't had major difficulties with their children after the marriage. I just decided that I didn't want to do that to my kids, so I've postponed my own remarriage for another two years. By then my youngest will leave for college."

A mother of a blended family described the following interaction between her teenage son and her new husband: "Before I married Jim, he and my son Paul were like best friends. I was so excited because I thought that now, after thirteen years of being by ourselves, Paul was going to have a father figure. The strangest thing happened, though. As soon as we got back from the honeymoon, I noticed my son acting a little strange around Jim. Within a few weeks they were barely speaking, and now, after three years of marriage, Paul and Jim can't even look at each other without getting in a fight. I don't know what happened when Jim and I married, but something obviously clicked off for my son."

That example is typical of many stories I've heard from stepparents who are horrified by what happens when they try to blend a family. It never seems to be easy, and the way everyone gets along before the wedding does not seem to be a very good indication of what to expect after. In fact, it's not unusual for the children to push you toward marrying Mr. So-and-So, and then to create havoc after the wedding, saying they never really liked him.

How can you increase your chances of blending families successfully? Here are a few guidelines.

✳ The potential stepparent needs to be introduced to the children in a gradual and natural way. In the beginning, fun outings are best, since they reduce the tension of "making conversation." Once the initial transitions are over, however, natural family activities are best.

✳ Don't expect instant rapport between your children and the new stepparent. Those relationships take time, usually many years. If the relationship seems to go well from the beginning, expect a strained transition later.

✳ Younger children usually adjust more quickly to a stepparent than do older children and teenagers.

✳ The stepparent should try to observe the family customs and traditions, including giving the children gifts on special occasions. Be careful to not overdo the gift giving, however, since children will tend to view it as a bribe.

✳ Don't push your children to participate in your wedding. They may feel intense pressure to be loyal to the other parent. Let them know of your plans, and tell them you would like for them to take part, but that you will let them decide for themselves. Then give them several weeks, if possible, to make up their minds.

✱ If new stepparents don't have children, they need to educate themselves about childhood development and parenting. Don't assume it will come naturally. They are taking on a big commitment and need to prepare themselves.

✱ Don't expect your children to love or respect their stepparent as much as they do their biological parent. To do so is unrealistic and sets the stepparent up for tremendous disappointment.

✱ Don't force your children to call the new stepparent "Mom" or "Dad." Find out what they would prefer, and then try to compromise on a name or nickname that's acceptable to everyone, including your former spouse. (Yes, even after your remarriage, the lines of communication need to stay open.)

✱ Continue to spend individual time with each of your children, and constantly remind them of your undiminished love for them. Keep in mind their fear that with each new person or child in your life, you will have less love for them. The feeling is particularly strong if there is a stepchild about the same age as your own child, or if a new baby is born into the blended family.

✱ While your children need to respect and listen to your new spouse, you need to remain their primary disciplinarian. Younger children can take correction from their stepparent more easily than older children and teenagers. Therefore, it is unfair to the stepparent for you to expect him or her to take on the major disciplinary role.

✱ Children generally try to play one parent against the other, but the practice is particularly intense in a stepparent relationship. Try not to get sucked into this "divide and conquer" strategy. Avoid taking sides with your children or your spouse. Instead, discuss the matter privately with your spouse, and then come back and tell the children your decision. Remember, they will take it best if it comes from you, their natural parent.

✱ You and the stepparent need to keep in mind that intense feelings of anger and resentment are normal in the blended family, especially among the teenagers. Try not to personalize the anger and respond in kind. You're probably bearing the brunt of years of perceived betrayal and disappointment. Be as patient and compassionate as you can, knowing this is a difficult transition for everyone—one that statistically will last five years.

If you are parenting as a single and your former spouse is remarrying. You also will have adjustments to make in your own attitudes and with your children as they report their feelings toward the new "creature" in their lives. It's probably a no-win situation for you. If they love their new stepparent, you will feel "replaced"; if they don't like their new stepparent, you'll have to hear the weekly reports of how "She did this, and she did that."

Here are a few guidelines to help you and your children cope with these changes:

✷ If you can't be accepting of your former spouse's remarriage, at least try to stay as neutral and emotionally uninvolved as possible. If you're really struggling with the whole issue, you probably need to talk with a counselor or adviser about your feelings. Otherwise, they will affect your children's adjustment.

✷ Give your children permission to attend or participate in the wedding. Forbidding them will only hurt their relationship with you in the long run.

✷ As hard as it might be for you to accept, you need to have at least a casual relationship with your former mate's new spouse. You will probably need to talk with him or her on the phone occasionally, and it doesn't help the children if they see you snarling at each other every time you speak.

✷ Give your children permission to talk about the times at the other parent's house. Listen to their stories about the other partner and the other children, but try not to make any judgments or offer your opinion. Try to remain detached when they complain about or praise the stepparent. Stay out of what goes on in the other household unless you have good reason for significant concern, such as "They don't feed us over there." Then, don't assume it's true. Try to take it up calmly with your former spouse. Only involve the stepparent if you find you get along with him or her better than you do with your ex-spouse.

Remarriage of either spouse is a difficult transition for the children. It . . .

    (1) ends the fantasy that their parents might get back together,

    (2) triggers the fear that the new spouse will take away the love their parent has for them, and

    (3) creates anxiety about whether they will get along with this intruder in their family.

Which of the following statements are true? Check all that apply.

☐ 1. I am rushing into another romantic relationship.

☐ 2. I'm getting involved in another romantic relationship but it's no rush. We're all ready for it.

☐ 3. I have avoided romantic relationships, largely because of the children.

☐ 4. I've been seeking a romantic relationship, primarily because my children need another parent.

☐ 5. My children have been encouraging me to find a new romance.

☐ 6. My children seem quietly resentful about the dates I have.

☐ 7. My children have expressed open hostility toward my dates.

☐ 8. My children seem too interested in the details of my romantic relationships.

☐ 9. My ex-spouse is trying to find out about my romantic relationships through the kids.

☐ 10. I am trying to find out about my ex-spouse's romantic relationships through the kids.

☐ 11. My children are still hoping my ex and I will get back together.

☐ 12. My ex-spouse has remarried. (If not, skip to #18.)

☐ 13. My ex-spouse's remarriage hit me harder than I expected.

☐ 14. My children were involved in my ex-spouse's wedding.

☐ 15. My kids get along fine with my ex's new spouse.

☐ 16. I get along fine with my ex's new spouse.

☐ 17. I'm secretly worried that my ex's remarriage will make him or her a better parent than I am.

☐ 18. I have remarried or will soon remarry. (If not, skip to #30.)

☐ 19. My new spouse gets along great with my kids.

☐ 20. I have encouraged my kids to call my new spouse "Mom" or "Dad."

☐ 21. My new spouse is strongly involved in disciplining my children.

☐ 22. My new spouse doesn't know much about raising children.

☐ 23. It's taking time for my new spouse to learn how our family does things.

❑ 24. The children are harboring resentment against my new spouse.

❑ 25. The children sometimes try to create disagreements between my spouse and me.

❑ 26. My new spouse has children of his or her own. (If not, skip to #30.)

❑ 27. Our families are blending very nicely.

❑ 28. The children seem to be competing with each other for our love.

❑ 29. Our two families have conflicting traditions.

❑ 30. I have communicated love and acceptance to my children throughout this whole process.

COMMENTS:
1. Obviously, not healthy.
2. Fine, if you are not carrying emotional baggage from the past. Check the chapter on reentry.
3. You need to avoid romance because it is best for you. Therefore, it is also best for your children.
4. Bad move. Watch out for it.
5. Common, but beware. Kids are not your counselors.
6. Common. Don't worry, but *communicate*.
7. Also common. Communicate with your kids, but be sure to express *your* needs.
8. Common. Don't divulge too much. Keep it private.
9. Common. Not much you can do.
10. Don't do this. It makes the kids spies.
11. Common. Gently wean them away from this hope.
13. Common. All sorts of emotions rise to the surface.
14. This can hurt, especially if you feel rejected and left out.
15. This is good. You are bound to feel jealous, but don't give in to your feeling.
16. This is good—uncommon, but good. For the kids' sake, at least, you need to be on good terms.
17. Common, but relax. Focus on being the best parent you can be.
19. Wonderful! But expect ups and downs.
20. Not necessarily a good idea. You don't want to displace their other parent. Find a suitable new term.
21. Not necessarily a good idea. At first, *you* should remain the primary disciplinarian (especially with older kids).
22. These issues should be explored before marriage. However, if

you are now married, you must invest extra effort in developing parental skills.

23. Each family has its traditions. It takes time to learn them and to make up new ones.
24. Common. But talk it through.
25. Common. Don't let it work. Present a united front to the kids.
27. If so, be thankful.
28. Common. Keep spreading the love around.
29. See #23.
30. This is the key. You will need to keep affirming your love for your children over and over.

Summary

In this chapter we have looked at some common areas of contention for single parents and then presented practical guidelines for helping your children over some of the difficult hurdles. The following is a brief summary:

Increases Negative Effect of Divorce	*Lessens Negative Impact of Divorce*
1. Children are involved in visitation and custody squabbles.	1. Parents work out custody and visitation arrangement cooperatively.
2. Children are asked to choose between the parents.	2. Parents help children avoid loyalty conflicts by encouraging the relationship with the other parent.
3. Parents use the children to send messages.	3. Parents keep lines of communication open.
4. Parents become too busy or distracted from their children.	4. Parents spend quality time with each child.
5. Parents use the children and money as leverage to get what they want.	5. Parents keep money issues separate and away from the children.
6. Parents isolate themselves and their children.	6. Parents seek resources and support from a variety of settings, including church, school, family.

7. Parents expect the children to take the place of the missing parent.

8. Parents deny feelings and do not facilitate discussion with children.

9. Parents push children into relationships with a series of dating partners.

10. A remarriage before the children have had time to adjust to the divorce.

11. Parents maintain angry, bitter feelings.

12. Parents speak negatively about the other parent in front of the children.

13. Absent parent loses contact with the children.

7. The child remains a child, even though increased responsibilities may be necessary.

8. Parents allow children to grieve.

9. Parents provide stable adult relationships with relatives and family friends.

10. Giving your children at least two years of adjustment before bringing a potential stepparent into their lives.

11. Parents recover and move on in a healthy, new lifestyle.

12. Parents show respect for one another.

13. Absent parent maintains consistent contact with children.

Action Point: In the summary above, which areas are still a problem for you? Set a goal, or perhaps several, for the areas you still need work on. Write those goals here and on page 287 (appendix A) for future reference.

_____

_____

_____

_____

_____

_____

_____

_____

_____

_____

CHAPTER 9

UNDERSTANDING YOUR PAST FOR PERSONAL GROWTH*

"I never wanted my family to go through the same things I faced as a kid," Cheryl confided. It was evident that she was carrying some deep feelings about her divorce and how it related to her family history.

"When I was growing up, I swore to myself that I would never get a divorce. Now here I am going through one. What a track record!"

While we talked, Cheryl expressed another concern that went beyond her background. It had to do with the basic idea of the family. "What is a family, anyway?" she thought out loud. "Is there such a thing as a 'normal' family?"

Cheryl was considering questions any of us could be asking. The family unit seems to be falling apart. She represents a growing segment in our society of people who realize they grew up in dysfunctional families.

THE FAMILY AS A UNIT

Years ago, a noted family therapist developed a helpful illustration of the family. She encouraged her clients to think of the family as a mobile:

---

*This chapter has been developed from material found in *The Adult Child of Divorce*, by Bob Burns and Michael J. Brissett.

pieces of plastic, metal, wood, or paper suspended from interconnecting wires. (See John and Linda Friel, *Adult Children: The Secrets of Dysfunctional Families* [Deerfield Beach, Fla.: Health Communications, 1988], p. 48.)

From a distance, the mobile looks like independent parts hanging alone in the air. However, as you come closer to it, you see the parts are connected by thin wires.

If you blow on any part of the mobile, all the individual pieces eventually respond to your breath because of the connecting wires. The mobile twists and turns. The parts are actually interdependent. Then the mobile slowly begins to settle until it regains stability. Each part has resumed its proper position.

As you walk away, the mobile again looks like individual parts from a distance. However, you know better. Your breath created a disruption that clearly showed how each part was bound to the others.

The family is like a mobile in that each member looks like a distinct and separate unit. Then some disruption occurs. It could be as simple as, say, a little sister "borrowing" a blouse without permission. Suddenly, all the parts are affected! Mom is interrupted while she listens to the offended parties. Brother can't do his homework because of the commotion. And Dad quietly (but resentfully) turns up the volume on the television so he won't have to get involved.

The family is a unit—a unit of interconnected parts—and each part responds and reacts to the others.

WHAT IS NORMAL?

Carrie grew up in a "typical" American family: Dad, Mom, a sister, a brother, one dog, and two cats. Everything seemed stable to the outside world. She worked hard to maintain that image. But Carrie knew differently. Her father was an alcoholic, and she was never quite sure when the next trauma would occur. To Carrie, the most-important thing was that her friends didn't know about her family problems. She felt she would just die if they found out.

It was a little different for Terry. Yes, his family was intact. His father was an outstanding businessman in the community. His mother was active in all the right clubs. Both parents genuinely seemed to love him and his little sister. Yet, his dad and mom lived in different rooms, slept in different beds, and maintained separate lives.

Louise thought she lived in a normal house. Though both of her parents were busy with their work, real warmth and love were evident in the family. Everyone seemed to pitch in together. Everyone, that is, except for her brother Ted, who was on drugs. She was surprised, and for some reason she felt guilty.

Finally, there's Kevin. Kevin's parents were divorced when he was eight. He lived with his mother until his fifteenth birthday. Then, in a decision that seemed quite sudden, he moved eight hundred miles to live with his father and stepmother. Unfortunately, things didn't work out the way Kevin expected, and he moved back with his mother a year later.

In the preceding paragraphs, we have a sampling of different family units. Are any of those families normal? No, not one of them!

That leads us to a vital question: Is there such a thing as a normal family?

Normal is an elusive term. Many people assume a normal family is an intact one in which Dad and Mom still live together. However, when we scratch beneath the surface of *any* family, we discover characteristics that may or may not be considered normal.

Instead of asking whether a family is normal, the better question is whether it's *functional*. That is, does the family function in a healthy manner within its own unique customs and characteristics?

To explore this idea, let's take a quick look at two families, the Millers and the Robinsons.

Don and Sally Miller were divorced when their daughter was four and their son was two. Although Sally has custody of the children, she has worked hard to involve Don in the task of coparenting. For example, Sally has carefully resisted talking about Don in a negative way around the kids. She has also labored to communicate clearly with Don. Sally and Don still have many disagreements, but when it comes to their children, they've tried to "work off the same sheet of music."

For his part, Don has been consistent with his alimony and child support. Even though he has remarried, he made it clear to his new wife before the engagement that he was committed to the welfare of his children.

Don's commitment goes beyond the financial. He calls his children daily, writes notes to them, and is available to baby-sit when Sally has a reasonable request. He has turned down two promotions that would have required him to relocate hundreds of miles from his kids.

Don and Sally Miller might not be providing a normal home by some definitions. Nevertheless, they are functioning in a positive, healthy fashion in the aftermath of their divorce.

Marv and Ann Robinson are not divorced. However, Marv is overcommitted to his job, working seventy or more hours a week. He assumes that as long as he provides financially, Ann can take care of the warm fuzzies for the kids.

When Marv comes home, the children have learned to clear out of the way. If they create a mess or talk too loud, Dad might start screaming at them. They do everything they can to avoid bothering him.

As for Ann Robinson, she learned a long time ago that Marv didn't want to talk with her. At best, he would say, "Honey, I'm too tired to talk right now." At worst, he would lambast her about her lack of gratitude for his hard work on behalf of the family. Ann has learned to put up and shut up.

Some would look superficially at the Robinsons and consider them normal. However, they are not functioning in a healthy manner.

MAKE IT YOUR OWN

➤ Have you thought of the family you grew up in as normal? Why or why not? _____

_____

_____

➤ Was your original family functional? Which of the following statements best expresses its situation?

❑ Yes, my family worked smoothly.

❑ We had some obstacles to overcome, but we did pretty well.

❑ We probably had our share of dysfunction, but nothing serious. We were moderately functional.

❑ We had serious problems. It's amazing we turned out as well as we did.

❑ We were severely dysfunctional, and that has caused numerous problems later in life.

❑ Other: _____

_____

➤ If you could change one thing about the family you grew up in, what would it be? _____

_____

➤ If you now have children, would you say your present family is more functional than your original family, less functional, or about the same? Why? _____

_____

_____

> *A family is like a mobile. If one part is moved, all other parts are set in motion as well. They are individual units, but they're tightly connected.*

THE DYSFUNCTIONAL FAMILY

The opposite of functional is dysfunctional. To be dysfunctional simply means that a person or family is not able to function in a healthy manner.

Over the past ten years, as I've met with individuals and families in counseling, seminars, and other programs, I have made a startling discovery: we're all dysfunctional to a certain extent! Let me explain what I mean.

I have never met a person who is not struggling in some area of his life. No one is perfect. We all wrestle with issues that keep us from doing or being what we want to do or be.

The same is true for families. Every family is dysfunctional in one way or another.

That fact was hard for my friend Byron to believe. He confided, "All I've ever wanted was a 'normal' family. I grew up in a home with a lot of problems. I dreamed of the day when I could be married and have a stable family.

"After two years of marriage—a marriage I thought was pretty good—Karen left me.

"Now when I come to church on Sunday morning and see all those families dressed in their fancy clothes, and all the kids looking happy and well-behaved, I just want to scream. Everyone else has his act together. I'm the one who is strange."

It took me a long time to convince Byron that even families that look "all together" on Sunday morning have their problems. "Just think," I said to him, "they might have been yelling at each other all the way to church. But are you going to see those problems? No way!" The masks we've learned to wear (especially when we're at church) can hide a great deal of the reality of our lives.

Byron's understanding of the truth ultimately came out of our discussion of two biblical passages. First, we talked about a verse from the prophet Isaiah: "All we like sheep have gone astray; we have turned, everyone, to his own way" (53:6). My father worked with ranchers and understood the nature of sheep. He told me that a sheep, left to itself, will wander off in any direction. And every human being has gone off course just like one of those sheep. Left on our own, we cannot function properly.

The second verse that helped Byron was Romans 3:23: "All have sinned and fall short of the glory of God."

When Byron heard that verse for the first time, he was taken aback. "Who, me, a sinner?" he said.

Learning that the word *sin* means "missing the mark" helped him understand. It simply describes one who has not been able to function according to God's standards. In many ways, the word *sin* could be considered synonymous with *dysfunction*.

With this understanding, Byron was able to grasp that all people and all families are dysfunctional to a degree. The level of dysfunction depends on many factors. But the reality of being dysfunctional is shared by the whole human race.

Divorce and Dysfunction

After hearing the elective at Fresh Start entitled "Dysfunctional Families," JoAnn came to me with a troubling question. "I really appreciated the information I received in the elective," she said, "particularly the comparisons of a functional family over against dysfunctional families. That's where my question comes in. Are all divorced families dysfunctional?"

As with Byron, I reminded JoAnn that all people and families are dysfunctional to a degree. Therefore, the basic answer to her question was yes.

However, JoAnn obviously had deeper concerns on her mind. She was burdened about her children. "I really want to protect my kids," she explained. "I don't want them to be hurt by my divorce. But after listening to your elective, I'm worried that they might be destined to carry the dysfunctional patterns of our family into their future lives."

I spent some time explaining to JoAnn that whenever there is a divorce, a serious dysfunction has led to it, and the divorce itself will always disrupt the family system. Divorce creates a state of crisis for each individual and for the family as a whole. When we face a crisis like divorce, we must draw upon all our resources to cope. Those coping methods can be healthy or dysfunctional.

As I explained to JoAnn, a few years before there had been a tragic airline accident. As the investigators studied the crash, they learned that the jet had a weakness at the point where the wing was connected to the body of the aircraft. Under the stress of the flight, the wing ripped off, causing the plane to crash.

A divorce crisis is similar to the atmospheric pressure applied to that airplane while it was in flight. Just as the jet's wings were tested by the stress of the flight, so a divorce tests our ability to handle life's stress. A crisis will push our ability to cope to the limits. If our coping mechanisms aren't healthy, a crisis can create significant dysfunction.

"The good news for you and your children," I told JoAnn, "is that while the divorce reflects significant problems, it can also provide an opportunity for you to discover your strengths and weaknesses. You can feel good about the things you're able to handle. And you can honestly face the areas that the stress reveals to be weak. Of course your children have experienced and will continue to experience losses associated with the divorce. But there are constructive responses that can help heal those wounds and help your children grow.

"Thus, your children are not destined to repeat past dysfunctional patterns. Your divorce can actually become the context in which those patterns are discovered and changed."

MAKE IT YOUR OWN

➤ How do you respond to the idea that *all* people and all families are dysfunctional to some degree? Why? _____

_____

_____

➤ Have you ever been surprised to discover dysfunctions in a family that you thought had it all together? How did you find out? _____

_____

_____

➤ As you look back now, how do you think the family you grew up in compared to other families in your church (or neighborhood)? More dysfunctional, less, or about the same? _____

_____

➤ How do you think the dysfunctions in your family as you grew up have contributed to your divorce, if at all? _____

_____

➤ If you have children, how do you think the divorce will affect the functionality of your home? _____

_____

_____

> *Every family is dysfunctional to some extent.*

FUNCTIONAL VERSUS DYSFUNCTIONAL
FAMILY PATTERNS

As I've said, there are degrees of functionality or dysfunctionality. Each family is like a tapestry woven with many colors. The threads of the family are its combined experiences, history, and background; the personalities of each member; and the strengths and weaknesses of the family unit. Added together, all those variables form the unique combinations that cause a family to act in a functional or dysfunctional manner.

No two family units are exactly alike. The colors of a family tapestry form a one-of-a-kind family unit that carries with it a unique set of functional and dysfunctional characteristics. And those characteristics vary somewhere between totally dysfunctional and totally functional.

I remember talking with Barbara, who grew up in a difficult home. Her father was emotionally abusive: sometimes screaming, sometimes ridiculing, but never encouraging or supportive.

Once, when she was eight years old, Barbara was playing at the home of a friend. During their playtime, the father of Barbara's friend happened to pass by and pay the girls a compliment. Barbara couldn't believe it! She was convinced her friend lived in a perfect family! She had never experienced such encouragement, and she immediately assumed her friend's father was always supportive.

Of course, Barbara's friend didn't live in a perfect home. But for years Barbara assumed that family was perfect and normal—after all, she had never seen any of their problems. Exposed to a family environment different from her own, Barbara could view it only in terms of the extreme. Because the father wasn't negative (in one instance), she thought he must always be positive. She didn't realize that every family has its problems. The truth is, no family has it all together.

I like to think of functional and dysfunctional characteristics as absolutes at either end of a continuum something like this:

100%   _____   100%

Functional   Dysfunctional

When comparing functional and dysfunctional traits, we often tend to think of our families as fitting into one side or the other: either we're totally functional in an area or we're totally dysfunctional. But as we have seen, that's never the case.

To convey a better understanding of the functional/dysfunctional variations within families, I want to describe six comparative characteristics of functional versus dysfunctional families. Remember, every family will have both characteristics to a certain extent. Your own family falls somewhere between the two extremes.

STEADY PARENTAL WARMTH AND TRUST VERSUS VACILLATING WARMTH AND TRUST

Parental warmth and trustworthiness are evident in Bernie's experience. He wouldn't describe the home he grew up in as demonstrative or gushy. He always understood, however, that his parents loved him—and each other. It was not unusual for Bernie's dad to give him a big bear hug. And Bernie never worried about sharing his concerns with his mom and dad. He knew they might disagree with him, but that didn't matter. They would listen to him anyway.

Dan also experienced parental warmth and trustworthiness. His parents divorced when he was almost eleven. After a few turbulent months, life seemed to settle down to a regular routine—as regular as life can be without having a dad around the house.

But Dan's dad never missed his times of visitation. And one memory stands out when Dan reviews those first few years of the back-and-forth life children face when they live "between" parents. It took place whenever his dad drove him to school. Every time they went through that uneasy transition at the end of visitation, Dan and his dad would kiss each other on the lips. It was an act of love that had gone on for years.

One time was different, however. Dan's friends were out in the schoolyard. What would they think if they saw him kissing his dad? Dan hesitated. His dad picked up on his fears.

"Dan," his dad said, "if you don't want to kiss me, that's okay. But son, I love you very much, and I want to have a way of expressing that to you. So you think about what you want me to do. A hug, a handshake—anything would be fine for me. But I want to tell you I love you in a special way."

After he thought about it for a moment, Dan leaned over and gave his dad a big smack on the lips! Dan is now twenty-five, but he still remembers that day, and he still kisses his dad.

That's parental warmth; that's parental trustworthiness. A sense of acceptance. A knowledge that home is safe, a place where one can trust and be trusted.

On the other hand, the corresponding dysfunctional characteristic is vacillating parental warmth and trustworthiness.

Take the experience of Louise. One day she told me, "As I faced the normal physical transitions of adolescence, I was embarrassed about sexual matters. I wanted to talk to my mother about it, but I was scared. I wondered how she would react."

Louise didn't have to wait long before she had an answer. She got a crush on a boy at school, and she revealed her feelings to her mother. Before she knew it, her mother had told the secret to her brother, her sister, her father, and her friends. To make matters worse, she teased Louise about it. Louise could discuss many things with her mother, but never again did she talk with her about boys or sexual issues.

"A funny thing happened just before I was married," Louise continued. "My mother said, 'All the other kids in the family would talk to me about sex. But Louise seemed to be afraid of it.' I knew the reason behind my refusal to talk with her about it, but I never told her. I didn't want her blabbing about it with others or making me the object of ridicule."

A functional home is a place where children feel the security of consistent parental warmth and trustworthiness. A dysfunctional home is not safe. Children want to place the full weight of trust in their parents. Yet experiences like Louise's make children question whether their parents can be trusted. And if children can't trust their parents, whom can they trust?

MAKE IT YOUR OWN

➤ As you evaluate the home you grew up in, where along the line below would you say it belongs? Place an X at the appropriate spot.

Parental Warmth and Trust

100% _____ 100%

Functional   Dysfunctional

If you have children, place an O at the appropriate spot for your present family.

➤ What can you do to make up for the effects of a lack of parental warmth and trust in your original family? _____

_____

➤ What can you do to improve parental warmth and trust in your present family? _____

_____

_____

CLEARLY DEFINED LIMITS VERSUS THE UNPREDICTABLE

I first learned about the importance of limits while working on the staff of a junior-high camp. If we set out the boundaries of acceptable activity at the beginning of the camp and then enforced the boundaries, things ran smoothly. However, if the kids felt they could move beyond the limits, the whole camp would be uncontrolled.

Families work something like that. Clearly defined and reinforced limits will breed stability and security.

Joseph understands this very well. He never was a rebellious child. Maybe that's why a little incident that happened when he was twelve years old stands out so clearly in his mind.

Joseph was at a store with some friends. One of his buddies challenged the group to steal some little metal cars from the toy department. The boys accepted the challenge, each taking one car and putting it in his pocket.

An observant clerk called security while the boys began to walk toward the door. Before they could even think of getting away, a guard had them in the store's security office.

Joseph still remembers how humiliated he was as his parents and the police were called. He also remembers the discipline his parents administered.

Joseph comments some twenty years later, "Now that I think about it, my parents were just as concerned about my responsible fulfillment of family chores as they were about my breaking the law. They were consistent—and fair—in their application of rules."

Joseph's sister states, "My brother and I could not divide and conquer our parents. If we asked Dad for permission to do something and he said no, we might go to Mother and say, 'Mother, may we do this?'

"Instead of saying yes, she would say, 'What did your father say?'

"We would respond, 'he said no.'

"Then she'd say, 'Why did you come and ask me?' We'd try to do the same thing to Dad. But it would never work."

The opposite situation is a family with changing or unpredictable limits. Nancy grew up in a home where, on one night, she was allowed to talk for hours on the phone. The next night she was told she had to get off the phone in three minutes. That rule might last for a few days. Then the rule would switch back to unlimited access for a while.

Ken also had changing limits in his home. "I could get pretty much anything I wanted out of my folks if I badgered them long enough," he confided. "First I would ask, and they would say no. Then I would keep asking, and they would get upset. Finally I would start crying or comparing them to other parents or something like that. I knew they would give in after a while."

Loraine wasn't so lucky. She lived with her mom, who as a single parent held down two jobs to make ends meet. Loraine set limits for herself. As long as she was home when her mom walked in the door at eleven thirty every night, things were all right. By the age of sixteen, she could bluff her way into any bar in town. She was also on her way to alcohol and drug dependency.

Tim didn't need absentee parents to get into substance abuse. His parents felt that "a kid ought to have the freedom to make his own choices." So they "chaperoned" a party where Tim and his friends got roaring drunk on the booze they bought for him. When Tim's girlfriend became pregnant, Tim's parents paid for the abortion and cooperated in keeping the information from her parents. When Tim got in trouble at school, his parents threatened the principal with a lawsuit. I came to know Tim while he was going through his third divorce—at the age of thirty-three.

Clearly defined limits provide a sense of stability in the midst of an unstable world and teach responsibility for one's choices. The lack of such limits forces children to turn to themselves for stability and control of their environment or to eventually suffer the consequences of living without sensible boundaries.

MAKE IT YOUR OWN

▶ As you evaluate the home you grew up in, where along the line below would you say it belongs? Place an X at the appropriate spot.

Clearly Defined Limits

100% _____ 100%

Functional   Dysfunctional

If you have children, place an O at the appropriate spot for your present family.

➤ What can you do to make up for the effects of unpredictability of limits in your original family? _____

_____

_____

➤ What can you do to improve the clarity of limits in your present family? _____

_____

_____

RELATIVE CONSISTENCY VERSUS CHAOS

A functional home will maintain relative consistency. By "relative" I mean flexibility within a pattern of structured daily life. For example, the standard bedtime for a child might be eight o'clock. However, in special circumstances the child might be allowed to stay up later. That's relative consistency, which is much different from a home where the child has no standard bedtime—he might be put to bed at seven thirty one night, eleven o'clock the next, nine the next, and so on.

Robert grew up in a relatively consistent home. He said he always had a good idea of what would happen on any given day: "At a seminar I heard you say that one way to discern how a family functions is to think about what you expect when you open the door and enter the house. I never really had a problem wondering what to expect when I came home. There was rarely a surprise."

When Lynn heard Robert tell me of the consistency in his home, she responded, "Boy! I grew up in a different kind of place! My mother was an alcoholic, and my father was a traveling salesman. I never knew what to expect when I came home from school. Dad might be home or on the road—I never knew. Mom might be coherent or totally wiped out. Every day it was something different."

A consistent home creates an atmosphere of security for a child, a stable environment for growth. A chaotic home creates a sense of anxiety; it's an unstable environment.

MAKE IT YOUR OWN

➤ As you evaluate the home you grew up in, where along the line below would you say it belongs? Place an X at the appropriate spot.

Consistency

100% _____ 100%

Functional   Dysfunctional

If you have children, place an O at the appropriate spot for your present family.

➤ What can you do to make up for the effects of chaotic conditions in your original family? _____

_____

_____

➤ What can you do to improve the consistency of your present family?

_____

_____

_____

CLEAR FAMILY ROLES VERSUS ROLE REVERSALS

Gina's father abandoned the family when she was three years old. By the time she was six, Gina was responsible to provide primary care for her two younger brothers. She never remembered a night when she was sure her mother would be home. She was the one who fixed the meals, gave her brothers their baths, and put them to bed. By the time she was in her teens, Gina also became her mother's caretaker. Debilitated by intense depression, her mother might stay in bed for days on end. Lots of kids grew up wondering what it would be like to be a mommy or daddy. Gina grew up wondering what it would be like to be a kid.

The idea of role responsibilities has become foggy in our society. Some families maintain traditional roles: children are to be children; parents are to be adults. However, in many homes the roles are reversed or modified.

Diane is the twenty-nine-year-old mother of seven-year-old Tony. She was divorced two years ago, and her former husband has moved across the country. He rarely has contact with his son.

Diane explains, "When my husband left me, I was devastated! I didn't know who I could talk to about it. Then one evening little Tony said, 'Mommy, what are you thinking?' Well, I dumped my whole load on him. Since then, my son has become my best friend and counselor. I know it might sound strange, but I would rather talk to Tony than to anyone else. I don't know how I would have made it this far without him."

Tony no longer has the opportunity of being a child in his home. His role and his mother's have been reversed. He is now a peer and a counselor to his mother.

Role reversals occurred differently for Vic. One day his father would be acting okay. The next day Vic might have to drive down to the bar and pick him up. Year after year he was his father's son and "parent." When he was sober, Vic's father resented Vic's parental actions. When he was drunk, he depended on his son.

Jackie grew up in a large family. She was the fourth of six kids. Her dad, a city policeman, was killed while on duty when Jackie was eight. Her mom had to work to supplement a meager pension. Yet Jackie remarks, "Mom never made excuses when things were tough. And she never took any guff. She worked hard to maintain a stable home. She also maintained the standards that she had established with Dad. We never questioned who was boss at home. But she loved us, and we loved her. We had respect for each other."

When there are clear family roles, a child has the security of knowing where she fits in. When roles are muddied, she's never really sure what she should be doing. Or even worse, she never has the opportunity to experience and grow through the stages of childhood.

MAKE IT YOUR OWN

➤ As you evaluate the home you grew up in, where along the line below would you say it belongs? Place an X at the appropriate spot.

Clear Family Roles

100% _____ 100%

Functional   Dysfunctional

If you have children, place an O at the appropriate spot for your present family.

➤ What can you do to make up for the effects of role reversals in your original family? _____

_____

_____

➤ What can you do to improve the clarity of family roles in your present family? _____

_____

_____

OPEN COMMUNICATION VERSUS CLOSED COMMUNICATION

Russ cannot remember a time when he was unable to talk with his mom or dad. "Oh, we had plenty of disagreements," he explains, "but I never felt put down or condemned. It was no holds barred. We just said what we wanted to say." That was true even in their physical gestures. "When one of us was talking," Russ continues, "he might be waving his arms or pointing his finger or describing his words with motions. It could be a pretty lively place."

Russ's wife, Corrine, grew up in a totally different environment. No one was allowed to talk or express opinions. If someone spoke, Corrine's father was quick with a ridiculing or sarcastic comment. It was always safer just being quiet.

Once, Corrine tried to express herself on an issue she felt was extremely important. Her father became angry, stood up, and screamed, "That's the most stupid thing I have ever heard in my life." Then, while screaming about how stupid she was, he walked over to Corrine, pinned her against the wall, and said, "I'm not going to let you go until you tell me how stupid you are. Tell me you're stupid." Corrine finally gave in to his demand in order to escape.

After fifteen years of marriage and a great deal of hard work, Russ and Corrine understand each other's communication styles. Russ expected open communication. When he and Corrine disagreed, he would raise his voice and wave his arms in the air—the norm for his family. Corrine would pull away and refuse to talk. She associated intensity and animation with her father and wanted, instead, a quiet, peaceful conversation.

Fortunately, Russ and Corrine have invested hours learning about each other. Both have grown as they've discussed past experiences and struggles.

For Melissa, it hasn't been that way. Like Corrine, she grew up in a home where talking was a mistake. "Shut up!" and "Don't you talk back to me!" were household cliches. Melissa learned that safety meant silence. So she has used silence all her life as protection from the things she didn't want to face.

A child who grows up in a home with open communication will learn that his ideas are significant and worth sharing. He will feel he has a place in the family and the world. And he will learn healthy communication patterns.

A child who grows up in a home with closed communication will learn it's safer to be quiet than to express his thoughts. He will learn silence as a method of coping. He'll stifle his feelings and concerns. Or he will lash out when emotionally upset. In any case, he'll feel isolated. And he'll take those unhealthy patterns into his adult life.

MAKE IT YOUR OWN

➤ As you evaluate the home you grew up in, where along the line below would you say it belongs? Place an X at the appropriate spot.

Openness of Communication

100% _____ 100%

Functional   Dysfunctional

If you have children, place an O at the appropriate spot for your present family.

➤ What can you do to make up for the effects of closed communication in your original family? _____

_____

_____

➤ What can you do to improve the openness of communication in your present family? _____

_____

_____

ACTIVE/RELAXED VERSUS CONSTANT CRISIS

"When I was growing up," Bruce explained, "both my parents worked. As a matter of fact, all of us had to work to make ends meet. But you know, dinnertime always sticks out in my mind. No matter how busy we all were, we knew we should never miss dinner.

"The meals weren't fancy. It wasn't food that made that time important. What made it special is that we would do things together. When we were kids, Dad would tell us stories or make up games. When we got older, it was a time to talk about—and debate—the latest news."

Bruce's family experience is a good example of what it means to have an active/relaxed pattern. Every family member was busy, but there was an ebb and flow to their lifestyle. At certain times, things were hectic. Yet there was always the dinner hour to give everyone an opportunity to let down and relax for a while.

Chris described a different kind of family background. "In my family, we never got anything done until the last minute. My mother lived in constant fear that I would invite a friend over to play, because the house was always a mess. I can still remember how we would run around the hour before guests arrived, trying madly to get the place clean. Then, when the guests came, we were almost ready to collapse!

"I guess I picked up the pattern," Chris continued. "I wasn't able to graduate from college until I finished three incompletes. One teacher let me hand in a paper three semesters after I had taken the course. And I didn't get it to her until the day she had to hand in the grades to the registrar. I wish I could say I've changed, but I always seem to need threats to get anything done."

Adults who grow up in a home that moves from crisis to crisis often consider themselves adrenaline junkies. They can never get anything done until the pressure is on. However, those who grow up in an active-relaxed home learn how to pace themselves and plan ahead.

MAKE IT YOUR OWN

▶ As you evaluate the home you grew up in, where along the line below would you say it belongs? Place an X at the appropriate spot.

Active/Relaxed Versus Constant Crisis

100%		100%
Functional		Dysfunctional

If you have children, place an O at the appropriate spot for your present family.

▶ What can you do to make up for the effects of constant crisis in your original family? _____

_____

_____

▶ What can you do to improve the active/relaxed nature of your present family? _____

_____

_____

Traits of Functional and Dysfunctional Families	
Functional	**Dysfunctional**
Steady parental warmth and trust	*Vacillating warmth and trust*
Clearly defined limits	*Unpredictability*
Consistency	*Chaos*
Clear family roles	*Role reversal*
Open communication	*Closed communication*
Active/relaxed tone	*Constant crisis*

FAMILY RULES

"You just do what you have to do. Life goes on," stated Marie with resignation.

Marie was forty-six and in a small group at a Fresh Start seminar. She was describing the way she dealt with the deaths of her mother, father, brother, and marriage, all within eighteen months.

She went on, "Besides, I've never had time to dwell on my feelings. Of course it's tough, but I'm used to going on with my responsibilities."

In spite of living forty-six productive, responsible years, Marie had enjoyed little of her life. She knew much about coping but nearly nothing about feelings or fun. In addition to being divorced herself, she grew up in a difficult home, and somewhere back in her early years she stopped paying much attention to her thoughts or feelings about life. One way she learned how to do that was by using the three "rules" of a dysfunctional family. In her classic book for adult children of alcoholics, Claudia Black identified those rules that prevail when families deny the reality of their problems and pain: don't talk, don't trust, and don't feel. (Claudia Black, *It Will Never Happen to Me!* [M.A.C. Publishers, 1981] pp. 24–48)

Don't Talk

"I have proof that in our family it didn't pay to be honest." Marty was chatting over lunch with others who had just completed the "Dysfunctional Family" session at one of our seminars. He was recalling an especially painful lesson in the don't-talk rule.

"When I was fifteen, my father and his second wife moved from Miami to Phoenix. When Dad first told us he planned to move, my sister and I were afraid we wouldn't get to see him as much, since we lived with Mom in Orlando. But Dad said he would be making a lot more money and promised us we'd get to fly out there every Christmas and summer. Well, the year after he moved, he called and told us he couldn't afford for us to fly out for Christmas. However, he told us we could ride the bus! We didn't mind riding a bus from Orlando to Miami. But a bus ride to Phoenix would have taken two or three days each way. And we only had two weeks off from school."

"I felt so betrayed—he had promised to fly us! So I wrote him a letter telling him I was angry and felt it was unfair. Before he got my letter, he called back to say we could fly out after all. I was too scared to mention my letter.

"When he got my letter, Dad called me in a rage. He told me he was really disappointed in me for having such an attitude, and he said the trip was off. I just couldn't say anything to defend myself. I couldn't even talk! But I went to my room and cried bitterly. In a few more days, Dad called back again, and we did fly out for Christmas after all. But I never told Dad what I went through over that incident. I don't think I told him any of my deep feelings again for twenty years."

Sharing feelings and thoughts can be costly in a home where parents don't demonstrate trust and understanding. The child discovers that sharing those things might bring a painful reply from her parents. One response could be denial: "Oh, everything will be okay"; "Just don't worry about it"; "We'll handle it." Another response could be anger and punishment, as we saw in Marty's case. Still another response could be depression and self-pity: "I know, I know, we've made your life miserable. I'm sorry you don't have better parents."

Those kinds of responses are threatening to a child. She often concludes it's simply better not to talk than to elicit a painful experience by voicing her concerns. By the time she's an adult, she has learned that it's better just to keep her mouth shut.

Don't Trust

Denise is in her early thirties. Tears started flowing as she described instances through which she learned not to trust her parents. "I guess it wasn't really a big deal," she said, "but it hurt a lot. I was in the fifth grade, and I had stayed after school to make up a big test I missed because of being sick. My mother had no car, and my father said he would pick me up at four o'clock. I waited and waited at the corner where he said he'd be. He never came. Finally, I started walking home—a forty-five-minute walk through a neighborhood that wasn't very safe. He never apologized. He never even mentioned it to me. I felt I just didn't matter to him. I remember thinking I couldn't count on my father."

Jim is another Fresh Start alumnus who remembers experiences that convinced him not to trust. "About a year after my parents split, my dad came to town to visit. I had just finished the fourth grade, and school was out for the summer. Dad took my sister and me out to eat. He asked us if we'd like to spend some time with him that summer (he lived 300 miles away). We said 'Sure!' Then he asked how we'd feel if he ever remarried. My sister and I both started crying; we had been hoping he and Mom would get back together.

"After we got over our tears, he said there was a lady he'd met and planned to marry. In fact, they'd be married by the time we visited him later in the summer. By the end of the meal, he admitted he was already married, and he wanted us to leave the next day to spend the summer with them. To top it off, he asked us not to tell Mom that he'd remarried until the end of the summer. All summer long, I felt like I was betraying my mother.

"I had never really known my dad before that summer. Yet I felt very uneasy about the way he revealed the truth. I even remember wondering if there were other surprises and secrets about his life. Years later, I discovered he had been having an affair with my stepmother while he was still married to my mother. My doubts about his honesty had been well founded!"

When people like Jim and Denise experience parental models who consistently let them down or betray their trust, they begin wondering if they can believe anyone. *After all,* they reason, *if you can't trust your parents, whom can you trust?*

Don't Feel

Anita's mother brought her for counseling because of her hostility, apathy in school, and general disobedience. While she was in counseling, her father moved out and filed for divorce. It took several months of counseling to crack the emotional shell of protection Anita had built up.

When she was finally able to face her pain, Anita discovered she was furious with her parents for the turmoil and disruption in their family life. But more than that, she felt an incredible depth of sadness and fear.

Anita was reluctant to share her feelings with her parents. "They won't care," she said bluntly. "They had to know how upset I've been, and they never even asked how I was." With the next breath she would argue, "I know Daddy will be furious. And Mama is already so depressed."

In a few more minutes, she would continue to talk herself out of the idea of breaking the silence by talking to her parents. She claimed, "It wouldn't change anything to tell them how I really feel. It would just make things worse."

Anita is like many who grow up in dysfunctional homes. She learned that you may be ridiculed, criticized, or rejected when you face your feelings. As a result, it's easier to deny all feelings and act as though everything is all right.

MAKE IT YOUR OWN

➤ To what extent were the three rules of dysfunctional families enforced in your home as you grew up? Try to come up with a percentage.

_____% Don't talk.

_____% Don't trust.

_____% Don't feel.

➤ How did they affect the way you behaved in your marriage? _____

_____

_____

➤ How can you overcome the effects of these rules? _____

_____

_____

➤ If you have children, do you see these rules at work with them? If so, how can you change that? _____

_____

_____

Breaking the Rules

1. *Encourage children to talk about what they're thinking.*
2. *Be true to your word, whether you're promising a treat or threatening discipline. If you mess up, apologize.*
3. *Urge children to be honest about their feelings. Never make fun of their emotions.*

Dysfunctional Patterning

In the preceding pages, we have explored varied family characteristics and rules. As I stressed before, every family is unique. The characteristics you experienced and the rules you learned make up the patterns of your own family system.

Our children will also learn from us. Often the patterns we have consciously or unconsciously picked up have been passed down from generation to generation.

Early in this chapter, I told about a recently divorced mother named JoAnn who asked me how her marriage breakup would affect her children. I answered that the divorce need not push her children into lifelong dysfunctional patterns. It's encouraging to know that a powerful God is ready to support us in our recovery. He says, "Fear not, for I am with you; be not dismayed, for I am your God. I will strengthen you, yes, I will help you, I will uphold you with My righteous right hand" (Isa. 41:10).

It's also important, however, to recognize the functional or dysfunctional characteristics of our background. We can use our past for personal growth if we understand the coping patterns we developed in childhood. Our own recovery and the maturity of our children will be impeded or enhanced by our recognition of those issues and by the energy we invest in maintaining the positive and reforming the negative.

DEVELOPING A POSITIVE SELF-IMAGE

by Tom Whiteman

Without question, one of the consequences of a divorce is a damaged self-image. We all go through the self-doubts, the second guessing, and perhaps even self-abasement. And there's good reason for us to feel the way we do. One of the most-important things in life was our marriage and family. When that has fallen apart, of course we will feel like a failure. And even for couples who have been fairly hospitable to each other, toward the end of the relationship, the name calling and accusations get pretty ugly.

So now one of your divorce recovery tasks is to rebuild your self-image. That may become one of the first things you work on, since it's critical for every other relationship you'll develop. As mentioned in several chapters in this workbook, your self-image will affect the way and speed at which you recover from your divorce. Examining and improving your self-image as quickly as possible is vital.

Prior to my divorce, there was a period when I was growing in confidence and comfort with myself and other people. I had grown up somewhat withdrawn and feeling as if everyone else was better than me, but after marriage, a few good relationships, and a fulfilling job, I really began to like myself. That gave me the confidence to reach out and take some risks I never had the courage for before.

Then I was hit by the trauma of divorce. Suddenly I was that awkward junior-high-school kid again, shying away from people and filled with insecurities. Divorce has a way of setting us back emotionally and undoing most if not all the progress we've made on our self-image over the past several years.

Why do we have such a hard time maintaining a proper self-image, and how can we rebuild it once it's been shattered?

ORIGINS OF A POOR SELF-IMAGE

The origins of our struggle with self-image certainly precede our separation or divorce. Those incidents merely undo much of the work we have done to improve our view of self. In some cases, self-image may be at an all-time low. Why is this such a struggle? Let me outline some basic reasons.

✱ *We're in a spiritual battle.* I believe wholeheartedly that one of the major reasons we struggle so much—and many times lose the battle for our minds—is that we're not battling flesh and blood or anything else we can get our hands on; we are battling a spiritual warfare or, as some would call it, "a battle against the evil one."

I don't intend to sound mystical or as if I believe there are demons lurking around trying to "get us." I'm merely referring to the fact that Satan loves to defeat us and keep us there. What better way to do that than to ruin our marriages and then have us believe we're no longer any good or useful to anyone?

God wants us to believe in Him, love Him, and then love others *as we love ourselves.* He says that's His most-important commandment (see Matt. 22:35-40) How can we love God and other people when we don't believe in ourselves and instead believe we are defeated and useless? God does not send us those messages. They come straight from the pit of hell. So the next time you start to think, *I'm no good, I'm not lovable,* or that God can't use you anymore, acknowledge to yourself immediately where those kinds of thoughts originate. *Then fight back.*

✱ *Our fallen state.* We can't always blame Satan for our having bad thoughts. (The devil doesn't make us do it.) We must recognize our own sinful nature, which basically means that left to ourselves, we are quite capable of making poor choices and thinking wrong thoughts. The Bible states that this is all part of being human. That's why I believe that if we don't *work* on our self-image, we will naturally gravitate toward a negative one—a self-centered one that focuses on me, me, me.

After all, aren't we all naturally selfish? And isn't our poor self-image a reflection of this preoccupation with self? We focus on how *we* feel, on how *we've* been hurt, and on how *we* come across. This "me" attitude is what I refer to as the "dance floor syndrome."

Are you self-conscious about dancing in front of other people? If you're like me and never really learned how to dance, it can be fairly traumatic to have to dance in public. Why is that?

You're probably convinced that everyone in the place is looking at you and laughing inside over your gyrations out on the floor. But the truth is that all the others are concerned only about how *they* look and are therefore too preoccupied with themselves to even notice what you're doing. So go ahead out there and make a fool of yourself, because no one else is watching.

So it is with our self-image and many of our insecurities. We're focused on ourselves and how we come across. This "me" preoccupation may lead us to shy away from people, from challenging new situations, and perhaps even from discussions if we believe we will make fools of ourselves. The truth is, no one is really paying that much attention to what we're doing or saying, because they're primarily concerned about their own image. So speak up!

✳ *Our background and experiences.* Our background and family of origin have a large bearing on our personalities, which includes self-image. And even if you were raised in the most-loving of homes, you probably still struggle for a variety of reasons.

Researchers estimate that about 85 percent of your personality is developed by the age of six. And what is your image of self at age six? Just about everyone around you is taller than you, stronger than you, smarter than you; in fact, you're probably pretty dependent on other people for just about everything. Those experiences help to form our personalities. Is it any wonder we grow up to feel inferior in many situations?

Then add to those experiences the criticism of a parent, the inevitable teasing of your peers, and the occasional failures we all face and you can see how our background and experiences can affect our self-image. And I need to point out that I have mentioned only *normal* childhood experiences. Your personality is affected even more if you've had to endure any type of emotional or physical abuse or other significant trauma.

HOW DO YOU EVALUATE YOURSELF?

We are constantly evaluating ourselves according to a variety of criteria. These are some of the more-prevalent:

✳ *The ideal self:* We evaluate ourselves according to our own standards. These are standards we set for ourselves for who we think we should be or who we would like to be. The degree to which you expect a lot or only a little from yourself is largely a reflection of the standards you grew up with. Carried to an extreme degree, they can actually make you your own worst enemy. You can set up a list of "shoulds" and "ought to's" that no one could satisfy. That type of perfectionism can cause an unending cycle of never measuring up.

✹ *Feedback from Significant Others:* Another important ingredient in your evaluation of self-image is the feedback you get from the significant people in your life. As mentioned earlier, in your early years, that was mostly your parents. While parents continue to have a significant impact on your life well into your adult years, your peer group gradually becomes more influential to your view of self. Eventually, your spouse and maybe one or two close friends become the largest influences.

What happens when divorce enters your life? Obviously, you lose the affirmation of your spouse and for many, even your best friends can grow cold and distant (which you probably interpret as another rejection).

✹ *Feedback from Our Society:* This last area of evaluation should not be underestimated. Our society has a large bearing on our self-image. How? By the subtle influences and hidden messages it sends us constantly about what's important and what is valued in life.

Our society affirms us in four major areas: beauty, brains, brawn, and bucks. We see those values in every TV show, every commercial, our schools, our neighborhoods, and, unfortunately, even our churches. As soon as you start to socialize, you quickly learn that if you're a woman, beauty is critical. You're brought up to believe you need to look like a Barbie doll. (What a drag!) If you're a man, beauty is okay, but you can get away with not being good looking if you're strong. (Then you can beat up anyone who makes fun of you.)

If you're not the school athlete or the cheerleader type, you need to be smart—very smart, in fact, because now you have to go on to be a doctor, lawyer, or corporate executive in order to be valued.

The final category, bucks, is one that becomes more and more important as we get older. That's probably because the older we get, the more we lose of the other three. If you have money and lots of it, let's face it—you don't need to be good looking, strong, or smart. You get instant respect when people find out what you're worth; that even includes how you're treated by the church.

If you're like me, on a good day, you consider yourself to be average in the first three categories. But when it comes to money, I'm still waiting. The problem is, though, that we face a losing battle, because we all know we're gradually losing what we have in the physical areas, and the money problem isn't getting any better. Those temporal measures of self-image are a no win proposition, because even if you're beautiful, strong, smart, or rich, what you eventually find out is that there will always be others who are more beautiful, stronger, smarter, and richer.

So how can our self-image remain stable? It can't be based on our own view, because we've seen that that fluctuates according to our moods. It can't be based on what others think of us. We've learned the hard way that other people can turn on us, which devastates our self-image. And society's values are a never-ending cycle of trying to measure up but never quite making it.

How should we value ourselves? Our self-image needs to be based on something constant and unconditional, and that's why it must be based on God and His love toward us. This is so important, yet I meet so few people who have a clear understanding of how the truth can revolutionize our self-image. My own self-image was devastated when I went through divorce, but as I rebuilt it, I tried to focus on God's love for me and who I was *in Him.* I knew enough theology to know that as a Christian, I was considered part of God's family. And with Him as my Father, I could be assured of His constant love and care. That understanding helped me to build a more-healthy self-image.

The Bible states that God *delights* in His children and that we have obtained His inheritance (see Eph. 1). Think about that. If you hear you've just received an inheritance, how do you react? Think about God delighting in *you* in that same way. That makes you feel pretty good, doesn't it? You've probably never had anyone who felt that way about you consistently. But that's what we need if we're going to learn to love ourselves and view ourselves the way God views us.

Please note, however, that this knowledge does not solve our problem, because it's an abstract concept, and we don't have a tangible Christ to hold onto and whisper in our ear when the world begins to beat us down. That's why we need to be reminded every day about who we are in Christ and to work on our self-image. It's like a fish swimming upstream. We need constantly to be swimming against the current. The current is what the world tells us about who we are and what we tend to tell ourselves, or what Satan wants us to think. As soon as we stop swimming, we automatically will go with the current.

Here are some steps we need to take:

1. View ourselves as God views us.

As outlined earlier, the way God views us is vastly different from the way society views us. In 1 Samuel, God reminds us that "man looks at the outward appearance, but the Lord looks at the heart" (16:7). When the men of Israel were looking for their king, they looked for someone who was tall, rugged, and mature. Yet after looking at all of David's older brothers, God drew Samuel to a small, scrawny kid named David whom God knew to be of good character.

Let's reject the standards of our world and not be so consumed with the pursuit of beauty, brains, brawn, or bucks. Instead, let's focus on developing Godlike character. By seeking God's guidance and allowing His love to flow through us, we can become very attractive to others.

As children of God, we know our worth to Him and, therefore, need to begin viewing ourselves as He does. If we could do that, we would believe we really are unique individuals, created in God's image and extremely valuable.

2. Renew our minds.

As we view ourselves in a more-godly way, and as we try to develop more-Christlike character, we must also transform our minds (see Rom. 12:2). We must stop the constant thoughts that invade our minds about how we don't measure up or how we really aren't very valuable, and we must force ourselves to think as God thinks. I suggest memorizing some passages like Psalm 139:14, which tells us we're "fearfully and wonderfully made." Second Corinthians 5:17 tells us that in Christ, we're "a new creation." Repeat these thoughts at least a dozen times a day.

Every time you look in the mirror, instead of thinking, *Ugh! What am I going to do with this?!* think, *I'm a unique individual, created in God's image, and I'm going to make the most of this day.* This is not the same as "the power of positive thinking"; it's merely retraining ourselves to think the way God would want us to think rather than dwelling on the garbage we have picked up from society.

3. Associate with healthy people who can help to build us up.

Let's face it, we all have some friends who build us up and some who don't do a whole lot to help us. Someone who feeds into our "victim mentality" or encourages our feeling down and out is not the type of friend we should be developing. You've heard that misery loves company, and if you're going through a divorce, there's an abundance of people and groups who will feed your misery.

Instead, we need to find some healthy friends—those who have perhaps been through a similar change but have moved on with their lives in a healthy way. They should have a good self-image, a mature view of God and His healing power, and the ability to reach out to us without expecting anything in return. (Mostly that's because we probably can't reciprocate for a while.) Eventually, as we begin to heal and develop a better self-image, this friendship can become more of a two-way street, or we can become instruments of healing for others.

4. Set some short-term goals that we know we can accomplish in order to experience success.

This point is important for those of us who need some real concrete evidence that we're worthwhile, just to get us off to a good start. As we work on our self-image, it would be wonderful if we immediately got a big raise and promotion or had a book published with our name on the cover, but that *rarely* happens. Many times, though, good things don't happen to us because we're not taking any chances. We're too timid or insecure, so we play it safe for a while. There's nothing wrong with that. It's certainly natural. But as we seek to move on with our lives, we need to start taking some chances.

At first these need to be small steps, and perhaps something we *know* we can accomplish. Why bother trying something we know we can do? As we start out, it's vital that we succeed in the beginning, because that motivates us to try again. We know we'll fail at something sooner or later, but if we have a string of successes under our belts, the failure is much less likely to set us back significantly.

If your goal is to write a book and have it published, for example, the way to go about it is to first pick something you know you can do. (If you just start sending out manuscripts, I can assure you that you'll experience a lot of rejection.) You can enroll in night school and take a course in writing. You can also start journaling some of your thoughts and ideas for a while. Once you've succeeded at those goals, perhaps a contact with a small local newspaper or a newsletter publisher would be in order. And you build from there.

What if you meet with failure? Anywhere along the way, you can back up and try again, or perhaps you'll want to rethink or fine tune your goals a bit.

5. Pray for God's help and strength.

Although this is listed last, it certainly is not least. The process of developing a positive self-image is not easy or natural, and it is best accomplished with God's help. Therefore, part of our thinking must include an attitude of constant prayer to God.

"Lord, I need Your help. I want to move on with my life, and I know I need to work on my self-image. Help me to see myself as You do. Give me the strength and the courage to move out in new directions. Guide my path, Lord, so that I can begin to experience success and see quickly the things I do well. Then help me to do those things to Your honor and glory.

"Protect me from the decisions that would set me back or perhaps even destroy my self-image. I need Your help in making wise decisions. Help me to change my thought life, Lord, from one that accepts the world's standards to one that focuses on You, Your love, and Your mercy. Thank You, Lord!''

HANDLING THE HOLIDAYS

by Tom Whiteman

While the holidays are joyously anticipated by the typical household, for the newly separated or divorced, they can be some of the most-difficult times of the year. All the expectations, stresses, and financial concerns that accompany most people's holiday season are greatly compounded for those experiencing a family disruption.

I remember my own first few Thanksgivings, Christmases, and Independence Day celebrations (if you could call them celebrations). To say they just weren't the same anymore would be a gross understatement. For me, they were dreaded. The familiar traditions became sources of pain; the stored decorations, a reminder of how much I had lost; and the family gatherings, a glaring indication that someone was missing.

I remember that for the first two Christmases following my divorce, I didn't put up a single decoration. Then, for my third Christmas, I set up a small tree. It wasn't much, but it was an indication I was beginning to heal.

If you have children, you probably go through the motions during the holidays, trying to keep things as consistent as possible, just for their sakes. You want their childhood memories to be nice, but the truth is that the holidays can be all the more difficult when children are involved.

If you've been married any length of time, you've developed your own traditions and celebration styles that the children will obviously miss once one parent is gone. So how can you handle the major holidays? Here are some guidelines you might want to consider:

✱ It's important (although hard) for you to talk with your ex-spouse well before the holiday in order to arrange a visitation schedule. Working through this difficult and emotional subject will do much to make the special days more enjoyable for you and your children. Once you've decided on a schedule, sit down with your children and tell them what they can expect. But once again, try to do this months before the actual holiday.

Be upbeat and supportive about the arrangements, and encourage their questions. Remember, they may not ask you questions in advance, but you can be sure they will be thinking about it regularly. And the more important the holiday, the more they'll think about it. So ease their fears, and tell them months in advance about what they can expect on that special day.

✳ If you don't have children or if the children are not going to be with you on the actual holiday, make sure you plan to be with family or friends. You don't want to stay home alone with the memories of how it used to be. And don't wait until someone invites you over. Make your calls well in advance, because as the holiday approaches, you may find you don't have the energy to make last-minute arrangements.

If your children can't be with you, plan a separate holiday for them around the time of the actual day. Over time, this can become a much-cherished tradition as the children look forward to their "celebration after the celebration." One eight-year-old recently told me that the best part of being from a divorced family was in having two birthdays and two Christmases!

✳ If you do have the children for the holiday, don't try to replicate all the old traditions. That will only remind your children that the other parent is no longer around. Part of the acceptance phase involves being able to move on to new traditions and family interactions. The sooner you begin new traditions, the earlier your children can begin healing and moving on to a new lifestyle. Be consistent and traditional, but include some new, special events that will grow into new traditions.

✳ Watch your expectation level. Many people expect a joyous time and therefore have a greater chance of disappointment and postholiday depression. On the other hand, don't go into the holiday expecting everything to be horrible. That will only contribute to the problem by making your attitude unnecessarily negative. Approach each event with a little anticipation, but be realistic about the difficulties you must face.

✳ Many newly divorced people take a break from sending out Christmas cards and baking cookies, or they may find they have to make drastic cuts in the amount of money they spend on gifts. That's perfectly understandable, so don't feel guilty for those setbacks. You hope to work through this drought quickly. But in the meantime, it's probably best to explain to your close friends, family, and children that things will need to be different for a while.

This can actually be a good time to refocus on the true meaning of the holidays, the values of friends, family—and where God is in the whole process. The difficult times are typically a period of soul searching and reevaluation of priorities. As painful as it might be, we can emerge from this as stronger, healthier individuals and families.

THERE'S NO SUCH THING AS AN EX-GRANDPARENT

by Tom Whiteman

The following article is designed for you to share with your parents or in-laws. Please feel free to make a few copies and pass them along.

"Mom, tell Dad to pick up the other phone extension, I've got something I've got to tell you."

All over America, people are hearing those words. Unfortunately, many times the call is to inform you of the disturbing news that your son or daughter is getting a divorce.

Immediately you're gripped with a flood of thoughts and feelings. *What will we tell our friends and relatives? Will I still be Mom or Dad to my son- or daughter-in-law? What will become of my grandchildren?*

When most people think about divorce, they usually conjure up images of the embittered parents, the emotionally torn children, or maybe even the crafty legal posturing of the lawyers. Yet another drama, also unfolds that we typically hear little about. It's the plight of the *parents* of the divorcing couple.

It's fairly surprising that we don't hear more about how divorce affects the previous generation. After all, there's hardly a mature family that hasn't been affected. Just think about it statistically; about 50 percent of all marriages end in divorce, and the typical family has just over two children. It stands to reason that sooner or later, most of us will be touched by this family tragedy.

So what can you expect when it does happen to you? First, realize that it's normal to go through an intense grieving reaction. You might be surprised by how much you actually hurt.

You might reason, *This is ridiculous. After all, it's not my marriage that's falling apart. Why am I getting so upset?*

The news that part of your family is breaking up is very much like hearing of the death of a loved one. For many, the end result will be the death of a relationship. Perhaps we will lose our in-law, the grandchildren, or the other set of grandparents. In all cases, we know the family will never be the same.

This is very difficult to hear and much harder to experience, especially since the emotional healing takes at least two years to complete.

Let's review some of the emotional stages of grieving as they relate to divorce so you can be better prepared for the emotional onslaught and be better able to help your family through the crisis.

THE INITIAL SHOCK OF DENIAL

As a parent, you probably feel a great sense of pride when your whole family gets together for a special holiday or reunion. You imagine others as thinking, *My! What a beautiful family.* After all, that's what you think. When this Waltonlike scene is marred by the dissolution of a marriage, most parents go into emotional shock.

Sure, you knew your kids were having problems. But you always assumed they'd work out their differences. Now, when you hear the news, you tell yourself, *They've just had a fight. I'm sure they'll get back together.* This denial is understandable. Your kids have probably kept the worst of the problems to themselves, not wanting to hurt or worry you. How can you be expected to absorb in a few days what it has taken your children months, if not years, to conclude?

The denial stage allows you to think life will go on as usual. It's a natural and necessary reaction when the news is too painful to bear. You want to pretend it really isn't going to happen or that life will remain unchanged. *I'll still see the grandchildren on the weekends. I'll still go fishing with my son-in-law.*

You move beyond this initial stage when your son or daughter begins to come by without the spouse. The more your child talks, the more you realize things really are different. This reality moves you on to the next stage in the grieving process, one that is much more emotionally charged.

SECONDARY EMOTIONAL RESPONSES

You enter this next phase with a flood of emotions, including anger, guilt, and depression. This phase is distinguished by your realization that the true ramifications of your child's divorce will be much more serious than you expected. It's typical to think, *This really does affect me. I knew our son had a temper, but I never dreamed he could go that far. My child really does have a drug problem. I don't think I will ever be able to forgive my daughter-in-law for what she has done.*

The circumstances surrounding divorce can tear you up inside. Yet you're powerless to bring about any changes. Perhaps you lie in bed at night thinking about your responsibility in the mess. Or you pace in anger over what you'd like to tell "that no good..." The range of emotions varies between anger, guilt, intense worry, and depression. Many vacillate between all these emotions over a period of many months, sometimes years.

You must move beyond those intense emotions to be helpful in the situation. Once again, it's certainly normal to have all the feelings, but in spite of your mental anguish, you must realize there's really nothing you can say or do that will change your child's decision. There is, however, much you can do to help. In fact, this crisis probably presents one time when your child needs you the most. But if you're to have a *positive* influence on the situation, you must first reach a point of acceptance in your own healing.

Acceptance

Acceptance is not the same thing as resignation. Resignation is giving up in utter frustration. That's more of a depressed response than one of acceptance. When you accept the situation as it is, you face the fact that *for better or for worse, this is my family, and now we just have to make the best of it.* You see, acceptance really depends on your attitude about what has happened. It doesn't help to blame yourself or someone else. Nor does worrying or depression improve anything. Your ability to rise above your emotions determines how helpful you'll be to your children and grandchildren.

Gaining objectivity in the crisis is a sign of acceptance. Certainly in most cases, your major loyalty will remain with your own flesh and blood. But loyalty doesn't mean you need to feed into the hatred or name calling, particularly when it comes to your grandchildren. Never put yourself in the position of bad-mouthing the other parent in front of the kids. He or she will always be their parent in spite of any wrongs that may have been done. If your grandchildren and your own child express criticism of the ex it's fine for you to listen and be supportive, but that doesn't include fueling the fire.

For example, it's fine to say, "Yeah, I know what you mean" when the family member is critical of the absent parent. But it's not helpful to take the next step: "Yeah, I know what you mean. You know what he did to me one day. Your father..." That kind of venting might help you when you're in the anger stage, but you need to find a neutral friend or counselor to vent to, not your child or grandchildren.

Acceptance also means accepting changes. If your child is now a single parent, he or she will be much busier and less attentive to your needs. You need to accept those changes and try to help wherever you can. The holidays will also be different, but different does not have to mean worse. Try to help your child plan holidays and special events well in advance. You need to be as understanding as you can of the time constraints. After all, there's now a whole new person who must share the holidays with the kids—the ex. That's why you need to be as objective as possible and not become just one more source of stress for your son or daughter.

How Can I Help?

Perhaps more than ever before, your children and grandchildren need your stability, your objectivity, and your wisdom. Here are a few suggestions on how you can provide those:

✷ If you can continue to love both your child and the ex without betraying your child, it can be one of the healthiest postdivorce arrangements. Just because your son- or daughter-in-law did not work out as a spouse doesn't necessarily mean he or she is a bad person, parent, or child. By having a good relationship with both parties, you can be a positive influence on the whole situation.

✷ If a relationship with both parties is not possible, try to be gracious toward the former spouse, particularly in front of the grandchildren.

✷ Encourage, your child and grandchildren to talk with you about how they're feeling. Listen without condemning them. If you find you can't do this objectively, admit your struggle and suggest they talk to someone more neutral.

✷ If you disagree with their decisions or lifestyle, it's all right to let them know how you feel. Tell them, but then let it go. If they ask for your opinion, let them know. Otherwise, try not to nag them or hold your will for their lives over their heads (as in "We'll support you if you do what we tell you").

✷ If your child asks for support, either financial or emotional, give what you can without allowing a dependency to develop. Set limits on what you can do. For example, "I can help you get settled in a new place, but I can only support you financially for the first few months." Or, "I can help you by watching the children, but only until the summer is over." You want your child to get back on his or her feet, but you also need to encourage independence and self-reliance. Dependence on you will only prolong feelings of despair, worthlessness, and hopelessness.

✹ Don't allow yourself to be shut out of the lives of your child and grandchildren. Other than their actual parents, grandparents are children's most-important relationships. If need be, speak up and request that your visitation rights be included in any custody arrangement.

✹ If you have a specific issue with your former son- or daughter-in-law, take it up directly with him or her. Don't put your child or the grandchildren in the middle by telling them, "Your father was supposed to bring you by last weekend and never did. Tell him that we said..."

✹ If your child or grandchildren seem to need additional help, encourage them to seek counseling, a support group, or other self-help materials. You might even want to provide the resources for them to get started in this direction.

Remember, the grieving process can take up to two years to work through. So be patient with yourself and your child. The sooner you can find yourself emotionally healed, the quicker and more effective you will be at supporting your child and grandchildren. They certainly need your help now more than when they were an intact family.

LETTER TO A HUSBAND

by Thomas F. Jones

Dear Husband,

I'm sure you will be surprised to get a letter from me. After all, we don't know each other. But I have a lot of concern for you. I'm concerned about your marriage. I want your relationship with your wife to be the best it can possibly be. I want your marriage to be filled with healthy growth and satisfaction. Of course, I'm being a little presumptuous. For all I know, your marriage might be just great. But still, I do worry about you. I'm afraid you might be like me.

You see, I was once like you. I was a husband, too, for twelve years. I thought I was a pretty good one. I know I did a lot of things right. I was faithful to my wife. I loved her dearly, and I frequently told her so. I would surprise her now and then with unexpected little gifts. I even helped around the house. (I was very good at things like doing dishes, scrubbing floors, vacuuming, even changing diapers!) I shared decisions about money with my wife. I was not demanding sexually. I really don't think I was very demanding in any way.

But that was all a long time ago. We've been divorced now for thirteen years. You'll probably ask, "What happened?" The strange thing is that I'm still not sure I know.

At first I would throw up my hands and put the blame all on her. What happened was that one day she left and didn't come back. She wasn't really able to explain herself to me. She just said she couldn't live with me anymore. I tried to understand her. I asked what I could do to make things right. But nothing seemed to make a dent in her. Her mind was set like concrete. I did everything I knew to do, but it was out of my control. She had been gone a long time already. Emotionally, she had left me before she packed her bag and physically left home.

Perhaps the most-staggering thing for me to remember is that I didn't know she was gone. Long before I was able to see it, my wife had made an emotional move out of our marriage, and I hadn't realized it! A few years ago, the singer Rita Coolidge had a hit song called "My Crew," and one of the lines in the song said, "I was gone so long before you missed me." Wow, did that line ever speak to me!

I suppose that's one of the main reasons I felt I should write to you. If I could be blind, maybe you could be, too. What a terrible thing it would be if you found yourself in the same situation I was in!

Perhaps you're thinking, *Who is this guy, anyway? And what right does he have to give me advice about marriage? After all, he couldn't keep his own marriage together!* If you're thinking such things, I understand. And you are certainly right—I did fail to keep my own marriage together. But it's that failure, and the subsequent years of reflecting on that failure, that make me think I have something useful to say to you. I've learned a lot by failing. Failure is, after all, a great teacher. Because of failure, we often take a good, long, second look at things to find out what caused the failure. I think I know how I failed, and perhaps what I've learned can help you. It's worth a try at least.

First of all, I was smug. From the very beginning, I had an It-can't-happen-here attitude about the inviolability of our marriage. I was so naive. I had dreamed of having the perfect marriage and being the perfect husband. For years before I married, I had read books on marriage, communication, and sexuality. I was well prepared for my role as husband. Even more importantly, I was a Christian. My wife and I were trusting Him, and of course, God would never fail us!

Of course, it's a good and important thing to believe in God and to have a deep sense of commitment to one's own marriage. But it's wrong to be overconfident. Smug attitudes actually can breed casualness and carelessness. If someone is certain the dam cannot break, he may disregard the little leaks that spring up. But little leaks are just the things that need attention if a dam is to be kept strong.

My point is that no marriage can be held together by mere confidence and commitment. It takes more than that. It takes attention to detail! Belief in God is of great importance. A sense of commitment to marriage is also of highest priority. But such high and noble attitudes are worth very little if they're not in turn transformed into practical "leak stoppers" such as attentiveness, responsiveness, communication, and problem solving. In retrospect, it's plain to me that my smugness blinded me to many things that should have demanded attention.

Second, I was preoccupied. Like so many others, I got married while I was still in school, preparing for a great career. My wife was fully aware of my goals at first. But as we got down to the hard business of married life, it was a fact that for all my idealism about marriage, I was too busy to be a good husband. In addition to my full days in school, I also worked nights. There was simply no time for my wife. But because of our mutual commitment to my career, we did what many others have done. We resigned ourselves to patiently wait it out, expecting that after graduation it would all get better.

The problem with that line was that while it was a genuine expectation of both of us, I was daily undermining our future by the way I was conducting the present. I wasn't just spending the great majority of my time apart from my wife. More than that, and far more serious, I am now certain, I was developing a mental world in which she was playing no significant part.

Even when we were together, my mind was generally somewhere else. I was preoccupied with high and wonderful things that I attempted to share with her. I wanted her to know all about the new and exciting things I was learning. Of course! Wasn't that as it should be? A loving and considerate husband ought to share such things with his wife, right?

But what I failed to see then (and for a long time afterward) was that I was doing all the talking. I was sharing me and my wonderful world with her, but there wasn't any room in me for what was happening in her world. It was quite one-sided, this sharing of mine. Actually, and this is hard for me to admit even now, her world was really not very interesting to me. That's what I mean by *preoccupation*. I don't think my primary failure was in not providing adequate time with my wife. The greater failure was that in the time we had together, I continued to be in "my world" and generally had no interest in hers. The signals I was sending to her became more and more clear. My world was important to me, hers was not, and it was becoming less and less likely that graduation would change anything of significance.

The most frightening part of all this, as I now look back on it, is that my preoccupation was able to peacefully coexist in my mind with a deeply emotional sense of how greatly I loved my wife. I missed my wife very much in those long days at school and evenings at work. I looked forward to our times together with eagerness. My emotions genuinely attached to her and longed for her. So I was convinced that my love for her was very real, while at the same time I was investing little of myself in her. What I have since realized but did not know then is that love requires far more than strong emotional attachment to someone. The deepest feelings in the world are worth little if they don't issue in attentiveness.

In fact, I think it may be said that deep feelings in themselves can never be a measurement of love. The only measurement that has any real usefulness is the measurement of how much of myself I'm willing to invest in the other person. The fact that I had deep, true feelings is not in question.

But the fact that I was able to be so preoccupied with myself and so blind to my wife's world makes it painfully evident that my love was inadequate. As I said earlier, attention to detail is what matters. Deep feelings, just like deep commitment to principles, are totally useless if they don't produce appropriate behavior. For all my depth of feeling, I made no moves, took no significant actions, to effect change.

Third, I was not responsive to the danger signals when my wife began to send them. I'm able to look back from my present perspective and recognize that there were a number of times when she tried hard to communicate to me the emptiness she was feeling in trying to relate to her "missing" husband. There were times when she would speak with me directly about the need she felt. In such times, I would listen to her complaints and genuinely view myself as being responsive. I thought responsiveness meant sitting down and talking together, showing concern and reassuring her with words. Today I see such things as only the merest beginnings of true response, which involves taking action to change those things that are causing the trouble. In other words, I needed to demonstrate that the concerns of my wife were also my concerns. Talking was simply not enough.

Once again, let me point out that my deep feelings were doing me in. When my wife complained, I felt bad, and those feelings were real. I felt guilt and sorrow and frustration, even anger, because our situation was causing her so much trouble. Those deep feelings in turn reassured me that I was in fact a caring, loving, responsive person. But I wasn't responding. I wasn't taking action. I wasn't changing anything. I was kidding myself, and the major way I did that was to avoid responsibility for what was happening.

Did you notice that I emphasized the words "our situation" in the last paragraph? You see, it wasn't our situation that was causing the problems. It was my unresponsiveness to her! I was, in fact, still the same preoccupied man I had been in school. Only now, I was preoccupied with work. We had thought that after graduation there would be more time. In some ways, yes, there was more time spent together, but I was still preoccupied with me and my work. I was now proving myself, becoming a success at what I had trained for. And I was also still failing to notice that I was giving her little of myself. One reason I didn't see that was that I thought the problem was time. It wasn't.

Through it all, I failed desperately to ever grasp what my wife had understood early in our marriage. I failed to see that my life, my priorities, my career, my personal growth had become the only things that mattered enough to cause me to take significant action. An example may help you understand. On a number of occasions, my wife wanted very much to go to college. In the end, I always felt we couldn't quite afford it, so she never got to do it. One time, years after our divorce, she reminded me of how we scraped and saved and worked (both of us) to send me through school. Could we afford it then? Yes, of course; that had been for my career, my growth, my advancement. But could we afford it for her? No, of course not. But what struck me hardest as I thought about it was that back when it was all happening to us, I was unable to see. I thought then that it was a matter of money. It wasn't—it was a matter of priorities, and my wife's personal growth was not high on my list.

That's what my wife was attempting to communicate to me in those days before she gave up. She could see she was not high on my list of priorities, but I couldn't. When she tried to tell me she needed more from me, I lapsed into my comfortable emotions of "love." Of course she needed more of me; I needed more of her, too. She said to me on a number of occasions, "Let's get married." I would always laugh at her and say, "What do you mean? We *are* married!" Now I know what she meant.

Fourth, I was weak. The time came when my wife began to make drastic changes in her behavior toward me. Even then, when it was so obvious that any village idiot could have seen that radical trouble had overtaken the marriage, I still took no significant action to remedy anything.

I see no reason to explain in detail the painful final days of our life together. But I do need to emphasize that I was entirely without strength to take significant and useful action even then.

My point is that by that time, I could actually see that our marriage was in great trouble. I was no longer smug or too preoccupied to see. The potential end of the marriage was staring me in the face, and still I took no decisive action. Even today, with all this perfect hindsight, I'm not sure why I couldn't act with strength. But I am sure that it had to do with a couple of intertwining patterns that had been developing within me for a long time.

The first I've mentioned before. It was my deep emotional sense of love for my wife. At that time it had become clear to me that she was hurting. It was also clear that I was the source of much of that pain. So, once again, I felt guilt and sympathy and concern. Now I was willing to do whatever I could to help her. But what could I do?

That was the second pattern. I had by this time spent many years developing a kind of learned helplessness toward "her problems." Because I had not truly shared myself with her through the years, I had also developed a kind of immunity to her problems. They were *her* problems, not *our* problems, and certainly not *my* problems. So what could I do? I felt helpless.

What I did do then was to yield completely to the requests she began to make of me in the hope that my easy compliance would prove to her, at this late hour, just how sincere was my love for her. In the end, it proved just the opposite.

An outstanding example of what I mean was my helpfulness when she decided to separate from me. She had obtained an apartment in a faraway city. She wanted to move there with our three children. Of course she needed help. She would need money to move about half of our furniture, and she would need monthly support. She didn't know if she wanted a divorce or not; she just had to do this.

My response? I would do anything to please. What would you expect? I "loved" her too much to oppose her in this very difficult time. So I pitched in, rented a truck, drove it five hundred miles for her, and began to send monthly checks dutifully.

Of course, my wife was quite unimpressed. Actually, she was decidedly impressed with how easily I agreed that she could go away. For her, my passive agreement to her departure was only one more evidence that I didn't need her and was going to survive quite well without her. If I had any real interest in continued life with her, she had reasoned, I would have shown it with action.

I did show pain. There was a sickening anguish in the pit of my stomach, and constant headaches and sleepless, aching nights before she left. I protested against her move. I begged her to stay. After she left, I missed her terribly and told her so. But in all that extreme emotional pain, there was not one time that I attempted any action to change the situation.

You might guess that by this time, there would have been little I could have done that would have helped, and you would probably be right. But I didn't even try! Some of my friends suggested things to me. I might refuse to move her. I might simply say no to her and insist that we obtain some counseling before any decision was made. Or I might insist that the children were staying with me. She could leave if she insisted, but I would keep the children. Or I might have resigned from my job and followed her, finding work in a location near her and the kids. I suggested none of those things or any other thing. I kept my job, sent her money, and justified it all to myself and my friends by saying I was helping her.

What I just could not see was that my helplessness was totally irresponsible. I was copping out entirely and refusing to consider any approach to the problem except my compliant helpfulness. Once more I was acting as if this was entirely "her problem." She had a problem, and I viewed myself as helping. How wrong I was! *I* had a problem, and I was doing nothing at all about it.

Of course, as I've said, all this served only to confirm my wife in her opinion that absolutely nothing she could do would really get my attention. Yes, I would run to help when "she had a problem." But I couldn't see, even at the end, that what was happening to her and within her was truly my problem and my responsibility as well. The fact is that in her opinion of me, she was largely correct.

By now you may have decided that I'm on some gigantic guilt trip and in need of catharsis for the sake of my soul. But that's not the case. I don't believe our divorce was entirely my fault. My wife made her contribution to the breakup of our marriage. But it's not important to me anymore to determine who was most at fault. I have no need to place blame on her or to carry blame myself. I have recalled these things as honestly as I'm able for one purpose only. I have done it with the thought that someone else may be out there somewhere struggling with the same kind of things I faced. I'm concerned for you, my friend. If anything I've written can be of any help to you, it will have been worth the pain of recalling my most-difficult experience.

Perhaps as you have read my letter, you've found nothing with which you can identify. Perhaps you don't see yourself in my experiences in any way. If that's the case, please do just one more thing before you forget what I've written. Give my letter to your wife, and ask her to read it. Thanks.

Your sincere friend,
Tom Jones

HOW TO PICK A LAWYER FOR YOUR DIVORCE CASE

by Robert H. Klima, J.D.

Laws concerning the family are changing rapidly in every state. The law is quite different from state to state. It has been said that the law follows changes in society by about ten years. The upheaval seen in the law is simply a result of the upheaval in attitudes about family relationships.

It's simply not possible for the large majority of people facing separation and divorce to go through it without competent legal counsel. But how does a person choose a lawyer? It isn't easy.

Legal specialties are not recognized like medical specialties. Professional review boards do not certify legal specialists in most states. Having passed the bar exam, lawyers are free to pick any area of law in which they want to practice, without further training in that area and without any experience in it.

Not long ago, in all but the most-urban areas, virtually all lawyers were general practitioners. Only recently have more and more lawyers chosen to restrict the number of areas in which they practice. The result is that fewer and fewer lawyers will handle a messy or complicated divorce. Those who will generally fall into four categories.

1. The new lawyer who has to take everything to make ends meet. Watch out for this fellow. He means well but has little experience and may be wrong in his projections. If he works for an experienced family law attorney, he has someone to fall back on. If you go to a well-known attorney who refers you to his associate, however, be careful. He is probably pretty much on his own. His boss is too busy to keep an eye on him and doesn't want to anyway.

2. The general practitioner. There are many left. Some are surprisingly good at handling divorce cases. Many are not.

3. The semispecialist. This is the lawyer who does only a few things,

and divorce is one of them. This lawyer will likely be up to date and highly competent. He may not know quite as much as the true specialist, but the difference will be minimal in all but a few cases. He will also be considerably less expensive than the true specialist.

4. The true specialist. This group is growing all the time. Specialists tend to be found in urban and suburban areas. They also tend to be the most expensive. While many true specialists are honest, reasonable individuals, there are also those who rarely try to really settle a case because they command the highest fees by projecting the image of a fighter. Too many people suffering the trauma of a divorce fall prey to the fighter image. After spending many thousands of dollars, they finally learn that a divorce is not a battle to be won but a complex circumstance to be settled fairly. When clients learn that, they often change lawyers.

What, then, are the qualities one should look for in an attorney to handle a divorce?

✳ First, there is no substitute for experience. Litigation, negotiation, and counseling are all skills learned by experience, not out of a book. Five years' experience in family law is a minimum.

Experience also breeds the right sort of reputation (i.e., how the lawyer is seen by other lawyers). It's very important that opposing counsel respects your lawyer's competence both in and out of the courtroom. If he doesn't, you're not negotiating with a full hand. Be wary of lawyers with big reputations among the public at large; that sort of reputation will cost you an arm and a leg and will probably not help you.

✳ Second, there is efficiency. The biggest source of malpractice in this field is the inability of a lawyer to get his work done on time. Many lawyers have piles of work on their desks and may be months behind. Their problem quickly becomes your problem. A good lawyer must have gained the ability to get a day's work done in a day. A corollary to this is communication. The client should receive a photocopy of every letter or document on his case that passes through the lawyer's hands, and it should be mailed to him within a day. The client should also be informed immediately of every telephone call or conversation in the hallway of the courtroom that relates to his case. Obviously, only an efficient lawyer can do this.

✳ Third, the lawyer should be committed to finding the quickest, least-expensive, and most-fair resolution of your case, by negotiation if possible. So should you. Get rid of the idea that going to court will vindicate your sense of justice. It almost never does. The sooner a settlement can be reached, the sooner your own level of emotional trauma and uncertainty will be brought under control.

✳ Lastly, the lawyer should be able to maintain his objectivity. Don't misinterpret this as a lack of compassion. In the same way that a surgeon would be of no use to the patient if he burst into tears upon entering the operating room, so a lawyer is of no use to his client if he assumes the same sense of a moral crusade that many clients have. A good lawyer must be able to cut through the whole dramatic circumstance to the 1 percent that has any legal relevance. The lawyer is not your pastoral or psychological counselor. He isn't trained to hold hands; he's trained to find solutions to legal problems.

So how do you find such a person? People seek lawyers in many ways, but the best way is to ask other lawyers. Nobody can better judge a lawyer than other lawyers who have tried cases against him and negotiated with him. If you call three lawyers who advertise in the Yellow Pages that they handle family law and ask each one who the most-competent divorce lawyers are in their locality, you will probably notice you're hearing the same names repeatedly. If the lawyer tells you that he himself is the best, he might be right.

Other ways of selecting a lawyer include state bar referral systems and referrals by professional organizations. The American Bar Association and state bar associations have family law sections. If you're seeking a true specialist, they may be the best source. The Christian Legal Society also maintains a list of member attorneys, including the areas of practice for each.

Word-of-mouth referrals may tell you a lot about an attorney's manner and apparent competence, but they probably will tell you little about true competence. Above all, don't compare your case to somebody else's. Most clients are left with inaccurate impressions and with many things they misunderstand.

Whomever you select, it's essential that you trust the individual and feel comfortable with him. It's one thing to insist on explanations, it's another to be constantly suspicious. The lawyer who knows his client trusts him will usually work harder than the one who feels his client doubts him.

Too often, those facing divorce only want someone to look after their own interests. Occasionally, parties can get past this and want a solution that's fair to both parties. Such couples should seriously consider mediation by an attorney-mediator. Where such an individual is available, he generally can guide the parties to a fair agreement very quickly and at a fraction of the normal cost. Because he's an attorney, he can answer questions about legal rights and draft a sound document. Because he's a mediator, he cannot offer legal advice. He can offer suggestions based on what has worked for other couples. Those couples in mediation still can have private attorneys, although that's rare. Not all divorce lawyers can or will mediate, and few have any experience with it. Many who are familiar with mediation are distrustful of it. The family law section of your state's bar association may the best place to look for an attorney-mediator.

A word about fees. Virtually all attorneys handle contested divorce cases on an hourly fee basis and require a retainer paid in advance. Rates do vary, and you should not be afraid to shop around. But you should remember that most often a lower hourly fee means a less-experienced lawyer, and a flat fee from a clinic usually means a secretary will know your case better than the lawyer does. The true specialist will have the highest fee.

Whomever you select should be able to provide you regularly with a detailed billing statement itemizing every action taken and the time and cost associated with it. It's wise to insist upon this and review it carefully. Do not expect a cheap divorce, and be prepared to pay what it costs. Many people have to borrow the amount of the retainer. Good legal advice can be worth many times its cost in property settlement or support figures. And what price can be put on those noneconomic factors concerning custody and visitation of minor children? It's far wiser, indeed, to pay what good counsel is worth than it is to seek a bargain and later question whether you made a big mistake.

Remember, however, that whatever you resolve on your own or mediate with a neutral party will mean less time your lawyer has to spend on your case. The deliberate escalation of the hostilities will bring with it a high cost to all parties.

THE SEPARATED AND DIVORCED SUPPORT GROUP

by Bob Burns

I received Ken's call late in the afternoon. "Things have gotten so bad that my wife tells me she wants a divorce," he explained. "I don't know what to do. Is there anybody at the church I can talk to?"

Ken had been exploring the claims of Jesus Christ for a number of months. It was in the midst of this spiritual journey that the problems in his family life went from bad to worse.

It would have been easy for me to set up a time to talk with Ken. Yet I sensed he needed more than an hour's conversation. He needed some friends who understood his circumstances and would walk with him through the painful days ahead. So I put him in touch with one of the Fresh Start alumni in our church. I didn't realize it, but Ken's telephone call was the beginning of a twelve-step support group for the separated and divorced.

Looking back, I'm surprised a twelve-step group for the separated and divorced didn't happen sooner in our church. We had been presenting the Fresh Start Seminar since 1985. Growing out of the seminar was a Sunday morning "community" (called Genesis) for the separated and divorced. This community sponsors socials, monthly "talk it overs," and Bible studies for its members and visitors. Presenting the Fresh Start Seminar twice a year attracted a continual flow of new people facing the realities of marital separation.

When Ken called, I knew he needed immediate and personal care. So I called Tom, one of our Fresh Start alumni who was also involved in our newly developing support-group ministry. That ministry sponsors seminars, workshops, and twelve-step groups to help people integrate their faith with their personal recovery.

I asked Tom if he would get together with Ken. "Perhaps you could share your own experience of divorce and personal recovery with him," I suggested. Tom readily accepted and set up a lunch with Ken for the next day. Coming out of this lunch was the suggestion that yet another support group join in our growing number of twelve-step offerings: a separated and divorced group.

When the group began, a positive response was immediate. Five people attended the first meeting. Next there were ten. Now twenty to thirty-five people meet weekly. At times the number is much higher.

WHAT MAKES THIS GROUP WORK?

Why has the separated and divorced support group quickly become so popular? A few distinguishing characteristics stand out.

Powerlessness

The new people who come to the group have a feeling of futility. They don't know anything else they can do, and yet they feel they must do something. In their personal sharing and in hearing the experiences of others, they begin to see the benefit in admitting that they are, in fact, powerless to control the outcome of their circumstances.

For years it has been recognized that this first of the twelve steps is the initial hurdle toward personal recovery. However, it's a point that has often been missed in divorce recovery literature. Yet we have discovered that acknowledgment of the first step is vitally important to understand and apply during this time of marital distress. We cannot be responsible for the decisions and actions of our estranged spouse; we can only be responsible for ourselves. By recognizing this important step, we begin to move out of the initial grieving process and learn to maintain during separation and/or move toward wholeness as we reenter the single life.

Honest Sharing with Open People

A second reason for the group's popularity is the opportunity for those who feel the hurt and rejection of marital loss to talk with others facing the same struggle. The group provides a chance to talk with these fellow strugglers in a context of openness and honesty.

As I wrote this last sentence, the phone rang. The caller was a man who told me that his wife had left him two weeks ago. "Bob," he said, "it's pretty lonely."

I was able to tell him, "Larry, I know a group where you can find some friends. And they're meeting together tonight."

When a man or woman enters the process of separation and divorce, it is often hidden from friends, family, and others as long as possible. When the facts do go public, the confusion and grief of the experience are often compounded by embarrassment. In the midst of the emotional roller coaster, a person genuinely wonders where to go to safely share the pain and gain support. You feel the need for people, but you're afraid to be with them! Whom can you trust?

Those who are in our separated and divorced support group have a safe haven for encouragement, coping, and growth. They find others who understand. They no longer feel like the only ones going through the loss of dreams and the destruction of what was once the most-significant set of relationships in their lives. They begin to trust, face the facts, face the future, and, most importantly, face themselves.

Trusted Servants

A third reason support group works is a core of "trusted servants" who faithfully attend the meetings and are responsible to facilitate the process. They are not members of a leadership hierarchy! Rather, to be a trusted servant, one must have six months of faithful involvement in working the twelve-step program. Further, the trusted servant is recognized by the church leadership as a responsible individual with a lifestyle commitment to Jesus Christ.

The job description of a trusted servant is simple: to regularly participate in the support group, to occasionally be the monthly chairperson for the group, and to serve as a speaker for the meetings as needed.

Meeting Format

A fourth reason for success in the group is the simplicity of its meeting format. Gathering on Tuesday evenings from seven to eight, the group begins with a few opening comments on its purpose made by the chairperson.

Using materials adapted from numerous sources, a handout is provided that includes portions to be read out loud by the participants. (Sources include the Rapha Right Step materials [*Right Step Facilitator Training Manual* (Houston: Rapha Publishing, 1990); *Rapha's 12-Step Program for Overcoming Codependency*, by Pat Springle (Houston and Dallas: Rapha Publishing/Word, Inc., 1990)]; Claire W's *God Help Me, I'm Still Hurting* [San Diego: Books West, 1988]; *The Twelve Steps for Christians* [San Diego: Recovery Publications, 1988]; and *The Twelve Steps—A Spiritual Journey* [San Diego: Recovery Publications, 1988]).

The meeting begins with a unison praying of the "Serenity Prayer."

That's followed by the entire group's reading a proclamation taken from the Rapha *Right Step Facilitator Training Manual*. It states:

THE SIGNIFICANCE

The first step was taken one day by the Savior Jesus Christ when He stepped down from heaven to demonstrate God's love for mankind. The step led to the cross, the grave, and ended in resurrected power. The Right Step is now up to you. He said if you will turn toward the cross and follow Him, He will give you the strength necessary for restoration, and you will be set free.

THE PERSPECTIVE

We acknowledge that we are living in a war zone...that the mind is a battlefield. The good news is that the war has already been won by Christ. Defeat comes only when deception is believed; victory comes when truth is substituted for deception. Absolute truth and authority is found in God's Word, the rock and the foundation of our restoration.

THE CHALLENGE

The challenge is to break the devastating cycle of deception by restoring our relationship to God and to one another.

THE PROVISION

Having taken the right step, I have been set free. I know God has provided His unconditional love for me. Regardless of the past, and no matter what the future brings, this fact can never change! (*Right Step Facilitator Training Manual* [Houston: Rapha Publications, 1990], p. 30.)

After that proclamation, two other readings are shared in the group: the twelve steps of Alcoholics Anonymous (adapted to a Christian format) and the group guidelines. (See end of article for these resources.) The steps and guidelines are usually read by individual group members going around in a circle.

Our group guidelines, familiar to many who participate in twelve-step studies, are designed to allow safe sharing without fear of interruption. They are as follows:

✳ Confidentiality may not be breached by any member or visitor of this group, for any reason, at any time.

✳ Trust is the basis for the success or failure of this group.

✳ Any person has the right to pass at any time when asked to share. No explanation is necessary; simply decline your privilege by stating, "I pass."

✲ Speak one person at a time. No side conversations. Listen attentively to the person speaking.

✲ Speak only from your own personal experience. Avoid generalizing by using the responsible "I" rather than the "we."

✲ Do not sermonize, moralize, or give advice. It is your responsibility to be compassionate, supportive, and understanding of each other.

✲ Again, confidentiality may not be breached at any time. It is all right to say you were here; it is not all right to say you saw someone else here.

All this reading might seem a little too much if you've never participated in a group like the one I'm describing. However, a weekly repetition of prayer, proclamation, twelve steps and guidelines reinforces the basic tenets of the support group: our commitment to Christ-centered, spiritual recovery, and our commitment to maintaining a safe, supportive environment.

Following those readings, the chairperson will ask all who feel comfortable doing so to briefly introduce themselves and state why they have come. Because of the low self-esteem experienced by many newcomers, assurances are given that no one should feel obligated to talk unless and until they feel safe and secure in the group. After this comes an opportunity for those who would like to make a donation to the ministry. Again, newcomers are encouraged not to contribute unless they feel comfortable in doing so.

Finally, the chairperson introduces the speaker. This speaker is a member of the group and is usually prepared to spend about five minutes discussing one of the twelve steps or a related experience in the process of recovery.

However, before the speaker begins, he or she always asks, "Does anyone need to talk about or share something?" That offer may very well change the entire format for the evening. But since the agenda is focused on support rather than on the presentation of content, such changes are viewed as an opportunity rather than a problem.

After this sharing time, the group breaks into two or more subgroups of six to eight persons. Ideally, this group breakout divides between the separated and the divorced when attendance is adequate to support such a division. In those subgroups (facilitated by trusted servants), every person is given the opportunity to describe his or her experience, strength, and hope in the midst of marital disruption.

The idea of breaking into distinct sharing groups for the separated and divorced developed over a period of time. In the early days of the group, both the separated and divorced met and shared together. While that was beneficial to all, there were unique needs that concerned some of the separated participants. A primary concern was their desire to talk about the struggles of working on reconciliation with their spouses. To encourage one another during that effort, a number of those participants requested a distinct sharing opportunity.

A "group conscience" was held to discuss their request. That's a time held after the regular meeting when participants discuss their thoughts and concerns about the group. Here every person is encouraged to openly state his or her ideas, disagreements, or suggestions.

At the group conscience, the need for distinct breakout groups for the separated and divorced was affirmed. The result has been an even more supportive and significant sharing experience for both groups.

After the breakout time, everyone gathers back together. Any announcements pertaining to the group activities are made. Then everyone rises and repeats the Lord's Prayer. Finally, that last sentence of encouragement is repeated: "Keep coming back. It works if you work it."

Supportive Church Program

One distinctive of our support group that makes it work is that it's nestled in a broader church program committed to recovery. This begins with the church leadership, which believes in meeting the real needs of people—a commitment that led the church to direct primary church resources into support ministries.

Another aspect of the leadership commitment to recovery is the decision to work with couples for the reconciliation of their marriages. The church believes that marital disruption falls into the context of broken relationships described by Jesus in Matthew 18:15-17. In that passage, Jesus teaches that there is a time when relational disruption is so bad that one must "tell it to the church." In response, the church must do what it can to bring about reconciliation. This has meant providing couple and group therapy, assigning elders to the couple for shepherding, and employing caring church discipline.

For the separated and divorced, this commitment also includes a growing singles ministry. That ministry is divided into three communities reflecting various age and experience levels. One of those communities, called Genesis, exists specifically for the separated and divorced.

As noted at the beginning of this chapter, the Genesis community sponsors a Fresh Start Seminar every six months. This seminar is designed to meet the needs of both the churched and the unchurched. Therefore, it provides a primary rallying point for support to church members and outreach to those in the community.

Recently the program was expanded to include a "Fresh Start for Kids" seminar for children of divorce. Growing out of that program is a twelve-step support group for children of divorcing homes; it meets at the same time as the adult separated and divorced group. The group uses a format similar to the one described in this chapter.

The Genesis class, which meets on Sunday mornings, is developed around a six month follow-up curriculum to Fresh Start. The Genesis community also sponsors a full range of ministry activities for the benefit of its members.

Therefore, the separated and divorced support group does not exist in a vacuum. It is one component of a varied ministry "menu" available for those experiencing the trauma of a broken or disrupted marriage.

At the same time, the divorced and separated group fits into the broader support group ministry context. The church sponsors group focusing on many issues, including groups for adult children, codependency, substance addiction, and survivors of rape. We have found that many who are going through separation and divorce are facing what are commonly called "cross addictions." That is, the circumstances that precipitate the marriage breakup often involve issues of one's past or matters of personal life control. We strongly encourage those who come to the divorced and separated group to consider attending one or more of these other groups. Many of our trusted servants come to two or more groups a week.

GROUP LIMITATIONS

As I interact with regular participants and trusted servants of the separated and divorced support group, I have discovered two primary limitations to the group.

The first is that the group meets only once a week. Participants who are experienced in recovery say that a daily meeting would be most conducive to personal recovery. That way, a hurting person could always know a meeting was available. While the once-a-week format is consistent, it does not provide the immediate encouragement many feel necessary.

Since we can't provide daily meetings at this point, we try to satisfy the need for daily support by strongly encouraging participants to share names and telephone numbers. Over and over in the group one hears, "Can I call you?" or "You can call me if you need to talk." Group members make themselves available because they know the need!

A second group limitation is our need for a better sponsorship system. Sponsorship takes place when an experienced member of the group commits to some level of personalized support for another member.

We promote sponsorship in our entire support group system. And we work with our trusted servants in the encouragement of developing sponsors. Where sponsorship occurs, it has worked well. However, we have a shortage of experienced, recovering participants.

CHANGED LIVES

In the beginning of this chapter, I told about Ken, whose phone call began the process that eventually led to our support group for the separated and divorced. Ken has been involved with our group since it started. I sat down with him over lunch recently and asked him what difference it has made in his life.

"The Twelve-step group does two things for me," he said. "First, it gives me a chance to listen to other people. When they share, I can pick up on their feelings and what's happening to them. That helps me with my own recovery. I grow by hearing their point of view. I relate to their experiences. And I learn to identify my own feelings by listening to them share.

"At the same time, I get to share my own experience with people who will listen, understand, and not criticize me. This sharing is real important to me. When I first started coming to the group, I only told the facts. But that didn't get to the core of my problems. As I have listened, learned, and developed trust, however, I have gotten in touch with my own feelings.

"Before I got involved with the support group, I never had been in touch with my feelings. I still struggle to understand them, because it's all so new to me. All my life, I have either stuffed my feelings or reacted to them. I was never in touch with them; never able to share them; and certainly never capable of responding to them in a healthy way.

"Another thing I have learned from the group is that I've got to work one moment at a time. If I start projecting into the future, that's when I crash and burn. If I can keep in focus today, I'm all right."

"Ken," I asked, "What has it meant for you to have a group to support you?"

He responded, "I couldn't imagine how I would be able to deal with the situations I've had to face without this support system. I just couldn't handle it. I probably would have tried to commit suicide or done something really crazy. I might be in a padded cell due to the amount of stress I've had with the divorce and the added hassles at work.

"Where I have been spiritually is a key, too," he continued. "Since I've been separated, I have accepted Jesus Christ. I've been learning how to turn things over to Him. That's another aspect of the group that has been important to me. Because this is a Christ-centered support group, I have not been held back in sharing my beliefs. It's been a tremendous encouragement to my spiritual development and growth."

Ken is one of many who have found the friendship and encouragement needed to grow through the experience of separation and divorce. I believe what Ken has discovered is a basic truth for healthy divorce recovery; you can't do it alone. However, with the encouragement of recovering friends, you can do more than survive. As a man in the support group put it, "I wouldn't wish my divorce experience on my worst enemy. But I wouldn't give up the personal growth I have experienced because of it. I hate divorce, but I'm a better person because of my recovery from it."

LEFT OFF THE ARK

by Bob Burns

Noah was loading the animals into his ark two by two. Imagine how it might have felt being an unpaired animal in line. There you would have been, alone and rejected, while the other animals entered the craft. You would have been left off the ark.

The Christian who is single again through divorce often feels left off the ark of God's church, where marriage is the socially acceptable status, even if the marriage is in shambles. When the single who has been married enters the church, he or she often feels like the odd one out.

When the Bible addresses the issue of divorce, it approaches the topic from two mutually dependent perspectives. The first is that of doctrine. This is extremely important, for doctrine must always form one's foundation for living.

In our day, it's crucial for the church to grapple with her theological convictions regarding divorce. The believer in the pew is looking for clear understanding and direction in the matter. With a national average of close to 50 percent of all marriages failing in 1990, each denomination and each local congregation must clearly explain its position on this nationwide epidemic. Such a clarification before God's people will solidify their conviction before a personal, congregational, or denominational crisis occurs. It will also fortify their ability to deal with problems when they take place.

At the same time, another biblical perspective coordinates with the doctrinal imperative. It is the relational side of divorce. By highlighting the relational concerns of divorce, I do not wish to create an implied barrier between doctrine and life. But it's far too easy to examine the theology of divorce while remaining isolated from persons involved in it. That, too, can create an artificial separation of doctrine from life.

The relational concerns of divorce don't refer simply to the way a couple handle their differences. They also refer to the way believers in Christ are called by the Scriptures to care for those who are going through or have gone through the wrenching death of a relationship.

The prophet Malachi says that God hates divorce (see Mal. 2:16). But does God call His people to treat those shattered by such a covenant breaking with the same hatred? My thesis is that both Old and New Testaments mandate God's people to give themselves in compassionate ministry to the separated and divorced. Because of that mandate, the church must take specific restorative action to maintain corporate health and an effective witness in the world.

THE OLD TESTAMENT MANDATE

In the Old Testament, divorce is neither encouraged nor condoned. Rather, it is viewed as the shattering of a commitment that was meant to be forever.

It was not a simple matter. The impact it would have upon the individuals involved and the community as a whole was taken seriously. A number of passages, including Genesis 3, Leviticus 18, Deuteronomy 24, Jeremiah 3, and Malachi 2, are normally cited with reference to the Old Testament perspective on divorce. Indeed, those tests must be considered in formulating a doctrinal position on marital separation. They state the moral context of divorce, describing it as the breaking of a marriage covenant, and also provide the legal context of divorce, with the steps of litigation necessary for proper regulation and protection of each party described in detail.

However, those passages do not provide us with the full understanding of the care and concern God required His people to give to those who were being divorced. Such a perspective can be clarified when we study the contextual use of the Hebrew word for widow, *almanah*. The word refers to a woman who has been divested of her male protector, usually—though not always—through death. But the *Assyrian Dictionary of the University of Chicago Oriental Institute* states that *almanah* does not simply refer to a woman whose husband is dead. It also applies to a woman who enjoys no financial support from a male member of her family. Such a woman is in need of legal protection. She is also able to exercise freedom by starting a profession or entering into a second marriage. Thus, the word can be used in the sense of bereavement (such as loss of a spouse) or for one who has been discarded or forsaken (such as a divorced person).

This interpretation of *almanah* as the widowed or abandoned fits several Old Testament passages. For example, when God forsook His people and their land, they were characterized as *almanah* (Isa. 47:8), and their situation as *almanuth* (Isa. 54.4). But Israel's "husband" had not passed away! Rather, He had written her a certificate of divorce (see Jer. 3:8). Similarly, when King David returned to Jerusalem after Absalom's revolt, "the king took the ten women [with whom Absalom had committed adultery]...and put them in seclusion and supported them, but did not go in to them. So they were shut up to the day of their death, *living in widowhood*" (2 Sam. 20:3, emphasis added). Technically, they were in widowhood while their husband was still alive. All this is to say that the Old Testament taught that the forsaken spouse was considered in the same category as the widow.

The implications of this connection between the forsaken and the widow are powerful indeed, because the Old Testament is full of God's concerns and commands for the widow. God declared that He would execute justice for the widow (see Deut. 10:18; Prov. 15:25), and He required His people to do so as well (see Isa. 1:17; Jer. 7:5-6; 22:3; Zech. 7:10). He would punish those who refused to do so (see Isa. 1:23-25; Mal. 3:5). His people were to provide for the physical needs of the widow (see Deut. 14:28-29; 24:19-22). God was clearly on the side of the widow (see Pss. 68:4; 146:9), and He expected His people to be as well.

The Old Testament also addressed the member of the marriage covenant who was initiating the abandonment. While it described the proper legal procedure those individuals were to take to obtain a divorce, it also provided for legal discipline within the community directed toward them.

It is beyond the scope of this appendix to explicate the detailed instructions in the Law given for specific offenses. It must suffice to say that God took a firm stand for justice toward the oppressed, and God expected His people to administer justice in a meaningful way. With regard to divorce, others have shown that legal stipulations encouraged a lengthy and systematic procedure that sought to ensure both justice for the forsaken spouse and public responsibility for the one taking action.

THE NEW TESTAMENT MANDATE

The New Testament carried on the tradition of the Old regarding the treatment of divorced persons. But it went further, clarifying how God's people were to deal with all parties in the divorce.

First, let's consider Jesus' attitude toward the divorced as seen in the story of the woman at the well (see John 4). Here we observe our Lord initiating a conversation with a woman who had been married five times and was currently living in an adulterous relationship with yet another man.

We find a balance in Jesus' ministry with this woman. On the one hand, we notice that He understood her circumstances and feelings. He knew of her previous marriages and her present adultery. But He didn't use those against her. Rather, Jesus' honest and open handling of her situation broke through her emotional and religious smoke screens of resistance, preparing her to hear the word of truth.

Further, Jesus demonstrated an honest concern for this woman by breaking significant cultural taboos in order to communicate with her. He spoke in the open with a woman whose husband was not present (a questionable act in the Middle East to this day). She was also a "despised Samaritan." And to make matters worse, she was a flagrant sinner! But Jesus did not allow those social matters to keep Him from sharing with her the good news.

On the other hand, Jesus never condoned the woman's sin. He brought up the topic of her loose morality. Perhaps He delved into more of her past than we read in the narrative, for she later reported He "told me all things that I ever did" (John 4:29). Our Lord refused to carry on a superficial conversation when both He and the woman knew her circumstances.

According to John 1:14, Jesus ministered with grace and truth. Revealing His understanding of the woman's condition, He spoke with candor and truth. Yet truth was couched in the grace of His power to cleanse and restore wholeness. This combination of caring acceptance and honest confrontation prepared her for the life change of conversion.

The response of this woman was phenomenal. She confessed her sin by returning to the town and owning up to her past. In addition, she urged everyone to come and see this man. It's obvious that significant healing had taken place in her life. Past failure and weakness provided the bases of ministry to others.

This entire scene took place because our Savior extended Himself to one who had been divorced. He initiated the conversation. He disclosed the truth of her circumstances. He led her to an understanding of lifelong fulfillment beyond the disappointment of a broken marriage or a new sexual liaison.

Following our Lord's example, a similar pattern of ministry to the rejected took place in the early church. In 1 Corinthians 6, Paul explained that some of the new believers had come out of a variety of backgrounds, including sexual immorality, adultery, thievery, and other sordid lifestyles. (He did not include divorce in that list, but his obvious concern with their circumstances in the next chapter must mean that many in this situation were within the fellowship.) Like the woman at the well, those people who knew they were sinners grasped for the gospel of grace with eagerness.

An examination of other New Testament writers highlights the same theme: spiritual rebirth extends hope to the rejected, healing to the brokenhearted, and opportunities for meaningful service to those who once thought their lives had little significance.

While the New Testament described the gospel as a source of renewal, it also provided for a specific framework for parties involved in divorce. It addressed the problem of mixed marriages between believer and nonbeliever (see 1 Cor. 7). It explicated the restorative role that church discipline should take in the life of God's people (see Matt. 18:15-20; 1 Cor. 5:1-5; 2 Cor. 2:5-11). It required the appointment of church leaders who were expected to provide a supportive context where difficult issues would be handled before God with objectivity and compassion (see Matt. 18:15-20; Acts 20:28; 1 Cor. 6:1-6; Heb. 13:17; 1 Pet. 5:2-4).

We have observed that the New Testament developed the expectation of the Old. God's people were to extend themselves to those in the agony of divorce. Although the church was never to tolerate sin, she was to provide a context where the conditions preceding (and following) divorce would be handled. At the same time, she was responsible to follow the lead of the Lord Jesus, who actively sought out and ministered to divorced persons.

THE MANDATE IN OUR DAY

Both Old and New Testaments affirm the church's need to actively involve herself in the divorce recovery process. To fulfill this role, the church must evaluate and implement change in three areas: her attitudes, her discipline, and her program ministries.

The last ten years have marked significant attitudinal changes in the church. Some believers have developed a tolerance of divorce for any reason. This "do your own thing" mentality does not square with faithfulness to Christ's lordship. Such "liberation" is not the attitudinal change needed among believers today. Neither is there a need for hardened insensitivity that writes off all persons going through divorce as sinners who no longer hold an equal position in the church.

Rather, the mind-set necessary toward the divorced individual is one of practical grace, the humility of recognizing that every believer stands before God in need of mercy. No one person is better than another at the foot of the cross.

While most Christians would affirm that concept of grace in theory, the practical side means applying the truth of godly acceptance toward our relationships with others. Developing an attitude of practical grace means we must beware lest we take on the attitude of the boasting Pharisee in Luke 18:10-14 who said, "God, I thank You that I am not like other men" (v. 11). It also requires that we treat the divorced person in the same way Jesus Christ has treated us: redeeming us from our past failures, forgiving us for our present sin, and challenging us to live and relate on the basis of the truth revealed in His Word.

Acceptance can never be based on anything less than our mutual submission to Jesus Christ. When that's the standard, a caring attitude toward the divorced should follow. Where divorced persons experience rejection simply on the basis of their single-again status, the church should examine herself regarding her understanding of justification in practical terms.

A partner of attitudinal change must be restorative discipline, which is the church's corporate responsibility to maintain the standard of God's Word as her lifestyle pattern. It's unfortunate that God's people tend to view discipline as either a method of punishment or a theoretical idea rarely put into practice. The scriptural imperative for church discipline is restoration: to bring a fallen member back to the full status of an active participant in the fellowship. Only with this restorative purpose in view can discipline be used as an effective tool in the reconciliation of marriages and in the care of those shattered by divorce.

Restorative discipline takes hard work. It is one of the most-taxing responsibilities of the church. The process is outlined in Matthew 18:15-20. It begins with reconciliation on a one-to-one basis. If that attempt fails, one or two believers are to be called on as objective arbitrators. If that's also unsuccessful, the final step is to bring the matter before the church (which requires the involvement of the leadership).

This process demands cooperation from the entire body of believers. When a member seeks the aid of a fellow believer to intercede in a divided relationship, the one requested must be willing to participate. It's one thing to express concern. It's quite another to diminish one's personal comfort through involvement with another!

If the situation continues to deteriorate, the church leaders must take action. Extended time and effort will be demanded if they're to properly understand, negotiate, and exercise authority. Such an oversight role is often much more than a typical board member expected when he agreed to serve. Yet this is vital care for those who turn to their church for help in a crisis.

If the problem comes before the entire congregation, each member needs to clearly understand and consistently follow through on the decision of the fellowship. And of course, with all these dynamics, there is the added requirement of keeping restoration, not vindication, as the purpose of the procedure.

✸ If discipline is so difficult, why is it necessary? First, it's necessary because it is God's provision for maintaining a healthy lifestyle in the church. If the body of believers is to take seriously its faithfulness to God's

284   ARTICLE 7

Word, it must deal biblically with circumstances that flagrantly violate scriptural responsibilities. Without that, all admonitions to faithfulness take the form of empty words with no moral authority to substantiate the exhortation.

✵   A second reason for discipline is to provide a supportive context for the ones involved in the marital dissension. Where will the battered wife turn when she desires to remain faithful yet fears for her life? Where will the believing husband receive counsel when he is struggling with a decision to contest his divorce? Where will the separated Christian turn when faced with the desire to date after the failure of his marriage seems a foregone conclusion? Conscientious Christians in these types of circumstances welcome the network of support and counsel offered by God's people when it is available. The painful fact, however, is that thousands of Christians who honestly desire such objective guidance and encouragement from the church receive the answer that other believers don't want to get involved.

In separation and divorce, there is rarely, if ever, a case where one party is beyond reproach and the other should receive total blame for the failure. Marriage is a shared responsibility, and those involved in church discipline must labor to maintain joint accountability as the issues are handled. At the same time, in most divorce cases only one partner seeks the aid of the church. For that person, the discipline should not create deeper guilt but should provide a healthy context for restoration so that the person can maintain the status of a fully functioning member of Christ's church in the process.

In the meantime, what is the purpose of discipline toward the one who lacks any desire for the church's involvement? It is to win the brother or sister back through a prolonged, concerned call for accountability to the lifestyle promises he or she acknowledged in church membership and in marital vows.

Jesus declared that He came to give abundant life. He expected His people to be part of this life-giving and life-restoring process. Restorative discipline means the use of the authority of the church for the purpose of bringing persons back to such a state of wholeness. It's difficult. It's exhausting. It demands a long-term commitment. But it is an imperative if the church is to fulfill her ministry to the divorced.

✵   A third change for the church to explore is in the area of program ministries. Distinct from the need for attitudinal change and restorative discipline, program ministries deal with the ongoing expression of the church in the form of her activities and schedule.

What is happening in the church regularly for the divorced and separated in the congregation? Planned activities can communicate to those people that the congregation cares for them and is ready to invest the effort necessary to meet their needs. Such programs validate the full role the congregation feels these persons have in the fellowship. Weekly Bible studies, single-parent support groups, classes for singles in the Sunday school curriculum, and divorce recovery seminars are examples of some useful programs. Some churches with multistaff capabilities are even beginning to hire full-time professionals to serve in the area of single adult ministries.

The church must also assume responsibilities to establish programs of outreach to the separated and divorced of the community. It has been observed that the divorce experience is a complex process during which further personality growth can take place. Old lifestyle patterns and goals that were once assumed are challenged during this time of transition. Such reevaluation provides an exceptional context for thoughtful consideration of the gospel if the church is prepared to contact such persons at their point of need. Creative programs must be explored on this point.

The form that any particular church would decide to use in a ministry to single-again persons is not at issue here. Rather, the concern is for the divorced and separated people in the congregation and the surrounding community to sense that a redemptive fellowship is prepared to take action on their behalf. When this concern is present and expressed, the details of specific programs will work themselves out according to the various situations.

ACTION POINTS

Throughout this workbook, you have been recording action points or things you need to work on over the next few months and perhaps years. You have also recorded them on this page "for future reference." Well, the future is now. You should have a list of goals on this page that you can refer to at a glance. If you haven't got anything out of this workbook other than this list of goals, it has been worth the price of the workbook. I say that because if you went to a counselor, the first session would probably be spent identifying areas you need to work on. That session would certainly cost much more than the price of this book. May God bless and strengthen you as you work through these issues.

_____

_____

_____

_____

_____

_____

_____

_____

_____

_____

_____

_____

_____

_____

TEST-RETEST ADJECTIVE CHECKLIST

You should have taken this test in Chapter 1. Fill this out again when you're done working through the workbook.

Place a checkmark next to all the adjectives that describe how you feel right now. Read through the list by reading across the columns from left to right.

❑ angry	❑ annoyed	❑ ambivalent	❑ amused	❑ attractive
❑ anxious	❑ bored	❑ apathetic	❑ brave	❑ bright
❑ ashamed	❑ cheated	❑ collected	❑ calm	❑ confident
❑ bitter	❑ confused	❑ hesitant	❑ contented	❑ delighted
❑ defeated	❑ dejected	❑ disinterested	❑ engaged	❑ excited
❑ depressed	❑ detached	❑ different	❑ funny	❑ fulfilled
❑ disgusted	❑ discouraged	❑ glib	❑ grateful	❑ glad
❑ foolish	❑ empty	❑ interested	❑ helpful	❑ happy
❑ guilty	❑ exhausted	❑ hopeful	❑ interested	❑ inspired
❑ hateful	❑ helpless	❑ impatient	❑ involved	❑ independent
❑ inferior	❑ hurt	❑ indifferent	❑ joyful	❑ jubilant
❑ insecure	❑ irritated	❑ judged	❑ loyal	❑ loved
❑ lonely	❑ jealous	❑ at peace	❑ optimistic	❑ overjoyed
❑ miserable	❑ misunderstood	❑ misguided	❑ neglected	❑ needy
❑ overwhelmed	❑ nervous	❑ neutral	❑ pleased	❑ powerful
❑ pessimistic	❑ phony	❑ preoccupied	❑ relieved	❑ resilient
❑ rejected	❑ puzzled	❑ quiet	❑ respectful	❑ satisfied
❑ resentful	❑ restless	❑ reluctant	❑ romantic	❑ secure
❑ sadistic	❑ sad	❑ sexual	❑ sexy	❑ smart
❑ stupid	❑ sorry	❑ shy	❑ supported	❑ strong
❑ suicidal	❑ selfish	❑ silly	❑ thankful	❑ touched
❑ terrible	❑ tense	❑ surprised	❑ tough	❑ trusting

□ ugly	□ unappreciated	□ unsure	□ useful	□ whole
□ unhappy	□ upset	□ weary	□ welcome	□ well
□ violent	□ worried	□ questioning	□ willing	□ wise

TO SCORE:

1. Add all the checks in vertical column 1, and then multiply the number by (-4).
2. Add all the checks in vertical column 2, and then multiply the number by (-2).
3. Add all the checks in vertical column 3, and then multiply by zero. (Total for column 3 will always equal zero.)
4. Add all the checks in column 4, and then multiply the total by 2.
5. Add all the checks in column 5, and then multiply the total by 4.

Total your score from the five columns to see if your overall feelings are overwhelmingly negative (indicated by a high negative score), basically neutral, or overwhelmingly positive. This score may not reflect anything more than how you were feeling when you took the test. But it's helpful to compare this score to the one you got earlier.

Enter your total score here: _____

What was your score the first time you took the test? _____

Did you make any progress? _____

Why or why not?

_____

_____

Would you be willing to share your results? Please drop us a line at the Fresh Start office, 63 Chestnut Road, Paoli, PA 19301, or call us at 1-800-882-2799.

MARRIAGE AND DIVORCE
Position Paper—Fresh Start Seminars, Inc.

I. WHAT THE BIBLE SAYS ABOUT MARRIAGE

A. Marriage is a DIVINE INSTITUTION.

Contrary to some contemporary opinion, marriage is not a human institution that has evolved over the millennia to meet the needs of society. If it were no more than that, then conceivably it could be discarded when it is deemed no longer to be meeting those needs. Rather, marriage was God's idea, and human history begins with the Lord Himself presiding over the first wedding (see Gen. 2:18-25).

B. Marriage is to be regulated by DIVINE INSTRUCTIONS.

Since God made marriage, it stands to reason that it must be regulated by His commands. In marriage, both husband and wife stand beneath the authority of the Lord. "Unless the Lord builds the house, they labor in vain who build it" (Ps. 127:1)

C. Marriage is a DIVINE ILLUSTRATION.

In both Old and New Testaments, marriage is used as the supreme illustration of the love relationship that God established with His people. Israel is spoken of as the wife of Jehovah (see Isa. 54:5; Jer. 3:8; Hosea 2:19-20). The church is called the bride of Christ (see Eph. 5:22-32). The Christian marriage is sort of a "pageant" in which the husband takes the part of the Lord Jesus, loving and leading his wife as Christ does the church, and the wife plays the role of the believer, loving and submitting to her husband as the Christian does to the Lord. Thus, Christian marriage should be an object lesson in which others can see something of the divine-human relationship reflected.

D. Marriage is a COVENANT.

From the earliest chapters of the Bible, the idea of covenant is the framework by which man's relationship to God is to be understood, and it also regulates the lives of God's people. A covenant is an agreement between two parties based upon mutual promises and solemnly binding obligations. It is like a contract, with the additional idea that it establishes personal relationships. God's covenant with Abraham and his descendants is summarized in the statement "I will be your God, and you shall be my people." Marriage is called a covenant (see Mal. 2:14), the most intimate of all human covenants. The key ingredient in a covenant is faithfulness, being committed irreversibly to the fulfillment of the covenant obligations. The most, important factor in the marriage covenant is not romance; it is faithfulness to the covenant vows, even if the romance flickers.

E. Marriage is a WHOLE-PERSON COMMITMENT.

God meant marriage to be the total commitment of a man and woman to each other. It is not two solo performances, but a duet. In marriage, two people give themselves unreservedly to each other (see Gen. 2:25; 1 Cor. 7:3-4).

F. "What God has joined together, let not man separate," declared our Lord (Matt. 19:6). "Till death do us part" is not carry-over from old fashioned romanticism but a sober reflection of God's intention regarding marriage (see Rom. 7:2-3; 1 Cor. 7:39).

II. WHAT THE BIBLE TEACHES ABOUT DIVORCE

A. Divorce is abhorrent to God (see Mal. 2:15-16).

B. Divorce is always the result of sin.

God's basic intention for marriage never included divorce; but when sin entered human experience, God's intention was distorted and marred. Under perfect conditions, there was no provision for divorce, but God allowed divorce to become a reality because of man's sinfulness (see Deut. 24:1-4; Matt. 19:7-8). To say that divorce is always the result of sin is not to say, however, that all divorce is itself a sin. It may be the only way to deal with the sinfulness of the other party that has disrupted the marriage relationship.

C. There are two conditions under which divorce is biblically permissible.

Since divorce is a sinful distortion of God's intention for marriage, it is an alternative of last recourse, to be avoided whenever possible. However, Scripture does teach that there are two circumstances in which divorce is permitted (though never required):

1. In the case of sexual unfaithfulness (see Matt. 19:9).

2. In the case of desertion of a believing partner by an unbelieving spouse (see 1 Cor. 7:15-16).

D. Divorce carries with it consequences and complications.

Divorce, because it is a violation of God's plan, carries with it painful consequences and complications. God has made perfect provisions for the complete forgiveness of all our sin through the death of Christ, even the sins of sexual infidelity and unjustified divorce (see 1 Pet. 2:24; Col. 2:13).

Forgiveness, however, does not remove the temporal consequences of our sins or the pain and grief involved in the death of a relationship. Divorced singles, single parent families, remarriage, and the problems of "blended" families are part of the consequences of God's intention being thwarted. The church is to minister to individuals and families suffering these consequences, and to seek to help them respond with maturity to their problems.

E. Reconciliation is to be preferred to divorce.

While divorce is permitted, it is never commanded. Forgiveness and reconciliation are always to be preferred (see 1 Cor. 7:10-11).

III. WHAT THE BIBLE TEACHES ABOUT REMARRIAGE

A. Remarriage is permitted where the former spouse is deceased (see Rom. 7:2; 1 Cor. 7:39).

B. Where a divorce occurred prior to conversion, remarriage may be permitted.

"If any one is in Christ, he is a new creation, old things have passed away, behold, all things have become new" (2 Cor. 5:17). When one becomes a Christian, all sin is forgiven, and all condemnation is removed (see Rom. 8:1). Thus, preconversion conditions do not necessarily preclude remarriage to a Christian mate.

If the former marriage partner has also become a Christian, remarriage to that partner should be sought. Where the former partner has not been converted and attempts to share the gospel with him or her are rejected, however, remarriage to that person would be disobedient to Scripture (see 2 Cor. 6:14).

Even though remarriage is allowable biblically, there may be consequences from past sins that continue or destructive patterns from the old life that can carry into new relationships. Thus, a new marriage should be entered into with due thoughtfulness and with the counsel of mature Christians.

C. Where a divorce has occurred on scriptural grounds, the offended party is free to remarry.

A person who has been divorced because of infidelity of a marriage partner or desertion by an unbelieving partner is free to remarry (1 Cor. 7:15).

D. What about desertion by a "Christian" spouse?

First Corinthians 7 deals specifically with the case of a nonbeliever who refuses to live with the believing spouse. The question then arises about the remarriage of a believer who was divorced by a partner who also professed to be a Christian. Such a situation ideally should involve the church in the steps of disciplinary action outlined in Matthew 18. A Christian who decides to walk out of a marriage without biblical cause is in violation of Scripture. Such a person who refuses the counsel and admonition of the elders and persists in following the course of disobedience ultimately is to be dealt with as though he or she is an unbeliever (see Matt. 18:17). The deserted spouse would then be in a position of having been deserted by one whose sinful behavior and unresponsiveness to spiritual admonition give evidence of an unregenerate heart, and thus he or she falls under the provision of 1 Corinthians 7:15.

E. Where a former spouse has remarried, remarriage is permitted for the other person.

Regardless of the reasons for the divorce itself, if one of the partners has remarried, the union is permanently broken and reconciliation is impossible, and thus the remaining partner is free to remarry.

F. Scripture does not absolutely forbid remarriage of a person who has caused a nonbiblical divorce.

Where there has been conversion (in the case of a person who was not a Christian when the divorce occurred) or the demonstration of genuine and heartfelt repentance (in the case of one who was a Christian at the time of the divorce), remarriage may be permitted for the offending party if (1) the former spouse has remarried or (2) the former partner refuses reconciliation (see 1 Cor. 7:15).

G. Scripture recognizes the possibility of separation that does not lead to divorce.

Because of mankind's sinful nature, couples can, at times, be involved in a marital relationship that is destructive, either physically or emotionally, to the two marriage partners and/or their children. It is possible that separation might become necessary because of the destructive nature of the relationship or the potential danger to one or more of the family members. Such a situation does not provide grounds for dissolution of the marriage and the establishment of a new marriage. Where no biblical ground for remarriage exists, a Christian is bound to seek reconciliation as long as there is a possibility of such reconciliation taking place (see 1 Cor. 7:11).

IV. ANSWERS TO SOME RELATED QUESTIONS

A. Is there ever a totally innocent party in marital discord or divorce?

No one is ever free from sinful conduct or attitudes, so in this sense there is no "innocent party." However, there are some sins that nullify the marriage covenant and some which, though they may be serious, do not. In any case of marital discord, both partners should be encouraged to try to understand how they contributed to the conflict.

B. Will divorced persons be allowed to participate in service opportunities in the church?

Spiritual, psychological, and relational maturity are primary qualifications for service opportunities. Divorce would be considered only one part of a much broader evaluation of a person's suitability for service. Divorce would not necessarily preclude serving. A primary consideration must be the reputation the individual has in the Body of Christ and the community (see 1 Tim. 3:2, 7; Titus 1:6).

C. What if there has been no sexual unfaithfulness in a Christian marriage, but two Christians decide to dissolve their marriage because they are incompatible?

The Bible does not recognize incompatibility as grounds for divorce. Reconciliation must be achieved, and every means possible should be considered, including individual and/or marriage counseling. If Christ is on the throne of two human hearts, conflict will cease. He does not fight with Himself.

D. A frequent reason given for seeking a divorce is that the original marriage was a mistake. The couple believe they got married for the wrong reasons and are asking why they should perpetuate a mistake.

God's promise is that He is able to cause all things to work together for good, even our human mistakes (see Rom. 8:28). The Bible does not recognize a "mistake" as grounds for divorce. A deliberate, knowledgeable violation of God's revealed will for marriage is never an appropriate response to a mistake made earlier in life. Two wrongs do not make a right.

E. What if a couple is separated or divorced, and both desire to have sexual intimacy with each other?

Sexual intimacy is the privilege of a marriage relationship. If the couple is already divorced, such intimacy would be classed as fornication. If the couple is not actually divorced, sexual intimacy might be appropriate (see 1 Cor. 7:4-7). However, serious consideration should be given by both partners to their personal motivation in the relationship. One of the considerations a couple must have is their reputation with their children and friends.

V. SUGGESTED BOOKS ON MARRIAGE, DIVORCE AND REMARRIAGE IN THE BIBLE

Adams, Jay E. *Marriage, Divorce, and Remarriage in the Bible.* Grand Rapids, Mich.: Zondervan Publishing House, 1980.

Atkinson, David. *To Have & To Hold.* Grand Rapids, Mich.: William B. Eerdmans Publishing Company, 1979.

Duty, Guy. *Divorce & Remarriage.* Minneapolis: Bethany Fellowship, Inc., 1967.

Ellisen, Stanley A. *Divorce and Remarriage in the Church.* Grand Rapids, Mich.: Zondervan Publishing House, 1977.

House, H. Wayne, ed. *Divorce and Remarriage: Four Christian Views.* Downers Grove, Ill.: InterVarsity Press, 1990.

Murray, John. *Divorce.* Phillipsburg, N.J.: Presbyterian and Reformed Publishing Co., 1978.

ANGER INVENTORY

Name_____ **Date** _____

Please answer by circling the appropriate number using the scale below. Choose the number that describes your feelings most accurately.

0-Never   1-Very Little   2-Moderately Often   3-Very Often

1. Are you irritable at work, school, or home?
        0   1   2   3

2. Do you lose your temper when driving or riding in a car?
        0   1   2   3

3. When asked to do something at home, work, or school, do you tend to procrastinate?
        0   1   2   3

4. When angry, do you give others the silent treatment?
        0   1   2   3

5. Do you have difficulty allowing people to become close to you?
        0   1   2   3

6. Are you tense or critical during meals?
        0   1   2   3

7. Are you frequently in a hurry or impatient?
        0   1   2   3

8. Do you lose your temper?
        0   1   2   3

9. Do you feel you could hurt someone if you expressed your anger?
        0   1   2   3

10. When angry, do you act as if you have forgotten what you've been asked to do?

     0   1   2   3

11. Does the expression of anger make you feel strong or give you pleasure?

     0   1   2   3

12. Do you have difficulty giving praise or expressing thanks to others?

     0   1   2   3

13. Do you have thoughts of punishing or hurting others by withholding your love?

     0   1   2   3

14. Are you often late for work, school, appointments, engagements, and so on?

     0   1   2   3

15. Do you have angry outbursts or tantrums?

     0   1   2   3

16. When angry, do you deliberately make mistakes or perform tasks slowly?

     0   1   2   3

17. Do you ever have thoughts of hurting yourself?

     0   1   2   3

18. During the evening, are you angry or critical?

     0   1   2   3

19. Do you think of punishing those who have disappointed you by hurting yourself; for example, through illness, alcohol, drug usage, dangerous behavior, or through failure in important areas of your life?

     0   1   2   3

20. Are you overly polite and apologetic when you're angry or provoked?

     0   1   2   3

21. Do you find yourself being very competitive?

     0   1   2   3

22. Do you isolate yourself at home, work or school?

     0   1   2   3

23. Do you experience thoughts or feelings of prejudice against others?

     0   1   2   3

24. Do you initiate quarrelling, or are you often argumentative?

     0   1   2   3

25. Is it difficult for you to give up your desire to seek revenge against those who have hurt you or someone you love?

    0   1   2   3

26. Do you drink excessively?

    0   1   2   3

27. Do you act in an aggressive manner with others?

    0   1   2   3

28. Are you manipulative?

    0   1   2   3

29. Do you have difficulty trusting people?

    0   1   2   3

30. Do you tend to overreact to minor events?

    0   1   2   3

31. Do you attract others and then push them away when you know they're attracted to you?

    0   1   2   3

32. Do you enjoy violent films or books?

    0   1   2   3

33. Do you feel angry about your responsibilities?

    0   1   2   3

34. Are you critical of those with whom you live in regard to their abilities or physical appearance?

    0   1   2   3

35. Do you fantasize expressing anger physically against those who have hurt you or someone you love?

    0   1   2   3

36. Do you find yourself trying to control others?

    0   1   2   3

37. Would you rather be with animals than with people?

    0   1   2   3

38. Are you disappointed with yourself?

    0   1   2   3

39. Do you have difficulty accepting your anger when you've been disappointed or hurt?

    0   1   2   3

40. Do you misdirect your anger?

      0   1   2   3

41. Do you provoke others?

      0   1   2   3

42. Do you become angry when you reflect on the events of the day?

      0   1   2   3

43. Do you have difficulty allowing people to touch you?

      0   1   2   3

Anger Inventory Guidelines

A. Calculating the Scores

1. Add the total for all the questions to arrive at an overall score.

2. Add the scores for questions 5, 22, 29, 36, 37, and 43 for the Trust score.

3. Add the scores for questions 3, 4, 10, 13, 14, 16, 19, 31, and 33 for the Passive-Aggressive score.

4. Add the scores for questions 9, 11, 17, 25, 32, and 35 for the Violent Potential score.

B. Interpreting the Scores

1. Overall total less than 45 - mild anger

                        45 - 65 moderate anger

                over 65 - high anger.

2. Over 6 on the Trust score is significant.

3. Over 9 on the Passive-Aggressive score is significant.

4. Over 7 on the Violent Potential score is significant.

FRESH START DISCUSSION QUESTIONS

The Stages of Grieving

➤ Describe the process of your separation and/or divorce. Where do you see yourself on the "slippery slope"?

➤ Have you experienced significant persons who have supported you? Who are they? How have they supported you?

Reentry into the Single Life

➤ What are one or two adjustments you have faced in reentering the single life?

➤ What are some ways you have sought to take responsibility for your future?

➤ How do you respond to the encouragement to go slow and seek friendships rather than romance?

Biblical Insights on Divorce

➤ How do you feel about the biblical teaching on marriage, divorce, and remarriage? How does it relate to your own circumstances?

➤ What help or support would you like to receive from God's people as you go through this process of recovery?

➤ How do you react to the idea that:
marriage for the wrong reasons is wrong.
marriage should not be used as an escape from single life.
you are ready for remarriage only when you don't need to remarry.

Working Through Bitterness: Learning to Forgive

➤ Describe some of the frustrations or bitterness you're struggling with.

➤ Forgiveness sounds like a big order to many. How do you respond to the encouragement to forgive? How might the forgiveness of God help you deal with your separation or divorce?

➤ Coming to Fresh Start has challenged me to . . .